The Kirwan Years, 1998–2002

The Kirwan Years, 1998–2002

CHRIS PERRY

Paper (ISBN: 978-0-8142-5745-6)

Text design by Sans Serif, Inc.
Type set in Minion by Sans Serif, Inc.

In the summer of 1999, I undertook several freelance writing assignments for the president of Ohio State. By January 2000, Lee Tashjian and Brit Kirwan had lured Nancy and me to Ohio. We had always lived on the East Coast, and our Columbus "adventure," as we called it, turned into a delightful introduction to the Midwest. This book is dedicated to the people of The Ohio State University and their supporters, as well as the many others who made our time in Ohio so memorable and such fun. Go Bucks!

William E. Kirwan, twelfth president of The Ohio State University.

Contents

Foreword ix

Good to Great

1 Context and Continuity 3

Changing of the Guard

2 The Brits Are Coming 9

3 Getting Started 23

The Academic Plan

4 A Plan Is Born 35

5 Building a World-Class Faculty 44

6 Developing Leading Academic Programs 53

7 Developing Leading Medical Programs 67

8 Enhancing the Teaching and Learning Environment 79

9 Serving the Student Body 90

10 Creating a Diverse Environment 111

11 Helping Build Ohio's Future 122

Managing the University

12 Paying for It All 141

13 Strength in Numbers 155

14 Crises Come and Go 174

15 Hooray for the Scarlet and Gray 188

Changing of the Guard: The Sequel

16 Time to Change Partners Again 207

Appendix 221

About the Author 232

Academic Plan 233

Index 255

Foreword

This is the thirteenth in a series of histories that recount the accomplishments and, to some extent, the tribulations of the university and its presidents. One covers the history of the university generally; the other twelve focus on various presidential administrations. Sponsored by The Ohio State University Board of Trustees, these volumes reflect not only differences of time, environment, and presidential personality but also the differing approaches chosen by a variety of individual authors. Taken together, these histories tell the story of one university while shedding light on higher education in general and on what exactly it is that university presidents do.

The information herein comes from about eighty interviews and a variety of written materials. More personally, it also comes from the author's experience as senior speechwriter to the president from January 2000 through June 2002 and as the primary writer—or, more accurately, negotiator—of the language in the Academic Plan.

The primary activity and achievement of the Kirwan years was the creation, adoption, support for, and early implementation of the university's Academic Plan. Much of this book is organized around that transformational document, with each strategy incorporating a "signature initiative" in which Brit Kirwan played an especially vital role.

Those expecting a complete recitation of all that happened during the four years of the Kirwan presidency will be disappointed. While a great many areas are covered, the approach is more thematic than comprehensive. Many specifics were deleted to keep the manuscript to a suitable length, and, except where deemed essential, the temptation to update the story after Kirwan's departure was resisted. Some additional facts can be found in the appendix, which also includes the complete text of the Academic Plan. Unless otherwise noted, photos are courtesy of Kevin Fitzsimons and his University Relations team, the University Archives, or other university or university-related offices.

Of course, many people contributed to this book in important ways, including those who submitted to one or more requests for interviews or reviewed part or all of the manuscript. I want to particularly thank David

Frantz, Maureen Sharkey, and Lucy Gandert in the Board of Trustees Office as well as General Counsel Ginny Trethewey for their assistance and sound advice. Also due major thanks are Jan Allen, Michael Hogan, and Bill Shkurti, who served as my advisory committee and made many useful suggestions. Finally, Robert Robinson, a graduate student in diplomatic history, provided invaluable assistance with research and in other ways. To all of them, and many others, I am grateful.

Good to Great

1

Context and Continuity

The Kirwan years were part of an ongoing mission to transform The Ohio State University from a good institution to a great one, an endeavor launched two decades earlier under President Edward H. Jennings and continued under President E. Gordon Gee. While each president brought a distinctive style and particular set of interests, each also advanced what is, in hindsight, a consistent drive for selectivity, quality, and national recognition for Ohio State students, faculty, and programs. All three men—Jennings, Gee, and Kirwan—aspired to match the school's reputation for football prowess with a reputation for academic excellence. Each built upon the legacy of his predecessors, which often blurred attempts to ascribe credit or blame and produced what appears to be a relatively seamless pursuit of higher academic standing.

President Jennings initiated the movement from open to selective admissions, which began to attract better-prepared undergraduate students. He implemented the first Selective Excellence programs created by the Ohio Board of Regents, which targeted resources to raise the academic bar at Ohio's public universities. He also strengthened the Honors Program and launched the high-tech research park on the university's West Campus.

President Gee supported and funded these programs and the thrust for academic excellence that they represented through such initiatives as Academic Enrichment and Strategic Investment. He also built the university's self-esteem, convincing folks, on campus and off, in Ohio and elsewhere, that The Ohio State University was in fact worthy and deserving of respect. He personalized the university and its mission, making friends for Ohio State everywhere he went. And he instituted the wildly successful "Affirm Thy Friendship" fund-raising campaign.

Toward the end of the Gee years, the Board of Trustees began seeking a

Gordon Gee and Brit Kirwan outside the President's Box at Ohio Stadium in the fall of 1998.

more strategic course for the university's future. At a leadership retreat, it occurred to Provost Dick Sisson that the year 2010 was not all that far away. Why not, he asked, adopt a 20/10 plan? The idea took root, and the resulting 20/10 Plan set a quantitative stretch goal of ten academic programs ranked in the top ten among public universities and an additional ten in the top twenty by the year 2010. It was among a handful of key goals, programs, and reports that were in place or in progress when Kirwan arrived.

Another was the highly acclaimed report from a research commission chaired by Bernadine Healy and strongly influenced by Ed Hayes, who then headed the Office of Research. Issued in August 1998, one month into Kirwan's presidency, the report proposed "[t]o improve the quality and volume of research and scholarship to the point that Ohio State will be recognized among the top ten public research universities in the U.S." Heavy on benchmarking and detailed comparisons with other institutions, its recommendations were bold and measurable, and many of them—such as its emphasis on interdisciplinary research—strongly influenced events to follow.

Other important influences included reports from the Committee on the Undergraduate Experience (CUE), the Graduate Quality of University Experience (G-QUE), the Inter-Professional Council Quality of the University Experience (I-QUE), the President's Council on Outreach and Engagement, the Campus Master Plan and various district plans adopted by the Board of Trustees, and annual leadership agendas instituted under President Gee and prepared by Provost Ed Ray. Another related activity was budget restructuring, begun in the mid-1990s (but not implemented until July 2002) to align budgets with academic goals and foster incentives and accountability to generate revenues and reduce costs.

Missing, however, was a strategy to tie these and other ideas together into a focused approach to implementing the 20/10 idea. "As a university we have identified many problems," Kirwan told the University Senate, "and we have a larger number of strategies, plans, committees, and dedicated individuals making daily contributions to our efforts. What we don't have, and what we badly need, is a unified, comprehensive, coherent strategy—a single plan, if you will—that articulates goals, strategies, and metrics."

And in fact, the major development of the Kirwan years, and the greatest legacy of Kirwan's own leadership, was the creation, acceptance, and initial implementation of the university's Academic Plan. Begun in 1999 and adopted by the Board of Trustees in December 2000, that plan became the centerpiece of Ohio State's agenda, with budget and other priorities emanating from its six strategies and fourteen initiatives. In a relatively short period of time, it became the university's battle cry in budget skirmishes with the state.

Looking back, the flow is more apparent than it was at the time. Perspective, like hindsight, is 20/20.

"Ed (Jennings) put things in place," says General Counsel Virginia (Ginny) Trethewey. "Gordon began to change people's attitudes. Brit took this sense of hope and enthusiasm and focused it via the Academic Plan and Diversity Action Plan." Using selective admissions as an example, Bill Shkurti adds: "Ed got the law changed; Gordon funded it; Brit institutionalized it." The Academic Plan became an active and transformational document, and when Kirwan left, the trustees sought a president who would follow through on the existing plan, not create a new one. Thus, in her first State of the University Address in October 2003, President Karen Holbrook characterized Ohio State's "unity of vision" as a great advantage and reported on Academic Plan progress.

But as successful as the plan was, it could not transform the social and political climate of Ohio, where the commitment to academic excellence in higher education—and the resources necessary to achieve it—was less substantial. Thus, counterbalancing the success of the Academic Plan during the Kirwan years was the struggle to maintain, and if possible expand, state support while seeking to increase other sources of revenue. Along the way, Ohio State progressed on many fronts and hung on through the glitches and crises that inevitably plague such a large university.

While Presidents Jennings and Gee came to Ohio State during fiscal crises, the Kirwan years began when things were going well. The economy was chugging along in the later years of the high-tech boom that would later be seen as a "bubble." Governor George V. Voinovich was in the final six months of his tenure while running for the U.S. Senate. His successor appeared likely to be another Republican, Bob Taft, holder of a famous Ohio name and then Ohio's secretary of state. In Columbus, Greg Lashutka was halfway through his second term as mayor, and his reelection looked likely.

As the university welcomed a new president, it was likewise fairly satisfied. Board leadership had been strong, with successful business and community leaders in charge. A basketball program in need of repair had been fixed, and head coach Jim O'Brien—with his pleasant manner, obvious ability, and strong values—was becoming a central Ohio favorite. While some controversy with the city lingered, a major new arena was nearing completion on Olentangy River Road. Ohio State felt proud to have attracted a president who brought stature to the position and was known to have turned down other, perhaps more prestigious institutions. The DeRolph school-funding case was a looming problem, but generally, times were good.

Changing of the Guard

2

The Brits are Coming

On December 20, 1997, members of the Ohio State Board of Trustees gathered at the Bexley home of George Skestos. What better way to discreetly host their high-profile guest, Skestos had suggested, than with a luncheon prepared and served by his wife, Tina. Thus, the trustees welcomed a tall and gracious southerner whom some of them were meeting for the first time. They became acquainted over veal stew, the questions probing but friendly.

"I sat four seats to his left," Michael Colley recounted later, "and asked about his commitment to Ohio State. As he answered, I could see all the heads nodding and observed that, 'I think you're hired.'" Later, when Development Vice President Jerry May took Kirwan on a tour of the campus, board members unanimously agreed that there was no need to talk again; he was their man.

Two weeks later, on January 5, 1998, it was announced that William English ("Brit") Kirwan would become the twelfth president of The Ohio State University. The Search Committee's bold strategy had worked. Ohio State had attracted one of America's leading university presidents, a man who had transformed the University of Maryland–College Park into precisely the kind of institution they wanted Ohio State to become. "You're lucky," an administrator at Maryland said. "You're going to love him."

The trustees were particularly pleased because Kirwan was considered to be unobtainable. He had turned down the presidency of the University of Washington and twice had declined to compete for high-level positions in the University of California system. One was the chancellorship at Berkeley in which the other finalists were reported to have been Condoleezza Rice, then provost at Stanford and later national security advisor and U.S. secretary of state; Laura Tyson, an economics professor at Berkeley who later chaired the Council of Economic Advisors; and Bob Berdahl, president of the University of Texas at Austin, who got the job. Word about the search had leaked, Kirwan says, and he inquired about his chances. When told he was among the top two, but was not necessarily the first choice, he withdrew.

Years before, while Kirwan was provost at College Park, Ohio State had approached him about becoming provost. He had dined in Washington with Ed Jennings and visited the campus, but was not ready to leave Maryland. Instead, Ohio State hired Myles Brand, who went on to become president of the University of Oregon and later the University of Indiana and the NCAA.

Big Shoes to Fill

Gordon Gee, the outgoing president at Ohio State, was considered a tough—some said impossible—act to follow. For seven and a half years, Gee had personified Ohio State in a larger-than-life way. Thus, the greater Columbus community was eager to meet its new leader. After all, next to the governor, the president of Ohio State may be Ohio's leading citizen.

In late June 1997, Gee had accepted the presidency of Brown University, a much smaller institution but a member of the elite Ivy League. He would remain at Ohio State until mid-December and assume his new position on January 1, 1998. On September 5, the Board of Trustees named a search committee headed by Alex Shumate, a respected Columbus attorney and chair of the Board of Trustees. The search committee also included three other trustees, five faculty, one vice president, two students, two deans, one alumni representative and two nonteaching staff. Assisting the committee was William Funk from the search firm of Korn/Ferry.

The committee worked hard to develop the kind of presidential profile that Malcolm Baroway described in *The Gee Years* as "messianic." Meanwhile, the search committee collected names and met with potential candidates in six cities during three days in November. Actual interviews were conducted in Columbus during the first half of December.

But other activity was taking place concurrently on an even less public track, with a process tailored to the needs of a reluctant candidate. Noting that few people were qualified to take on this complex job, Gee had offered a short list that included Kirwan, who, when approached by the search consultant, declined to participate.

"We consulted with many people regarding the nation's top presidents," said former board chair David Brennan. "Brit was on all the lists, with a notation saying you would never get him. But he was the consensus best choice, so I said to Alex, 'Let's not fool around. [Let's] go after him.'"

And go after him they did. On November 4, Shumate traveled to College Park on the ruse of talking to Kirwan about a Kellogg Commission report. He brought along Bernadine Healy, dean of the College of Medicine and Public Health, as well as Funk and board secretary Bill Napier. Healy made a big impression on Kirwan, who also made a big impression on her. After interviewing him, all she could say was "Wow!" She later described the process as "love at first sight." Ten minutes into the meeting, Shumate changed the subject, popping the question that was on his delegation's mind: Would Kirwan consider coming to Ohio State?

"I was so impressed by their audacity," Kirwan remembers, "I couldn't help but be flattered. And I was absolutely captivated by Alex, who was so eloquent about the Ohio State vision and its future." He went home and told Patty, "You're not gonna believe what those folks did."

Kirwan agreed to meet again in mid-November in Crystal City, Virginia, at a dinner meeting in a room reserved under a false name. This time Shumate brought a larger contingent from the search committee that included trustees Ted Celeste, Jim Patterson, and Tami Longaberger. The search committee members liked what they saw, and Brit's name kept topping their short list. However, since they didn't know if Brit would accept, all the finalists received serious attention.

Shumate next informed Kirwan that he was their top candidate and invited him to Columbus. "I was so sure I wasn't going to accept the job that Patty didn't come—nor did she want to—but I felt that they had been so nice that I should go," Kirwan recalls. That became the critical December 20 visit, with lunch at Skestos's home.

"First, I went by the president's house, where the search committee was gathered on the porch," he continued. "Then I talked with Gordon. I did not realize that my lunch with the board was the interview. My head started to swim. Then Jerry May took me on a tour, and we hit it off immediately. I was so impressed with their aspirations, their huge capital campaign. I could feel the affection the community had. We went back to the house. George Skestos and Alex made an offer that got my attention, very generous by the standards of the time. Then they took me to meet Governor Voinovich.

"They could not have done the courtship better," Kirwan added. "I flew out as a courtesy but got back on the plane thinking, 'How am I going to explain this to Patty?' I had not made up my mind, but my thinking had changed radically. Also, I was in my tenth year as president at Maryland . . . and could not help wonder if it wasn't time for someone else. I was very disappointed in the level of support the university was getting. Plus I was sixty years old, and this was energizing."

The more Kirwan learned, the more energized he became. He liked the fact that Ohio State was a complete university with a single campus culture. In contrast, Maryland lacked medical and law schools, without which a research university was limited in the stature it could achieve, and as part of the University System of Maryland, it was not a freestanding institution. And then there was that matter of legislative support. "What concerns me about Maryland as a state," he told the *Baltimore Sun* in words he would later repeat in Ohio, "is that there isn't a spirit, a culture, a constituency that insists on a greater level of funding for higher education." (At least partially in response to Kirwan's departure, the legislature increased state support by 33 percent.) His meeting with Voinovich encouraged him to believe the grass might be greener in Ohio.

Patty facetiously suggested another reason for the move. "When people ask me why we're leaving," she joked, "I tell them that my husband wanted to go to a bowl game before he dies."

In fact, the decision was wrenching. The Kirwans are a close family, and all their family and friends live in or around Maryland. The kids did not even go away to college, living at home while attending College Park. Every Sunday they gathered as a family for dinner. They had never been separated.

Daughter Ann Elizabeth by nature is curious and outspoken. She abhors stereotypes, especially about women's issues and feminism. She has influenced her father on this topic and others, just as he has influenced her. A freshman at Maryland living at home and sharing a car with her father, she once filled up the Honda with gas and was charged $1.50 for what should have been an $11.50 purchase. She told her dad, who, concerned that the error might come out of the attendant's paycheck, made her drive back to College Park that night and pay the additional $10.00.

"That changed me," she said.

Son William E. Kirwan III considers himself a mixture of both parents. Bill spent many hours at home drawing, encouraged by his mother, who was herself artistic and had once aspired to become a fashion designer. Setting out to study engineering, he developed doubts that this field was for him. After many conversations, his father suggested he try architecture, where he later found his life's work. "He can listen and analyze problems," Bill says of his father. "He is very fair, presents both sides. He brings a clearness of mind to sort things out." Today Bill and wife, Chris, are both architects.

The Kirwans pose in the fall of 1998 with their daughter, Ann Elizabeth, and her then fiancé and now husband, Brendan Horton. The couple was married in Columbus in the summer of 1999.

On the plus side, the Kirwans' home on Deep Creek Lake in western Maryland, designed by their architect son, was located midway between Maryland and Ohio. Living in a university-provided residence, Deep Creek was Patty's hidden retreat, where she could do the cooking that she loved but seldom got to do and decorate the house as she wished. In contrast to the Williamsburg-like decor in the official residence, Deep Creek featured Shaker simplicity and overstuffed chairs looking out at lovely mountain and lake views. Another positive was that Patty's mother, who was getting along in years, and a sister lived in relatively nearby Lexington, Kentucky.

Nonetheless, Patty did not want to move. Ann was not yet married, and Bill had just gotten married. One night in bed, Kirwan told Patty, "We really have to talk about this." "Okay," she replied, "but I'll only go if they pay me," figuring that would make it go away. "There was no pay at Maryland," she explained. "I could not even use Brit's car. I would have to give up seventeen years' seniority

Patty and Brit Kirwan enjoy a football game in 1999 with son Bill, second from left, and his friend Greg Lyons.

in the public school system to go there [Columbus], and my role would constitute a full-time job. That's why I said what I said to Brit. Brit told Alex, who immediately said that would be no problem. They called my bluff!"

And as it turned out, Patty enjoyed Columbus and her full plate of activities. She tutored staff members working on their GED as part of an adult education program. She hosted teas at the residence at which fifth graders practiced their manners. She pursued her interest in the arts, joining boards for Opera Columbus and BalletMet. She tutored in the public schools and participated in the Ohio Hunger Task Force, the "I Know I Can" program, and the Critical Difference for Women program. Patty was an honorary board member of the Seal of Ohio Girl Scout Council and, as a breast cancer survivor, she enthusiastically supported programs to find cures for that disease.

"The people of Columbus are warm and gracious," she says. "There's a love affair the community has with the university, almost a reverence."

An animal lover—she still has a dog named Carmen Ohio—Patty developed a great fondness for the chimpanzees with which psychology professor Sally Boysen worked at the OSU Chimpanzee Center. Among those who eased Patty's entry into town was Deborah Eschenbacher, who in August 1998 took her on a women's donor tour that incorporated the veterinary school. There Patty met Sally, falling in love with her and the chimps.

"Had that been available when I was in college, I probably would have majored in it," Patty Kirwan says today. She often took visitors to see the chimps and helped raise money for Sally, who named one chimp Harper, Patty's maiden name.

Throughout the search, Kirwan remained under the media radar. Had the offer leaked earlier, he says, the pressure at Maryland might have kept him from leaving. Negotiations continued through the Christmas holidays and were sealed during Sugar Bowl week.

"Alex called me every day from New Orleans," Kirwan recalls. Then on Saturday, January 3, a story by editor Mike Curtin appeared in *The Columbus Dispatch* that for the first time named Kirwan as the leading candidate to replace Gordon Gee. "That night I attended a basketball game with Duke at Cole Field House," he remembers. "It was a strange feeling. Governor [Parris N.] Glendening asked me at halftime, 'What can we do?' 'Nothing,' I said. 'It's too late. I've decided.'"

On Sunday, Maryland officials confirmed that Kirwan was leaving, and the deal was announced on Monday. Kirwan would earn an annual base salary of $275,000, well above his $217,000 salary at Maryland and larger than Gee's salary of $231,000. He deferred increases of $16,000 in 1999, $11,640 in 2000, and $396 in 2001, and his actual salary when he left in 2002 totaled just over $303,000. He also served on paying corporate boards such as Wendy's and Les Wexner's Intimate Brands. Patty would receive an annual honorarium of $25,000, paid from unrestricted gift funds.

The Kirwans' Monday began with a press conference in College Park. Later, the couple flew to Columbus, where at 5:30 PM the Board of Trustees elected him president. At 7 PM, Shumate publicly introduced the Kirwans at a reception at the Fawcett Center for Tomorrow. "Once or twice every century," Kirwan said, "a university has an opportunity to move to a higher level of excellence. I believe, because of the base of strength here at this university, the excellence of the people, and the commitment of the community, this is such a time at Ohio State."

At the reception, Kirwan ran across Athletic Director Andy Geiger, who had left Maryland for Ohio State in 1994. After feigning mutual disbelief, the two embraced. "I am the person that ripped him away from Stanford," Kirwan told

Board Chair Alex Shumate shares a laugh with the president-elect at the January 1998 announcement of Kirwan's appointment.

the audience. "Then I held onto his leg as Ohio State took him away." They were together again, this time with the nation's largest intercollegiate athletic operation. Interviewed incessantly because of his Kirwan ties, Geiger predicted that Kirwan would want to be known as an academic leader and would "want us to win with values."

"This is the most enthusiastic presentation of a public figure I have seen in years," TV 10's Penny Moore told her viewers. "One can only wonder how long the honeymoon can last."

"We have created a vision and a strategy for Ohio State—a vision of what a complex public university can be, and of how it can contribute to the larger community," Shumate said. "Dr. William Kirwan is the individual who can take us to the next level."

A Presidential Couple

Who was this man in whom a unanimous search committee and Board of Trustees had entrusted the university's future? Born in Lexington, Kentucky,

Kirwan was the son of a football coach and history teacher who briefly served as president of the University of Kentucky, where two high-rise residence halls are known as Kirwan Towers. Calling UK his "playground," Kirwan accompanied his father to football practice and donned his own miniature Wildcat uniform. He played football and basketball and ran track in high school, then attended the university on a football scholarship as a tight end. Years later, his children would also attend a university where their own father was a major presence.

In his seventh-grade homeroom, Brit sat behind Patricia Harper, learning to admire her independence and later noting that "[s]he didn't necessarily go with the flow. She did things her way." When the class embarked on its senior trip to Washington, DC, Brit arranged to sit with her on the bus. Later, Patty also enrolled in the University of Kentucky, where she majored in nutrition. Her grandfather was a doctor whom Patty and Brit adored, and she hoped that her husband would be a doctor also. In fact, Brit was a pre-med student until he faced organic chemistry. "I realized," he said later, "that as a doctor, I would make a great mathematician."

And a mathematician he became, as well as Patty's husband, the couple marrying after their graduation in 1960. At the time, the United States and

Patty Kirwan served as an active partner with her husband.

Soviet Union were competing in a race for space, and Kirwan landed a National Defense Education Act fellowship. He enrolled at Rutgers, where he earned master's and Ph.D. degrees in math, and in 1964 was hired by the University of Maryland as an assistant professor. The Math Department was good then; it later became one of the top ten among public universities and in the top twenty overall. He excelled as a teacher and researcher and in 1977 was named chair of the Math Department, an appointment he saw as a temporary detour from his academic duties and which his faculty colleagues jokingly called his "fall from grace."

"I never dreamed I was embarked on a permanent career change," he says of that move. Daughter Ann believes that he would have been perfectly content as a faculty member, interacting with students, but had been "propelled onward." He went on to become vice president of Academic Affairs and provost, acting president, and president of the university. In total, he spent thirty-four years at College Park, one of the thirteen institutions that comprise the University System of Maryland.

While Brit was at Rutgers, Patty worked in the Chemistry Department at nearby Douglas College before taking a teaching position in the New Brunswick Public Schools. Following the birth of their children, she volunteered until the children were in school, then returned to education as a teaching assistant in the public schools, working with learning-disabled middle school students.

A Passion for Excellence

In nine years as president of the University of Maryland–College Park, Kirwan compiled a noteworthy record. Support from research grants increased two and a half times, while the number of faculty elected to the prestigious National Academies of Science and Engineering and the Institute of Medicine rose from one to fifteen. The number of departments the National Research Council considered "distinguished and strong" went from six to sixteen. While in 1993 *U.S. News & World Report* found no Maryland departments worth including in its top twenty-five, five years later it found forty-five.

Further, freshman SAT scores at College Park increased 200 points to 1,200. Kirwan also strengthened undergraduate honors programs and created additional related programs, and by 1998, approximately four in ten incoming freshmen were admitted to one of these selective endeavors.

Kirwan also became widely known for his commitment to diversity and his effectiveness in raising minority participation, and under his presidency Maryland became a national model. Minority faculty increased from 10 to 15 percent of total faculty, minority students rose from 19 to 29 percent of the overall student body, and degrees awarded to minority students went from 15 to 28 percent of all degrees. "More blacks graduated from College Park under Kirwan than from any other university, not including historically black colleges," the *Washington Post* wrote when he left. And while the U.S. Supreme Court invalidated Maryland's minority scholarship program, Kirwan's impassioned advocacy of the initiative gained him loyalty and support from the minority community.

In addition, Kirwan expanded the land-grant agenda to make it relevant for the twenty-first century, while Maryland's endowment rose from $23 to $208 million and its private gifts increased from $14 to $88 million. He also launched a $350 million Campaign for Maryland, which was more than halfway complete when he left.

"It is absolutely the case that when the history of the University of Maryland is written, his name will be written in capital letters," said Dan Fallon, one of Kirwan's provosts.

Kirwan's energy and passion were widely recognized and applauded, and one example became legendary. Winning a nationwide competition, Kirwan had lured the prestigious American Center for Physics to College Park—or he thought he had, until the local city council threatened to quash the coup in a midnight vote. Kirwan, who had been watching the proceedings on cable television in his pajamas, soon appeared in the hearing room, still dressing himself as he arrived. His plea electrified the audience, and the center was saved.

When Kirwan elected to leave Maryland after thirty-four years, the reaction on campus was one of shock and sadness. Praise for his work at Maryland was widespread. National education leaders also chimed in. "He is passionately committed. He really cares about the academic enterprise. He believes in it, he values it, and he demonstrates it," said Peter Magrath, president of the National Association of State Universities and Land-Grant Colleges.

"We got the guy nobody could get," Shumate said later. "He had a proven track record and the perfect personality. He was the right person to follow Gordon Gee." "I didn't think we would ever find anyone to succeed Gordon," adds trustee George Skestos. "It was perfect timing because he was just perfectly right for Ohio State at the time. They're entirely different. Gordon is more a man of ideas, 'We're going to do this and that,' and Brit makes it happen. It was the kind of continuity we were seeking but never expected."

Karen Hendricks, who joined the Board of Trustees after Kirwan became president, also views Kirwan as a complement to Gee. "It is sort of like the conductor of a symphony," she says. "At times you need the flutes and at times you need the drums. Brit brought excellence and discipline. Gordon was a visionary, a PR guy par excellence."

Kirwan had transformed Maryland into a much higher quality university. Could he do the same for Ohio State?

Interregnum

To smooth the transition at Maryland, Kirwan offered to remain there through June 30, 1998, while visiting Columbus as often as he could. In February, for example, he sat next to Governor Voinovich's wife at the State of the State message to the General Assembly, during which the governor introduced him as the new Ohio State president. In the lobby afterward, television crews lined up seeking his reaction to the speech.

"I can't imagine such a thing happening in Maryland," Kirwan later told the *Baltimore Sun*. "Nobody here [*sic*] would ask me what I thought of a State of the State speech. It's not a matter of respect for me as a person. It's a matter of respect for this institution."

Through such early experiences, Kirwan learned that his new position made him a celebrity. The sudden visibility took some getting used to, and at times it cost the Kirwans privacy that they would have preferred to retain. When his candidacy first hit the papers, he answered the door in Maryland one Sunday morning in his bathrobe and was greeted by a *Dispatch* reporter who had traveled to Maryland to track him down.

Among the new president's first priorities was to work with Jerry May on the university's "Affirm Thy Friendship" campaign. He also began introducing the campus community to the four major goals that would form the foundation of his presidency. Together they would build Ohio State's national reputation by selectively investing in its most promising academic programs, enhancing the educational quality of the undergraduate experience, realizing a commitment to diversity, and better serving the needs of Ohio communities.

Off campus, he offered another, companion message. Ohio, he said over and over again, was falling behind economically. The state that had enjoyed so much success with agriculture and manufacturing had to make the transition to a knowledge economy, and the key to that transformation was education.

Bottom line: Ohio had to better support its colleges and universities, especially research institutions such as Ohio State.

Wherever he went, the new president's enthusiastic, easygoing style was well received. While he did not "work a crowd" like Gee, who made sure to shake hands and say a word to everyone, Kirwan's sincerity was obvious, and those who spoke with him agreed with a comment by Maryland education professor Willis Hawley. "What he brings is a real openness," Hawley said. "There are no hidden agendas. When you sit and talk to him, you think you're the most important thing on his agenda." Someone described it as Kirwan's "front-porch" style. Kirwan took pains to put people at ease. "I don't think of myself as [wanting to] remake Ohio State," Kirwan told a reporter for *The Lantern*, the campus newspaper. "I want the school to attain its own aspirations." He also heaped praise on his popular predecessor. "I admire Gordon tremendously," he said. "In many ways, having the opportunity to follow him . . . is the best opportunity that can happen to a person. People will find that we are both different," Kirwan predicted, "but we share many values in common."

The relatively long transition period from January through June allowed the new president to absorb a new culture, get up to speed on issues, and become acquainted with his leadership team. At an Alumni Association dinner in the Washington, DC, suburbs, he was amazed by the turnout, passion, and enthusiasm for Ohio's only statewide university. It also allowed his teammates to get to know him, and most found this "mathematician with charisma," as a *Baltimore Sun* columnist described him, up to the job. To trustee Alex Shumate, these six months provided a very important opportunity for the new leader to mentally and programmatically assume the new job. As a result, Shumate said, "We didn't miss a beat."

At the same time, the year between Gee's departure announcement in June 1997 and Kirwan's arrival in July 1998 encouraged some confusion about who was in charge. There was Provost Dick Sisson, who served as interim president for six and a half months. There was Kirwan, who spent what time he could in Columbus. There was Shumate, determined that the university's momentum be maintained. And there was Gordon Gee, who reportedly was finding it difficult to leave. The challenge, Sisson says, was to maintain stability, maintain the momentum behind the university's major academic and development initiatives, and keep all balls in the air while paving the way for Kirwan's arrival.

Meanwhile, when the Board of Trustees created a search committee in September 1997, it also created a transition team headed by Sisson. In December, Sisson became interim president, withdrawing as a candidate for president at the University of Texas at Austin, where he had been a finalist. Simultaneously,

Former interim president and provost Dick Sisson and Patty Kirwan listen as the new president responds to a media query during his first day on the job in July 1998.

the trustees named Ed Ray, then senior vice provost and chief information officer, as acting senior vice president and provost.

Sisson had come to Ohio State in 1993 from UCLA, where he had been a faculty member and administrator for twenty-five years, serving as senior vice chancellor for Academic Affairs in his last two years. A native of Gallia County, Ohio, with a bachelor's degree in international studies, a master's degree in political science from Ohio State, and a Ph.D. degree in political science from the University of California–Berkeley, Sisson was a nationally distinguished scholar and held leadership positions in numerous national organizations.

Ray, a member of Ohio State's faculty since 1970, chaired the Department of Economics before joining the Office of Academic Affairs in 1992 as an associate provost. His research interests included foreign investment, trade barriers, protectionism, income tax, and social security, and as part of the state's trade delegations, he had served as counselor to Governor Voinovich on trade missions to China and the Pacific Rim. At the time of his appointment as provost, Ray had primary responsibility for budgets and resource issues. He is now president of Oregon State University.

3

Getting Started

On July 1, 1998, Kirwan was greeted at Bricker Hall by an official welcoming party. After remarks by Ted Celeste, now board chair, and from Dick Sisson, Mayor Lashutka, and Undergraduate Student Government president Josh Mandel, the Men's Glee Club sang the fight song and "Carmen Ohio." Kirwan promised to say "Go Bucks!" every morning upon arising and, *the Lantern* reported, seemed to know all the words to the songs. After lunch at the Faculty Club, he toured the Ohio Union and at the Student Advocacy Center met director Mary Basinger, who had worked for Presidents Jennings and Gee. Six months later Basinger was back in Bricker Hall as Kirwan's administrative assistant, responsible for the president's overflowing calendar.

Ten days after his arrival, at his first Board of Trustees meeting, Kirwan cited "a remarkable congruence between the issues I feel most passionately about and those this university has identified as among its highest priorities." Those priorities, a restatement of his four goals, were to

> strengthen our efforts to elevate the quality and status of undergraduate programs;
> target investment that would help the university achieve its 20/10 Plan;
> become a national model in diversity; and
> expand the scope of the land-grant mission to address the important social, cultural and economic issues of today and tomorrow.

The Rhodes Report

Noting that a university's upper-level administration evolves over time, Kirwan expressed a need "to look and see if this is the structure we need now." To

Board chair Ted Celeste helps welcome Kirwan to Bricker Hall while Columbus mayor Greg Lashutka looks on.

do so, he asked Dr. Frank Rhodes to head a consulting team to review the university's upper-level administrative structure.

As a professor of geological sciences and a former president of Cornell, a former chair of the American Council on Education and the Carnegie Foundation for the Advancement of Teaching, as well as a member of the National Science Board and the President's Educational Policy Advisory Committee, Rhodes's credentials were impeccable. More important, he enjoyed Kirwan's confidence. Assisting him in this Washington Advisory Group review were health care consultant Carolyne Davis and UCLA Chancellor Charles Young.

Their September 30 report, based on discussions with seventy-one people and a review of key written documents, found "a widespread feeling that The Ohio State University is better than most of the public believes it to be" and "a more-or-less widely held belief that the administration could be more effective . . . if lines of responsibility were . . . clarified, decision-making simplified, and accountability required. There is a sense, shared by many," the report continued, "that the university is ready to respond to strong presidential leadership." Further, the consultants reported, the university's administrative structure was seen as "large, clumsy and ineffective," "not organized for success," and "skilled at failing." Decision making was viewed as "episodic, piecemeal, well-intentioned, but rarely effective." Eighteen people reported to the president, three times the number management consultants considered optimal.

The Rhodes team made twenty-five recommendations, many of which Kirwan endorsed in a November 12 communication to campus leaders headlined "Organizing for Success." The new president also decided to forgo a search and elevate acting provost Ed Ray to executive vice president and provost. The move clearly established the provost as the university's second in line, chief operating officer, and chief architect of the university budget, while enhancing the budget's stature within the academic community.

Provost Ed Ray shown presenting a Selective Investment Award to Political Science Department chair Paul Beck in 1999.

Some saw the absence of a national search as a missed opportunity. Others felt that Kirwan was putting too much responsibility in the hands of one person. Still others felt that the reorganization created additional bureaucracy. Perhaps, they thought, an institution as large and complex as Ohio State needed two provosts, or even three. Still others recognized that Kirwan had himself been a provost and knew what the job entailed. Kirwan noted that he had "consulted broadly" before reaching this decision.

Next, to recognize the importance of finances and better integrate administrative, business, and financial functions, Kirwan elevated Bill Shkurti from vice president for Finance to senior vice president for Finance, Business, and Administration. In a resulting consolidation, Janet Pichette (later Janet Ashe), vice president for Business and Administration, reported to Shkurti rather than directly to the president.

Kirwan also made a key change within his personal staff, naming general counsel Ginny Trethewey to the added position of executive assistant to the president. In this, he followed another recommendation in the Rhodes report, the only instance in which an individual was mentioned by name. "The president could benefit greatly," the report advised, "from the remarkable talents Virginia Trethewey provides and the particular blend of legal counsel, unique experience, and general advice that she can offer."

The executive assistant position was then held by Bill Napier, who had served as director of governmental relations and executive assistant to President Harold Enarson and, briefly, to President Jennings before joining state government and, later, the Ohio Board of Regents. Napier returned to the university in 1996 as secretary of the Board of Trustees and executive assistant to the president. When Trethewey assumed the executive assistant position, Napier remained as board secretary while becoming special assistant to the president for Government Relations.

Following another recommendation from the Rhodes report, Kirwan created a new position—vice president for University Relations—to better coordinate public and media relations, including development of a communications and marketing strategy. And he directed the provost to recruit a senior, nationally recognized expert as the university's chief information officer.

One week after the release of Kirwan's memo, Ray reorganized the Office of Academic Affairs. He named Alayne Parson senior vice provost for Academic Administration, Nancy Rudd vice provost for Academic Policy and Human Resources, Martha Garland vice provost and dean of Undergraduate Studies, and W. Randy Smith vice provost for Curriculum and Institutional Relations. Ray also created a new position, vice provost for Budget and Planning, which

Ginny Trethewey, shown here with Kirwan and her son, John McCorkle, served the Kirwan administration both as vice president for Legal Affairs and General Counsel, and executive assistant to the president.

was later filled by Alayne Parson, and launched two national searches—one for a permanent vice president for Research; the other for a chief information officer.

On December 4, the Board of Trustees approved the organizational and personnel changes that required their imprimatur. Besides those already noted, these included the appointments of Jim Davis as interim chief information officer and Mac Stewart as associate provost for Undergraduate Studies and dean of University College.

Six months later, Nancy Harden Rogers became vice provost for Academic Administration, and in June 2001 she was named dean of the law school. She was replaced in the Office of Academic Affairs by Carole Anderson, the former dean of Nursing. Later, when Nancy Rudd retired, she was replaced by Barbara Snyder, who left her position as associate dean for Academic Affairs in the law school. Under President Holbrook, Snyder served as interim vice president of University Relations and interim executive vice president for Academic Affairs and provost, eventually holding the latter position on a permanent basis.

Working Style

Whereas Gee liked large group meetings, Kirwan transacted much of his business through a series of weekly, biweekly, or monthly meetings with his key lieutenants.

"Brit had tremendous ability in one-on-one conversations," Trethewey explains. "He would get the result he wanted in one meeting, then use that to advantage with the next person, building as he went. He kept a lot in his head, kept many balls in the air, and was religious about holding those one-on-one meetings."

"He was very smart and aware of details," Ed Ray recalls. "He did not micromanage but neither did he forget anything." Others noted that whenever they ran into the president, Kirwan would ask—oh so nicely—how various projects were coming. "He could be pointed and never forgot an assignment he'd given," says Trethewey. "He nicely but relentlessly pursued his goals. And there was an absolute refusal to quit or give up." "Focus was key," adds Shkurti.

Because he preferred to limit group meetings to major policy discussions, Kirwan welcomed a Rhodes recommendation to modify primary decision-making forums. Rhodes had found "widespread complaint" from participants of the coordinating council and president's executive committee that the issues these groups addressed were misaligned with the level of participants.

"No meeting was too large for Gordon," Trethewey recalls, noting that he had a coordinating council for nuts-and-bolts that met weekly, an executive committee that met twice a month for higher-level policy, a third group that included those on the executive committee plus thirty or so others that met monthly "for dog and pony shows," and a "kitchen cabinet" that met for dinner at the president's house.

To streamline and focus the existing committee structure, Kirwan created two groups. One was a planning cabinet chaired by the president at which he and the provost, vice presidents, executive assistant to the president, and secretary of the board determined university priorities and major initiatives, recommended budget requests and policies to the trustees, and oversaw progress toward university goals. The other was a coordinating council chaired by the provost that included the vice presidents, executive deans, and executive assistant to the president. It discussed major items coming before the planning cabinet, monitored current-year budgets along with progress on the annual leadership agenda, and proposed initiatives to advance university positions. It also interacted with the University Senate, Faculty Council, Council of Deans, University Staff Advisory Committee, and the three student government organizations.

Kirwan's working style also included the heavy use of e-mail. "You cannot underestimate the importance of e-mail during those years," Trethewey says, explaining that besides an "overwhelming volume" there were ongoing iterative sessions during which she and Kirwan would "discuss" a topic day and night for forty-eight hours. Provost Ray recalled similar "conversations," noting that their offices were fifty feet apart and they could have "pulled back the curtain" and conducted a live conversation.

Why did Kirwan like e-mail so much? "I genuinely like to get advice before making decisions," Kirwan explains. "I allow myself to be overscheduled, and e-mail allows the opportunity to converse at nonbusiness times. Also, I find it difficult not to respond to messages." He also gets by on five or six hours of sleep, offering lots of evening and early morning time to fire up his laptop computer. Trethewey adds that Kirwan found e-mail an efficient, "cut-to-the-chase" vehicle that he could utilize at all hours and that allowed him to control the conversation with sometimes wordy colleagues.

It was not unusual for Kirwan to send messages at midnight or 5 AM, and his e-mail traffic accelerated during halftime breaks of basketball games. "I had to check in over the weekend," Bill Shkurti says, "to be sure that some important decision had not been made [without his knowledge]."

The president was also a communications maven and technology junkie. He loved high-tech gadgets, even though he often found the technology challenging, and he made continuous use of desktop and laptop computers, a Palm Pilot, and a series of ever-more-sophisticated cell phones. Commenting to Mary Basinger that Andy Geiger had a new phone, the president soon had one also. He was seldom out of touch and became anxious when cut off from e-mail and cell phone contact.

Most of those who worked with him enjoyed the experience. "He is easy to get to know, sincere, amazingly attentive and interested; a straightforward,

Some members of the president's staff at a farewell event in 2002. Left to right: Diane Toogood, Michelle Compston, Herb Asher, Kirwan, Lynda Farrell, Mary Basinger, and Dick Stoddard.

honest, caring person," says Basinger. "He was everywhere. He had as much energy as Gordon Gee but was less hyper. When tired, more from the pressure than from the hours, he would drag his feet. And he was always late. He wouldn't cut off an intensive conversation; he wanted people to feel that he cared. And he was a gentleman who would apologize if he said 'Damn.'"

"He brought enthusiasm and sincerity," adds Trethewey. "It was his style not to seek credit. He had as little ego as a powerful person can have."

Kirwan's relations with faculty were generally good. It helped that he was the first permanent Ohio State president to come from the arts and sciences—rather than from law, business, or the ministry—and bring comprehensive teaching and administrative experience.

"I watched them unpack his office and saw that he had brought his math books," says fellow mathematician and senior vice provost Alayne Parson. "It was a good sign. Then, at his first senate speech, I heard someone comment, 'He's one of us.' He appealed to the faculty. He went to the Math Department and was introduced as a faculty member."

"What I liked," says Keith Alley, interim vice president for Research, "is that he came in as a scholar and faculty member, waiting to get the lay of the land and to understand the culture before trying to move things."

"He made us very comfortable," says philosophy professor Dan Farrell. "You could see the guy was an academic."

Finally, and perhaps most important, Kirwan's style was marked by an overwhelming desire to get things done, preferably by consensus.

"To me, Brit was a very atypical university president," comments Ora Smith, former president of SciTech. "There is not a stuffy bone in his body. Further, he did not micromanage. He brought an executive mindset. He worked on general principles, was not involved in details. He did a good job of surfing, skimming atop the waves, in a good way. You have got to surf in a job like that or you'll drown. And he was very interested in getting consensus. I never saw him butt heads; instead, he would nudge. And if things were going in the right direction, he would sit back and allow it to happen."

While Gordon Gee had been gone from campus for more than six months when Brit Kirwan officially took up his new duties, Gee's dynamism and high profile inevitably invited comparisons between the two men that lasted for at least a year or two. Those working with the new president liked him immediately. Those who saw little or nothing of him at first wondered what he was up to, why he wasn't spending the night in dormitories as his predecessor had done or why he did not work the crowd as widely and intensely as Gee. After all, his predecessor had often been cited as a potential candidate for governor.

While Kirwan's stock rose strongly with the passage of time, those early days were not easy. "I underestimated the emotional drain of leaving Maryland," Kirwan says in a bit of self-analysis. "It took a toll. When I got on the job, I wasn't prepared for the fact that I didn't know anybody. I knew everybody at Maryland. Suddenly, it struck me, how alone I was, following someone known by all. It took awhile to adjust. The presidency of any university is lonely. There is no group of peers, no one to talk to."

The Academic Plan

4

A Plan Is Born

Dimon McFerson, a former CEO of Nationwide who joined the university Board of Trustees just as the Academic Plan was being finalized, asked his colleagues how this plan compared with its predecessor. Told it was the first of its kind, he exclaimed, "You've got to be kidding!" To a business leader like McFerson, it was inconceivable that one would operate a $2 billion institution without such a blueprint.

As noted in chapter 1, what was original about the Academic Plan was not so much the plan's elements—many of which were in place or had already been proposed—as the fashioning of this material into a comprehensive and coherent planning document. The combination and focus of the material and the specificity of the initiatives, resources, and timetables made the plan workable and credible. "Plans often become the document that formalizes what's been happening," says McFerson, "but you have to go through the exercise."

And what an "exercise" it proved to be!

In fact, nothing significant happened until the summer of 1999, toward the end of Kirwan's first year. "The idea evolved," Trethewey says. "Brit did not walk in the door and say, 'Let's develop a plan.'"

"We began to talk at planning cabinet about whether we should merge the various documents we had," Kirwan recalls, an approach that supported his desire not to reinvent the wheel and to move as quickly as possible.

Committees worked on various sections of the plan, and at a retreat on September 30, 1999, the trustees and deans were brought into the process. The president defined the current environment in stark terms:

An academic reputation as a "second-tier" public research university.

A slowly improving reputation as a center of learning, but with unacceptably low retention and graduation rates, especially with underrepresented minorities.

Improving recruitment from underrepresented groups, but with too many departures from underrepresented faculty and too few minorities in leadership positions.

Recognition as one of the nation's major research centers, but with an underachieving research portfolio.

A national leader in carrying out the traditional land-grant mission.

Goals, aspirations, and accomplishments that are not understood among key constituencies.

Intensifying competition for outstanding faculty, students, and research dollars.

"We are trying to go to a very high place," Kirwan cautioned the participants. "There is no map because we haven't been there. We need an internal map to keep us focused and that lets us measure our progress. We need fewer, bigger ideas, and we need 'Oh, wow!' people." He took the same message around Ohio, hammering at the need for a top-tier university to rejuvenate Ohio's economy in the information age and plugging the key elements of a strategic plan. With Dave Bhaerman preparing PowerPoint presentations to illustrate the message, Kirwan devoted some of his enormous energy to educating audiences on campus and off.

The challenge was real enough, especially considering the resource gap between Ohio State and the nine universities it had identified as its aspirational peers: the University of Arizona, UCLA, University of Illinois at Champaign–Urbana, University of Michigan, University of Minnesota, Pennsylvania State University, University of Texas at Austin, University of Washington, and University of Wisconsin–Madison. In FY1997, for example, Ohio State ranked 19 percent below the benchmark average in current funds revenue per student FTE (Full Time Equivalent). Only four of its academic doctoral programs ranked among *U.S. News & World Report*'s top twenty-five in 1999, compared with twelve for Michigan; eleven for Wisconsin, UCLA, and Texas; and nine for Illinois, Washington, and Minnesota.

Based upon past efforts and information from the retreat, the administration circulated a draft Academic Plan within the campus community and to a few off-campus groups on November 19, 1999. A memorandum from the president and provost asked readers to consider such specific questions as, Is

The Academic Plan was all about excellence in teaching, research, and service. This photo was taken in the Department of Electrical and Computer Engineering's Brillson Lab.

the plan visionary enough? Does the plan support our commitment to academic excellence? and Is there support for the 20/10 goal?

In the words of Ed Ray, readers "applauded the effort but damned the product." Responses came from a broad cross-section of the campus constituency, representing input from

the deans of fifteen colleges representing 2,244 faculty members; chairs of two departments representing 65 faculty; and additional individual letters;

major university faculty committees: University Senate Steering Ad Hoc Committee, University Research Committee, Faculty Council and Faculty Cabinet, and Senate Fiscal Committee;

multiple student committees: Council of Graduate Students, Undergraduate Student Government, and Inter-Professional Council; and

university staff: University Staff Advisory Committee and multiple education and student service areas.

Suggestions included an even greater emphasis on academic excellence, a more passionate and compelling vision, a focus on fewer initiatives (a few big ideas), and a linking of financial resources to individual plan initiatives. The Council of Deans argued that the plan, budget, and annual goals should be aligned. A University Senate Steering Ad Hoc Committee proposed that academic excellence be not a component of the plan, but its backbone. It suggested a table of contents that was close to what was finally adopted—the sort of responsiveness that led to the plan's broad acceptance and the enthusiasm it aroused.

The intention had been to collect feedback through February 21, 2000, and present a finalized plan to the Board of Trustees on March 3. Given the quantity and nature of the reactions, however, the process took a detour. Kirwan and Ray distributed the feedback—thoroughly analyzed and categorized by ACE presidential fellow Dr. Lois Nora—to the leadership team, requesting brief descriptions of each plan initiative, including an implementation timeline and cost estimate.

The team gathered for another retreat on May 3 to prioritize a long list of existing initiatives into approximately ten considered important enough to "clearly and unequivocally advance us toward our overarching goal of being a truly great university." That retreat, facilitated by Vice Provost W. Randy Smith, did its job, and ultimately the plan included fourteen initiatives—more than ten but well below the two dozen or so that were on the table and the scores that were included in the November 1999 draft. Also reviewed were new drafts of a revised vision statement and an "environmental scan" that candidly illustrated the university's strengths and weaknesses, as well as the key challenges to be met.

The Defining Moment

Meanwhile, the plan had been moving forward in other important ways. Soon after his July 1, 1999, arrival to assume the new position of vice president for University Relations, Lee Tashjian attended an Academic Plan retreat at Darby Dan, the Galbreath family farm. He remembers "a lot of thrashing around" about what the plan should include. "At one point," Tashjian recalls, "Bobby Moser said it would be a lot easier to contribute if he knew what the vision and so forth were, a profound moment that consumed the rest of the meeting, without a conclusion being reached."

Driving home, Tashjian thought of Jim Collins, who had led a vision exercise at ARCO, where Tashjian had worked before joining Ohio State. Collins is a management educator, with experience at McKinsey & Company, Hewlett Packard, and the Stanford University Graduate School of Business, who authored *Built to Last* and, more recently, another leadership book, *Good to Great.*

Sandra Harbrecht, president of Paul Werth Associates, a Columbus public relations agency, also knew Collins from her work with Andy Geiger in the mid-1990s. She had suggested to Tashjian that Collins would be a great resource for Ohio State to use and had even called Collins to ascertain his possible interest.

"There is no question that the defining moment came about because Lee Tashjian kept referencing books by Jim Collins," Kirwan says. "Lee came to my office one day and suggested we get Jim to come and talk with us. We were struggling. I called Collins and said we were an example of a very good institution trying to become great." Collins laughed, explaining that "you can't afford me" and that he had no time. However, he added, if the Ohio State group—which had to include the president and provost—would come to Colorado Springs, he would give them a day and a half. The deal was struck, with Collins charging one-quarter of his normal corporate fee, and twelve to fifteen university representatives making the trip in two rented corporate planes on January 4 and 5, 2000.

"I will never forget what happened," Kirwan continued. "We started, and Collins's initial question was, What are your values? We looked at each other. Not a sound was uttered. 'You need values and a mission,' he explained, so we engaged in developing these fundamentals and returned to Columbus with a clear sense of direction."

"I'm new," Tashjian remembers thinking. "These folks are doing this on my word. If this doesn't work, I will look like a buffoon." Fortunately, Collins immediately established rapport with an hourlong discussion of what was necessary for a good institution to become great.

"The Collins trip was probably the turning point in the plan's development," says Trethewey. "We started over in a sense. We had been writing and rewriting the same old stuff. From February 2000 through the summer into early fall, there was intense effort and progress."

The planning process was replete with creative tensions. There were heated discussions at planning cabinet meetings and in smaller meetings about the vision and values statement that had been constructed in Colorado, as well as about language on diversity, whether an idealized description of the future would be taken seriously, tensions between recruiting "star" and regular faculty, the availability of resources, and other matters large and small. At one point, Kirwan, egged on by Dick Stoddard, introduced another important concept. The plan, he suggested, should be externally focused, as much about the people of Ohio and their future as about Ohio State. Otherwise, only insiders would care.

With the debate that followed the Colorado experience and extensive comment from the campus community, drafters went into high gear. The May 3 retreat formalized core content for the plan, although debate over the number and wording of plan initiatives continued for some time.

Toward the later stage of the process, Brad Moore arrived from Berkeley as the new vice president for Research. Moore pushed for greater emphasis on multidisciplinary research initiatives and for substantial additional research space, arguing for half a billion dollars over five years, double the amount in the final plan. Other out-of-the-box thinkers also helped shape the final document. Joe Alutto, dean of the Fisher College of Business; Fred Sanfilippo, senior vice president for Health Sciences and dean of the College of Medicine and Public Health; and Judith Koroscik, dean of the College of the Arts, were among those who urged boldness rather than timidity. Then, when the plan was taking its ultimate shape, Kirwan posed the $64,000 question: Was everybody on board? "Brit gave them their marching orders," Randy Smith recalls, adding that "it's unusual to be that forceful in academia."

Under the day-to-day direction of Ed Ray, the rewriting, editing, and revision of various kinds continued through the spring and summer and into early fall. On October 5, 2000, the administration released the Academic Plan with a five-year price tag of $750 million. Two days later, it was the focus of Kirwan's annual State of the University address to the University Senate. Some faculty thought the senate should formally vote on the plan, but Senate secretary Susan Fisher concluded that their input had been adequately reflected and that the process was okay as it stood.

The revised plan addressed many of the concerns that had been raised during the venting process and was well received—not only among campus constituencies but also by editorial writers for Ohio's leading newspapers. The plan's combination of vision and specificity, as well as its candor, differentiated it from many other similar documents. Strengths and weaknesses were assessed bluntly. One-time and continuing cost estimates were provided for each initiative. Revenue sources were outlined in some detail.

"In twenty years of university administration from the center," Kirwan said in an e-mail to colleagues, "I have never experienced a better example of

Arts dean Judith Koroscik chats with Annie Glenn (left), wife of U.S. Senator John Glenn.

people working together constructively on a major project than was demonstrated by all of you and others in our effort with the Plan. I feel proud to be part of a team that can do such work."

Later, Purdue president Steven Beering told Kirwan that it was "the best planning document I have ever read."

A Plan . . . at Last

On December 1, 2000, Kirwan formally presented the plan to the Board of Trustees, which in Resolution No. 2001–62 unanimously approved it and urged the administration to move forward with implementation and report annually on its progress. Now came the dicey matter of implementation, day-to-day responsibility for which fell generally to Provost Ray.

The Academic Plan begins with a new university vision—purpose, core values, overarching goal, and future—before addressing bedrock questions that offer a rationale and context for the document. It next outlines six strategies and fourteen initiatives along with several facilitating actions that are necessary to successfully implement the plan. It concludes with a summary of preliminary cost and revenue estimates for the first five years—the plan was

Board of Trustees photo taken at President Kirwan's investiture in February 1999. Left to right: Board secretary Bill Napier, Dan Slane, Tami Longaberger, Jim Patterson, George Skestos, Mike Colley, Brit Kirwan, Ted Celeste, Zuheir Sofia, Judge Robert Duncan, and student trustees Soraya Rofagha and Allyson Lowe.

intended to last much longer—and an academic scorecard that compares Ohio State's performance with that of its nine benchmark universities.

The six strategies, which along with the initiatives are covered later in the book, were no surprise given its predecessor documents and the goals of President Kirwan. They were to

1. build a world-class faculty;
2. develop academic programs that define Ohio State as the nation's leading public land-grant university;
3. enhance the quality of the teaching and learning environment;
4. enhance and better serve the student body;
5. create a diverse university community; and
6. help build Ohio's future.

Experienced in corporate planning, McFerson complimented the result. "It had stretch in the plan, it had vision in the plan, it had attainable results, with timelines," he said. "And most importantly, it had performance measurements. . . . I thought it was very well thought out."

No sooner was the plan finalized than University Relations began promoting it widely. Written copies were distributed far and wide, and the plan was posted on the OSU Web site. The president and provost visited various OSU colleges as well as the media and alumni and community groups, presenting the plan and highlighting its importance. The idea was to make people aware of the plan and build enthusiasm for it. To an unusual degree, the strategy worked.

Over the remaining eighteen months of Kirwan's tenure, there were ups and downs in implementing the Academic Plan. The "ups" consisted largely of positive implementation steps; the "downs" from hopes dashed by state budget actions. Both are described in this volume.

In his final board meeting on June 6, 2002, Kirwan referenced a first-year progress report on the Academic Plan that coincided with his departure. After reciting a list of accomplishments, he expressed the view that the plan's greatest impact came in two other ways. One was that "the focus and discipline of the plan allowed us to make substantial progress at a time of incredibly restrained resources." The other, he said, was that the plan "helped create broad acceptance for our vision inside and outside the university."

"Over the past two decades," Kirwan went on, "a debate has pitted two opposing visions of Ohio State against one another. Were we to be the university that focused on size and tried to accommodate everyone knocking on our doors, or were we to be the nationally recognized, top-tier university that Ohio has heretofore lacked? Today, thanks to the efforts begun by Ed Jennings and continued by Gordon Gee, and with what we have been able to accomplish over the past four years, I think that debate is over. This is a university that is now on a trajectory to realize the aspirations of the Academic Plan and enter the ranks of the nation's very best teaching and research universities."

Finally, the plan was never intended to be a static document. Work soon began on additional improvements, and a modest plan revision was completed without fanfare by Ed Ray and posted on the university's Web site during the spring of 2003.

5

Building a World-Class Faculty

In preparing its report, the research commission queried senior faculty and administrators from peer institutions on which strategies most improve the quality of research and scholarship. "The response was clear and unanimous," the commission wrote. "Their number one priority is hiring and then supporting exceptional faculty members. This strategy so out-distances all others that we could not get them to name a second." While "universities do not exist for faculty," the report added, "[they] certainly thrive because of them."

Ohio State had far to go to match its peer institutions in the number and concentration of eminent faculty or in academic programs ranked in the nation's top tier. Thus, the Academic Plan's first two initiatives were to recruit, over three to five years, "at least 12 faculty members who have attained or have the potential to attain the highest honors in their disciplines, concentrating these appointments in areas of strategic focus," and to "implement a faculty recruitment, retention and development plan—including a competitive, merit-based compensation structure—that is in line with our benchmark institutions." These steps were intimately linked with the Academic Plan's second strategy, which was to increase the number of world-class academic programs. Although more could have been achieved in a less restrictive economic environment, there was progress on both fronts.

What's more, the president worked successfully with the University Senate on a host of touchy and, in at least one case, controversial issues.

Signature Initiative: Compensation

Recruiting, retaining, and motivating about three thousand regular faculty and sixteen thousand staff requires competitive compensation. But even though the faculty received average salary increases of 3.5 and 4 percent during Kirwan's first two years as president, with some departments adding another half a percentage point from their own funds, average salaries remained about 2.5 percent below the benchmark average. Ohio State's ranking among benchmark institutions had slipped from above the median some years ago to eighth out of ten. Staff salaries were below market by 7 to 10 percent.

An optimistic budget forecast in the fall of 2000 deteriorated, and by the late spring of 2001 it was apparent that not even a typical salary increase was realistic for Kirwan's third year. With FY2002 fast approaching, the administration granted a flat $395 annual increase to all regular faculty and staff whose performance met expectations—enough to cover only cost increases for health benefits and parking. It was the equivalent of 0.8 percent, furthering the disparity with peer institutions.

The $395 increase was unusual not only in amount but also in structure, since for more than a decade, raises had been given on individual merit rather than across the board. Individual increases normally ranged from zero for those failing to meet job performance expectations to more than the average amount for those who excelled. This year, however, everyone would get the same small amount.

"We are painfully aware of the inadequacy of these compensation gestures," the president told the trustees in June 2001, "but it's the best we can do at the moment." Going forward, he said, Ed Ray and Bill Shkurti would prepare a compensation strategy to raise faculty and staff compensation "to the mean of our benchmark institutions within three or four years." A Competitive Compensation Oversight Group would be formed to assist in this process.

The president also emphasized that reaching compensation parity with inadequate state funding would require cuts to existing programs and that some other objectives be sidetracked. "I do not underestimate the difficulty of this task," he said. "However, if we really believe that academic excellence starts with a top-quality faculty and staff—and we do—then this is the right step to take, and we must take it."

"At first employees begrudgingly understood," says Human Resources associate vice president Larry Lewellen. "Then, as they learned that other Ohio colleges had given more normal increases, resentment built. There were more contentious Faculty Council meetings, forums, and so forth." While the move was not popular, Shkurti adds, it helped position the university to protect its academic programs when additional budget cuts hit later in the year.

Given that fiscal restraints did not permit the university to implement the Academic Plan as aggressively as it had intended, Kirwan identified four primary initiatives for the short to medium term. Topping the list was compensation, which became a test of Kirwan's commitment to excellence and of the Academic Plan's credibility.

In May 2002 the trustees approved a salary budget increase in the range of 4.5 percent, which was 1 percent above market. "This is the first year in our plan to provide salary budgets of up to one percent above comparable institutions," Ray said. "We hope that within the next several years, Ohio State will again be offering competitive salaries." This did not mean that the eventual goal was merely median performance. Rather, the goal was considered a way station en route to even more competitive compensation.

This action was taken—and the promise kept—during a year of severe budget reductions. When the dust finally cleared, faculty salaries went up by 4.8 percent, more than 2 percent above market. However, a major challenge remained. Benchmark salaries had risen more than 23 percent over the past five years, compared with just 15.8 percent at OSU.

Stars Shining Bright

Initiated in 1993, Academic Enrichment was an early initiative to encourage excellence by awarding dollars—usually matched by the recipient departments—to high-potential faculty programs. The initiative was intended to build such programs, with a special emphasis on interdisciplinary collaboration. In the seven years between 1993 and 2000, when the program was discontinued, about one hundred awards were made to programs in fourteen colleges and other university units totaling about $7.8 million in continuing funding and about $3.9 million in onetime payments.

Among the faculty supported by Academic Enrichment funds were Len Brillson and Winston Ho in the Center for Materials Research; Karen Bell, then chair of the highly regarded Department of Dance and later dean of the College of the Arts; Mauro Ferrari, who was hired on one of the health sciences awards and who, as director of the biomedical engineering program, later participated in an award fund position in nanotechnology; and Maria Palazzi, associate director of the Advanced Computing Center for the Arts and Design. These awards also provided seed funding for additional undergraduate honors courses and supported the recruitment of graduate students.

With Gee's blessing, Dick Sisson and Ed Ray took the next step in initiating Selective Investment for Academic Excellence. The program, just starting when Kirwan arrived, was designed to raise already strong departments to the very top of the national academic ladder. The initiative was so compatible with his goals, Kirwan said, that he promptly championed the idea. The first four awards were made in September 1998, with each department matching $500,000 in additional continuing university funding ($1 million total) over a period of years. Four additional awards were made in 1999 and five more in 2000, for a total of thirteen. Recipients were: Electrical Engineering, Materials Science and Engineering, Physics, Psychology, Chemistry, History, Neuroscience, Political Science, an interdisciplinary proposal in cardiovascular bioengineering from the Colleges of Medicine and Public Health and Engineering, Economics, English, Mathematics, and Law.

In addition, at the suggestion of David Brennan, the Board of Trustees created the $8.5 million President's Strategic Investment Fund to help jump-start Academic Plan priorities. (Of that total, $5.5 million was freed up when the Development Office began to support its operations out of fund-raising receipts rather than the General Fund, while $3 million came from the State of Ohio's Research Challenge.) Kirwan used this fund to help establish the MicroMD Laboratory in the Science Village, Medical Informatics,[1] and the Biomedical Research Tower, as well as to enhance the undergraduate experience, technology transfer, and pharmacology.

In July 2001 the Ohio Board of Regents awarded Ohio State four of the state's seven new Eminent Scholar positions, providing up to $750,000 per position in endowment support to be matched by new university fund-raising. And during the winter quarter, in accordance with the Academic Plan, a faculty committee recommended pursuing proposals for nine distinguished faculty positions, five of which were filled by Alastair Minnis, English; Ann Hamilton, Art; Wolfgang Sadee, Pharmacology; Joel Saltz, Bioinformatics; and Roger Ratcliff, Psychology. Among other outstanding individuals recruited to play prominent roles in the success of the Academic Plan were Martha

Chamallas, The Robert J. Lynn Chair in Law; Chris Hammel, Physics; and Jay Zweier, Davis Heart and Lung Research Institute.

One key indicator of progress in attracting eminent or "star" faculty are memberships in the ultraprestigious National Academy of Science, the National Academy of Engineering, and the Institute of Medicine as well as the American Academy of Arts and Sciences, an organization founded in 1780 by John Adams and other scholar-patriots. When Kirwan arrived, Ohio State boasted fourteen such faculty. When he left, there were twenty-three—still well behind such universities as Penn State (34), Michigan (132), and UC–Berkeley (404).

The university also continued its tradition of designating a small number of faculty as Distinguished University Professors. During the Kirwan years, the university added seven DUPs to the ten that had already been named. Many other faculty and staff were honored by campus, state, national, and international organizations. A new tradition, Faculty Recognition Day, took root in 2001 at the Northwestern game in Ohio Stadium, where a halftime ceremony recognized recipients of the year's most prestigious faculty awards. The Best Damn Band in the Land created six star formations around which the honorees clustered, with Kirwan and Ray visiting each group.

At halftime during the Northwestern game in the fall of 2001, the university held its first Faculty Recognition Day event. President Kirwan and Provost Ray are shown here with thirteen faculty members.

Distinguished University Professor Matt Platz, Chemistry, applauds as the Best Damn Band in the Land entertains at the 2001 Faculty Appreciation ceremony recognizing recipients of the year's most prestigious faculty honors.

Senatus Universitatis

In his annual address to the University Senate on January 10, 2002, Provost Ed Ray stirred the academic pot by announcing three important actions. The first, covered in the next chapter, was the appointment of an ad hoc group to study the future of the Colleges of the Arts and Sciences, including the possibility of consolidation.

The second was a request from the senate for enabling legislation to permit colleges outside the health sciences to propose the appointment of clinical faculty—highly qualified, nontenured women and men who utilize their real-world experience to teach but do little research or service. The Moritz College of Law and the Fisher College of Business had requested approval to establish such positions, leading the provost and the president to request enabling legislation and the subsequent consideration of such proposals on their individual merits. Enabling legislation was enacted in June 2002, after which the law, engineering, and business schools submitted specific proposals.

The third item in the provost's senate address was the announcement of his decision to extend the probationary period for regular tenure-track faculty in the College of Medicine and Public Health (COMPH). Knowing that tenure was the "third rail" of campus politics, the provost had worked extra hard on this section of his remarks. "This has got to be right," he told a colleague he asked to review a draft of his remarks. But while Ray achieved his goal, his relations with the senate—which had been pretty good until this point—were damaged as a result.

The saga began when Fred Sanfilippo expressed a desire to extend the probationary period during which medical faculty could earn tenure from the sixth to the eleventh year. (A companion proposal would allow COMPH to make promotions to associate professor in advance of a tenure decision.) The argument was that medical faculty have extensive duties that other faculty do not; for example, tenure-track faculty who also maintain clinical practices devote many hours to patient care as well as teaching and research. Thirty-seven of the nation's top medical universities, as ranked by *U.S. News & World Report*, had such provisions.

Colleges seeking this change had to gain the support of their own faculty, then petition the provost for approval. Sanfilippo obtained his faculty's approval, then took the proposal to Ray, who expressed his willingness to extend the probationary period. He also agreed to uncouple promotion and tenure decisions for tenure-track faculty with patient clinical service responsibilities, but not for faculty in the basic sciences. Sanfilippo submitted a revised petition, which Ray approved.

The rub was in the interpretation of senate rules. Buttressed by an opinion from university attorney John Biancamano, Ray contended that he was obliged only to consult the Senate Rules Committee, after which he could make the decision on his own. The senate, in contrast, believed it retained the right to vote on such changes and that a sacred principle of university governance was at issue.

"Important issues centering on tenure, such as the length of probationary periods, absolutely must, in our opinion and in keeping with the totality of the University Rules, be the purview of the University Senate," wrote Marilyn Blackwell, chair of the Faculty Council, who also expressed the view that "had the proposal gone to the Senate, it would have been approved." Senate secretary Susan Fisher, who succeeded Gerry Regan in 2000, says the issue could have been resolved "if Ed had been flexible."

Others saw it differently.

Brit Kirwan chats with senate secretary Susan Fisher and treasurer Jim Nichols before a senate session.

"This was a major decision, and I was deeply impressed with the care and consideration Ed gave to the proposal and the extent of his consultations across the University," President Kirwan wrote in a widely circulated letter. "Further, I am in complete agreement with his decision and admire the forthright manner in which he addressed the topic at last month's Senate meeting."

Nonetheless, the president had worked hard to build good relationships with the senate, and this dispute was damaging those relations. Thus, Kirwan worked with Fisher and Vice Provost Barbara Snyder to change the rules so they could vote in the future. The rule change was passed unanimously at Kirwan's final senate meeting.

"Early on, Ed had been amenable to having the senate vote on this," Snyder says. "He is a big believer in shared governance. He tried throughout to do the right thing. Brit did all he could to support Ed. The medical faculty wanted this, of course. Fred was impatient; he wanted this done quickly but was told it would take some doing."

The Kirwan years also featured renewed discussion of the pros and cons of switching from an academic calendar based on quarters to one based upon semesters. President Kirwan made the case for semesters in his 2000 State of the University address, and the proposal was incorporated into the Academic Plan.

"I felt very strongly about quarter to semester conversion," Kirwan says, citing a national trend toward semesters, a difficulty in collaboration with other universities, academic limitations of a ten-week quarter, a "credit creep" for graduation which made it tough to compare Ohio State with other institutions, and the tendency of students in a quarter system to rationalize dropping "briefly" out of school. At his request, Susan Fisher impaneled a leadership group chaired by Professor Grady Chism whose members eventually cast an affirmative straw vote on the controversial issue. Then, citing the budget crunch and the need to install a $30 million student information system before such a conversion could take place, Kirwan asked the senate to defer the matter, which it did. "I feel the stage is now set [for eventual conversion]," Kirwan said.

The president also asked the senate to consider a companion issue, which was to revise the General Education Curriculum (GEC). An ad hoc Undergraduate Curriculum Review Committee chaired by Marilyn Blackwell undertook this assignment, issuing a report on July 30, 2002, that was distributed within the senate for review.

At a senate reception during his transition, Kirwan referenced a process in Maryland in which the senate had benchmarked itself against other similar bodies at other universities. He suggested that Ohio State's senate might want to do the same. Later, he reiterated the idea, which was also mentioned in the Rhodes report. Eventually, Caroline Whitacre chaired a Kirwan-appointed Presidential Commission on University Governance to undertake the university's first-ever overall review of senate operations. The group worked for eighteen months to produce a report, plus another six months on implementation. Views differ on how much was finally accomplished. Susan Fisher notes that fifteen of seventeen recommendations were implemented, while a proposal to add staff as voting members was defeated. Others say the major achievement was a decision to hold senate meetings on Thursday afternoon rather than Saturday morning.

Note to Chapter 5

1. This is a knowledge base of techniques and applications for healthcare delivery and information management in support of patient care, research, and education. Medical informatics is in the Department of Biomedical Informatics.

6

Developing Leading Academic Programs

Closely linked to the strategy of building a world-class faculty is developing outstanding academic programs—in this case programs that define Ohio State as the nation's leading public land-grant university. With the 20/10 Plan as the university's longer-term goal, and focused investment as the way to reach it, the Academic Plan continued the targeted approach that began in the 1980s as Selective Excellence and continued in the 1990s as Academic Enrichment and Selective Investment. The plan also focused on increasing space dedicated to funded research.

Further, the plan called for a series of multidisciplinary initiatives to leverage Ohio State's unusual breadth of offerings and talent. Two especially significant multidisciplinary initiatives were inaugurated during the Kirwan years. One was the Biomedical Research Initiative and Tower, which is covered in the next chapter. The second was the Institute for the Study of Race and Ethnicity in the Americas, which is covered here.

The university advanced programmatically in many ways during the Kirwan years. Examples include dramatic increases in research funding, major progress in such professional colleges as business and law, and the formation of new centers and institutes such as the John Glenn Institute for Public Service and Public Policy. Finally, the university laid the groundwork to strengthen the Colleges of the Arts and Sciences.

Signature Initiative: Institute for the Study of Race and Ethnicity in the Americas

As chair of the History Department, Mike Hogan sought to convince Colin Palmer, a faculty "star" at the City College of New York, to take a senior position in African American history at Ohio State. Enthusiastic about the idea, Kirwan joined Hogan in flying to New York, where Palmer expressed interest in working at an institute devoted to racial studies. Hogan drafted a preliminary institute proposal for Palmer's reaction, which he also shared with Humanities dean Kermit Hall, and, in an effort to broaden the funding base, broached the idea with the College of Social and Behavioral Sciences (SBS). Hogan and Paul Beck, chair of Political Science and the lead SBS representative, prepared additional drafts.

Palmer eventually declined the offer (he is now at Princeton) and Hall left to become provost at North Carolina State. Hogan, then interim dean of the College of Humanities, assembled another drafting committee that included law school dean Greg Williams, who became a strong ally in Hogan's negotiations with SBS. Eventually, Kirwan and Ed Ray blessed the proposal. So did the Office of Research, which was assessing competitive proposals to fund the new multidisciplinary centers and institutes called for in the Academic Plan. The funding came from the participating colleges, matched by money from the provost.

Among the institute's several unique features are its focus on ethnicity as well as race, its emphasis on the Americas, and the fact that it began with more than $1 million in annual institutional support—funds set aside prior to budget cuts and expected to stimulate grant activity. The initiative was intended not only to prepare students for a more diverse life, but also to provide useful information and policy guidance for the community. Located in Mendenhall Laboratory, the institute was also expected to encourage top-notch scholarship and stimulate international research in the important interdisciplinary field of race and ethnicity while enhancing local, national, and global outreach and engagement. It became an Academic Plan priority because of its positive role in recruiting and retaining women and people of color, as well as enhancing scholarship on diversity issues.

In spring 2002, following a national search, the university recruited as director john a. powell (who does not capitalize his name), a nationally known scholar then directing the Institute on Race and Poverty at the University of Minnesota. Jacqueline Royster, associate dean of Humanities and professor of

john powell heads the Kirwan Institute on the Study of Race and Ethnicity in the Americas.

English and African American and African Studies, played an informal role in establishing the institute and keeping it going until powell arrived in January 2003.

At its farewell dinner in 2002, the Board of Trustees surprised Kirwan by naming the institute for him. "When Jim Patterson began citing my commitment to diversity and the institute, I thought, how nice of him to mention that; it shows great sensitivity," Kirwan recalls. "I was proud of that accomplishment, but I had no idea that the next sentence would be the naming. Quite frankly, I was overcome with emotion. It was one of those instances in life when you heard words, but the words are disconnected from reality—like a dream or fantasy."

At its June 7, 2002, meeting, the Board of Trustees made the naming official—the kind of action normally taken months or years after a presidential departure.

"During your tenure, the university has made great strides in becoming more diverse and more welcoming," board chair James F. Patterson said. "While we have a long way to go, you should feel good about the progress we have made under your leadership. Given your role in bringing the institute to where it is today, we have decided to name it in your honor."

"To have my name associated with this great institute and university touches me in a way that nothing else has in my life," Kirwan said in his highly emotional response. "It means there will be an enduring bond for me to this university, something that is very, very important to me."

Arts and Sciences

The creation of the institute was consistent with the provost's long-held view that the arts and sciences could be strengthened through more collaborative operations, a belief strongly supported by the president. Thus, in his annual address to the University Senate in January 2002, Provost Ray named an ad hoc Committee on the Status of the Colleges of the Arts and Sciences—chaired initially by former President Ed Jennings and later by Joseph Ferrar, chair of the Department of Mathematics, when Jennings was named interim president.

The Colleges of the Arts and Sciences include the Colleges of the Arts, Biological Sciences, Humanities, Mathematical and Physical Sciences, and Social and Behavioral Sciences. As Jennings and others have noted, they comprise the core of the undergraduate curriculum, accounting for 60 percent of all credit hours taken annually and about 75 percent of all honors credit hours. Representing about 40 percent of all faculty, Arts and Sciences have received over 70 percent of the Distinguished University Professorships in the last decade, about two-thirds of all Distinguished Scholar Awards, and about three-fifths of all Alumni Distinguished Teaching Awards. They have likewise received the majority of the university's Selective Investment and Academic Enrichment awards.

Both Kirwan and Ray felt that the university had not taken maximum advantage of the synergies that can exist among those units and programs, and Kirwan believed that a single college of the arts and sciences would help those disciplines compete with the larger professional schools. Thus, Ray charged the study committee with examining whether the Arts and Sciences colleges "are appropriately configured for implementing the Academic Plan and for working collaboratively to strengthen our national reputation." After studying configurations at various benchmark universities, the committee recommended that existing administrative units remain intact but that an executive dean and vice president for the Arts and Sciences head a federation of Colleges of the Arts and Sciences.

Reporting four months after Kirwan's departure, the committee essentially implemented the president and provost's vision. There would be a substantial reintegration and unification of the five colleges into a single federation. Deans would report to the executive dean and through him or her to the provost. The executive dean would receive budget authority across the Arts and Sciences, as well as authority over the Honors and Scholars programs and authority to administer the curriculum approved by the faculty. The executive dean would also be responsible for reviewing the deans, naming search committees when openings occur, and recommending the appointment of deans to the provost. In addition, the executive dean would be responsible for centralizing undergraduate advising, development, space and facilities, communications, and outreach and engagement.

Research

When vice president for Research Ed Hayes died in March 1998, Dick Sisson named William "Bud" Baeslack III, an associate dean in the College of Engineering, as interim vice president. Baeslack served until he accepted a job as dean of Engineering at his alma mater, Rensselaer Polytechnic Institute. He in turn was succeeded in the interim role by Keith Alley, a professor of oral biology, who held the interim position until July 1, 2000, then served as senior associate vice president for Research until June 2002, when he left to become vice chancellor for Research and dean of Graduate Studies at the University of California–Merced.

Meanwhile, a search committee was established under the leadership of chemistry professor Terry Miller, who had chaired the committee that found Hayes in 1991. One name to crop up was that of Brad Moore, who had chaired the Chemistry Department and served as dean of the College of Chemistry at the University of California–Berkeley.

Moore was Kirwan's first big hire. The president badly wanted someone with top-notch credentials, and Moore was a member of the National Academy of Sciences and the American Academy of Arts and Sciences. What's more, Kirwan and Moore had an existing relationship. In the early 1990s, Kirwan had served on a committee on undergraduate science education that Moore chaired for the National Academy of Sciences' National Research Council, and they served together on a National Science Foundation committee.

Ed Ray (left), Brit Kirwan, and Brad Moore (right) present John King, English, with the Distinguished Scholar Award in 2001.

Moore was also a faculty representative on the committee seeking a new chancellor at Berkeley, the search in which newspapers listed Kirwan as a finalist.

Ohio State's Chemistry Department did work that was close to Moore's field in physical chemistry, and he was eager to bring his lab with him on any potential move. Moore was also impressed with what Kirwan had accomplished in Maryland and pleased that Brit went out of his way to court him during the search process, once taking Brad and his wife, Penny, to dinner and the symphony.

The search committee looked at roughly one hundred candidates and, Miller said, "nobody's combination of qualifications in several areas came even close to Brad's." Thus, Moore's appointment as vice president for Research was rolled out with considerable fanfare. Kirwan trumpeted the appointment whenever possible, always emphasizing Moore's national academy membership. Fanfare notwithstanding, however, Moore's tenure lasted less than three years. He had intended to complete his career at Ohio State and was "deeply disappointed" at Kirwan's departure for Maryland. Nine months later, he accepted a position as head of research at Northwestern University.

During his time at Ohio State, Moore pushed hard to raise research standards, recruit top-level people, and encourage multidisciplinary collaborations. Seeking to invest in areas showing the greatest potential, Moore redirected several million dollars in research funds that had been going to colleges on a formula basis to promote instead multidisciplinary initiatives and help support start-up packages for such prominent recruits as Wolfgang Sadee, Pharmacology, who was recruited from the University of California–San Francisco and is playing a critical role in Disease Intervention. There were winners and losers in this exercise, which resulted in grumbling and discontent in the colleges. Later, under budget restructuring, a portion of the Office of Research funding used to support these initiatives was added to the college budgets.

"Brad's focus was to get as much flexible investment money as possible so as to foster interdisciplinary, multidisciplinary activity," says Keith Alley, who was his deputy in the Office of Research. "He was totally committed to the goals and aspirations of the Academic Plan."

"Brad helped us to think big, build centers of excellence," says Alayne Parson. "We hadn't thought that way."

"It's difficult to overstate the value of somebody who's been at the mountain top, so to speak," says Kirwan. "There was no question of the symbolic value of Brad's NAS credential."

Research Accomplishment

In response to a call in November 2000, faculty submitted 110 proposals for multidisciplinary programs that led to eight trial initiatives: Biomedical Research, the Institute for the Study of Race and Ethnicity in the Americas, Environment, Human Learning, Information Technology, Nanotechnology, Nutrition, and Transportation. While only the first two became top priorities under the Academic Plan, Moore and Alley worked with leaders of all eight to set project directions and develop proposals for external funding. The Information Technology initiative ultimately became the Knowledge Bank discussed in chapter 8.

Then, after the 9/11 terrorist attacks, Kirwan and Moore concluded that homeland security could qualify as a major multidisciplinary initiative. They approached the Battelle Memorial Institute, which, despite its location adjacent to the university, was not a significant partner institution at that time. The result, announced in the spring of 2002, was the Program for International and Homeland Security headed by recently retired air force major general Todd

Stewart. It is a collaboration, with the university focusing on basic research and Battelle offering its expertise in applying and commercializing university discoveries.

Kirwan was delighted with this move. When Battelle began to reinvent itself, changing its business model to focus less on federal R&D and more on intellectual property and commercialization, he saw an opening. Battelle also had a new CEO, Carl Kohrt, and Kirwan set up a series of meetings to map out areas for collaboration. "Partnerships were being created," Kirwan says. "We had turned a corner. I got feedback from the community that people were pleased with this. Maybe we now could realize the potential."

Another exciting opportunity was the Ohio Plan, designed by the Ohio Board of Regents to leverage additional state support for high-technology economic development activities. Governor Bob Taft adopted much of the same material in his Third Frontier initiative, a potential $1.6 billion, ten-year plan to enhance the state's economic future. Of the total, $500 million was to come from a bond issue for high-technology development. A key part of the Third Frontier and the major source of new money, the bond issue was voted down in November 2003. The other $1.1 billion came from state capital spending, the state's General Fund, and tobacco settlement funds for grants and loans for research facilities at state universities. Moore viewed the governor's co-option of the program as an "awesome achievement" for which "Brit deserves 90 percent of the credit."

Originally, Ohio's share of the settlement from tobacco companies was aimed chiefly at smoking prevention and cessation and K–12 education. Kirwan advisers Curt Steiner and Jan Allen recall vividly the Saturday morning in the summer of 1999 that Kirwan reached them by cell phone in the Big Bear parking lot in Muirfield. "How about," he asked, "if we get the Cleveland Clinic, Case Western Reserve, the University of Cincinnati, and Ohio State—institutions unaccustomed to working together—to form a coalition to seek tobacco settlement money for biomedical research?"

It was late in the game to devise a proposal, convince the others, then sell it to the task force that was making recommendations to the General Assembly. Nonetheless, within a few weeks, all of this was done, and the legislature earmarked 20 percent of the state's $10.1 billion settlement—$1.8 billion over twenty-five years—for biomedical research and biotechnology. In September 2002 tobacco funding provided $6.5 million for a cardiovascular bioengineering enterprise led by Mauro Ferrari and $6 million for a biomedical informatics synthesis platform led by Joel Saltz, Medicine, who had been recruited

Marte and Rick (second from right) Denman talk with student participant Ben Basil and President Kirwan at the 1999 Denman Undergraduate Research Forum.

from Johns Hopkins. Eventually, seven medical facilities were part of the consortium.

Another major research accomplishment was National Science Foundation funding for the nation's first Mathematical Biosciences Institute in the College of Mathematical and Physical Sciences. Ohio State had used Selective Investment funds to recruit Avner Friedman, Math and Physical Sciences, from the University of Minnesota, and Kirwan had used his Strategic Investment Fund to support the $10 million NSF proposal. It was also among the large-scale initiatives to which the Office of Research made significant multiyear commitments. Others included the Bioinformatics and Drug Delivery initiatives in the College of Medicine and Public Health.

"Only several such centers are created every four or five years," Kirwan notes. "This was a significant statement for Ohio State."

Thanks to the efforts of many people, external research awards rose by 80 percent in the five-year period ending in FY2002, reaching $426 million as faculty wrote more and bigger proposals and enjoyed a higher success rate. Ohio State ranked fifth among U.S. universities in research support from industry, behind only Duke, Penn State, MIT, and the Georgia Institute of Technology.

And while rankings are not nearly so strong in federal research support, the 2001 National Science Foundation expenditure survey showed Ohio State rising from fortieth to thirty-second in federally financed research and development expenditures and from twenty-first to seventeenth place versus other public universities competing for federal funding.

Professional Schools

Ohio State's professional schools also made important progress during the Kirwan years. Most dramatic was a $30 million gift from Michael E. Moritz, for whom the College of Law is now named. It was the largest gift in university history—possibly the largest-ever cash gift to a U.S. law school—and at the presentation on June 29, 2001, Development vice president Jerry May noted that Moritz would join "names like Mershon, Gerlach, Fisher, Wexner, Solove, Schottenstein, Knowlton, Davis, and Ross."

Moritz held Ohio State degrees in business administration (1958) and law (1961), graduating at the top of his law class. He was a Dublin resident and a

At this 2001 meeting Michael Moritz signed the papers for his landmark $50 million gift to the College of Law. Shown (left to right): Ed Ray, Jerry May, Greg Williams, Moritz, and Kirwan.

partner in the Columbus law firm of Baker & Hostetler and was Bob Walter's lawyer in the creation of Cardinal Health Care. His gift created the Michael E. Moritz Scholars Program, which provides full tuition and a stipend to thirty Ohio State law students. It also financed leadership awards to three students each year, established four endowed faculty chairs, and created the Gregory H. Williams Dean's Fund for Excellence. The gift will help the law school, which received a Selective Investment Award, continue its climb in the national rankings, where it ranked fifteenth among public law schools.

The gift was a high point for Williams, who had served as dean since 1993 and would soon become the eleventh president of the City College of the University of New York (CUNY). He was replaced as dean by Nancy Hardin Rogers, vice provost of Academic Administration and holder of The Joseph S. Platt-Porter, Wright, Morris & Arthur Professorship in Law. She now holds The Michael E. Moritz Chair in Alternative Dispute Resolution.

During his final year as dean, Williams talked with Moritz about making a major gift that would transform the law school. As time went by, Williams outlined his vision for what the school could become, explained that it would require about $30 million to make that vision a reality, and expressed the university's interest in naming the school for Moritz. Finally, Williams invited Moritz to his home for a Saturday lunch at which Moritz agreed to make the gift. Knowing that Williams was preparing to leave Ohio State, and admiring what Williams had accomplished, Moritz wanted to complete the gift before Williams's departure. Thus, in the summer of 2001 the stunning $30 million gift was revealed.

Sadly, the following year in Florida, after leaving a Winter College dinner, Moritz died of complications following a hit-and-run automobile accident. He was sixty-eight.

"The legacy of his gift to Ohio State will touch the lives of people for as long as this university exists," Kirwan said in mourning Moritz's passing. Later, Moritz's wife, Lou Ann, told Williams that her husband's last year was the happiest of his life because he was so involved with the law school and was so pleased he could make this gift.

Law was only one of the professional schools to make significant progress during this period. Between 1998 and 2001 the Fisher College of Business completed and opened its building complex—the largest multibuilding project ever undertaken in Ohio State history. The 380,000-square-foot, $120 million complex contains the latest instructional and communications technology in a six-building, fully integrated management education campus. It includes satellite uplink capabilities, video hookups, and nearly four thousand

President George H. W. Bush spoke at the Fisher College of Business in 2001. While there, he met with (left to right) Joe Alutto, Max Fisher, and Les Wexner.

computer ports; tiered classrooms and breakout rooms for team projects; and quiet, comfortable study and multiuse gathering spaces. Named for industrialist Max M. Fisher, who donated $20 million to the school, the buildings all carry the names of prominent Ohio State supporters.

With strong support from Max Fisher, Gordon Gee, and others, under the ongoing leadership of Dean Joseph A. Alutto, and with its new buildings and programmatic approaches, Fisher College continued to move up in the national rankings. Its fifteen-month Executive MBA program combines long-distance and on-site learning and involves executives from all over the world. Closer to home, an undergraduate business minor was created on the Columbus campus, and it is now possible to earn a business degree from a regional campus. With Kirwan's support, the college began to set tuition on a market-pricing basis.

Finally, Fisher College proves that rankings have their benefits. In early 2000, the Roy F. and Joann Cole Mitte Foundation of Austin, Texas, issued a grant proposal to the nation's top twenty-five business schools. Quickly hopping onto a plane, Fisher College's Jim Miller was among the first to apply, and nine months later, Fisher College had an additional $8.2 million in scholarship money—the largest onetime scholarship gift from a single source at Ohio State and a source for seventy-five scholarships valued at $5,000 each.

Glenn Institute

On September 18, 1998, Kirwan and former Ohio U.S. senator and astronaut John Glenn announced the creation of the John Glenn Institute for Public Service and Public Policy, designed to provide expanded academic and service experience for students and practical educational opportunities for citizens and policymakers. Activities included Washington, DC, internships, lecture series, and much more, and a $20 million fund-raising goal for the Glenn Institute was incorporated into the "Affirm Thy Friendship" campaign. Herb Asher, professor emeritus of political science and the institute's interim director, was succeeded as permanent director by Deborah Jones Merritt, holder of The John Deaver Drinko–Baker & Hostetler Chair in Law.

U.S. Senator John Glenn signs an autograph at a student event in 1998.

A year before, it had been announced that Glenn's papers—his official senate papers as well as papers and artifacts from his NASA and military careers—would be donated to Ohio State. Glenn later said that while he had been approached by the Kennedy School at Harvard and informally by Stanford University, the National Archives had suggested Ohio State—a suggestion he followed even though he and his wife, Annie, had attended Muskingum College in their hometown of New Concord, Ohio.

The idea made a great deal of sense in terms of Ohio connections. "When I heard that the senator was shopping his papers," recalls Dick Sisson, "I remember thinking: Wright Brothers; first guy on moon; Neil Armstrong; first guy to orbit the earth. . . . It was a no-brainer for Ohio. The question was money. How would it be funded?"

Discussions began under President Gee in 1997, the same year in which the Board of Trustees named Glenn a University Honors Distinguished Fellow and an adjunct professor in both the School of Public Policy and Management and the Department of Political Science. The senator's wife, Annie, became an adjunct assistant professor of speech and hearing science at Ohio State. Then, during the presidential transition, Kirwan had a conversation with Gee and the trustees. "He was a national icon, and this presented an incredible opportunity," Kirwan says. "We had to make it happen. The trustees wanted me to see Glenn very early on, and I made several trips to his office to convey my and our excitement. Nothing had been settled at that time. He had a passion for public service and the order of words in the institute's name—'public service' before 'public policy'—was very important to him."

The September 1998 institute announcement came just weeks before Glenn's return to space aboard the space shuttle *Discovery* to conduct experiments on the process of aging in the human body. Glenn was seventy-seven at the time.

7

Developing Leading Medical Programs

One element that attracted Kirwan to Ohio State was the medical school, which the University of Maryland–College Park did not have. Apart from the good such a facility can do to improve the human condition was the contribution a top-rated medical school can make to a university's reputation. However, becoming the truly great university envisioned in the Academic Plan required that Ohio State's already good medical college and related facilities become significantly better in quality and stature. And that could only happen with a cutting-edge initiative in today's hot field of biomedical research.

Signature Initiative: Biomedical Research Initiative and Tower

Nothing better exemplified the benefits of the Academic Plan strategy than the Biomedical Research Initiative and the Biomedical Research Tower that will provide its visual identity. This multidisciplinary initiative was intended to make Ohio State a national leader in the biomedical revolution that is transforming medicine and health care as well as key aspects of the economy. After all, says Fred Sanfilippo, senior vice president for Health Sciences and dean of the College of Medicine and Public Health, "It is perhaps the most exciting period in the history of medicine."

Given its existing interdisciplinary programs and its broad research interests ranging from cancer and heart disease to agriculture, biological sciences, and pharmacy, Ohio State was well positioned to pursue this growing national priority brought about by the sequencing of the human genome. Biomedical research would provide the groundwork, officials said, for improvements in patient care while advancing programs in such fields as cardiothoracic bioengineering, nanotechnology, cancer and cancer genetics, renal transplantation, minimally invasive and robotic surgery, neurodegenerative disorders, pharmacogenomics, biomedical informatics, and high-field imaging.

The core of the initiative was a biomedical research plan to facilitate and leverage discovery across seven catalytic components or "nodes," each representing one component of studying and treating disease: mechanisms of health and disease, biomedical informatics, technology, risk factors, assessment, intervention, and health outcomes. The goals of the plan are to create synergies across disciplines, link basic science researchers with clinicians, and apply new technology and information to medical problems.

Kirwan asked Sanfilippo and Brad Moore to put a plan together, and Caroline Whitacre, associate vice president for Health Sciences Research and vice dean for Research in the College of Medicine and Public Health, was later named to coordinate the effort. Besides tapping into the vast expertise of current faculty, several new faculty members are playing key roles.

To provide the necessary space and equipment, it was agreed to build the ten-story, state-of-the-art Biomedical Research Tower off West 12th Avenue adjacent to the University Medical Center. Expected to open by 2006, the

Things to come: A rendering of the Biomedical Research Tower.

tower will nearly double the university's assignable square footage devoted to biomedical research and will house approximately one thousand people. Its location should also facilitate collaboration among researchers as well as with clinicians at the medical center and in various university hospitals. Further, based on internal analysis and various medical center and university reports, the $151 million tower is expected to provide a major payback to the Ohio economy, producing $3.7 billion in research-related spending during its first decade of operation and creating nearly seventeen thousand new jobs.

Sanfilippo had arrived at Ohio State expecting the building to be funded with state money from the Ohio Plan. Within months he learned that the Ohio Plan was dead in its present form and that there was no short-term state money for such a biomedical research facility.

"We would go nowhere without the building, and the normal capital process would not work," Sanfilippo said later. "The pipeline was full, so how do we fund it? We did it the way it's done at Hopkins and Duke, through extramural support from grants and bonds. To his credit, Brit was open to this [approach] and ran interference with the Board of Trustees." The initiative is consistent with the high level of growth in the National Institutes of Health research budget and could perhaps receive funds from the state of Ohio's tobacco settlement fund and the governor's Third Frontier Project.

"The approach to funding the Biomedical Tower was very important," adds Brad Moore. "It says we are willing to look at new ways of doing things and really compete with Michigan, Duke, and Johns Hopkins. This is not a risk-free strategy, and Brit was cautious about going into it, which was appropriate. More than the tower was involved. It was an integrated financial plan to build research programs: hiring one hundred faculty, start-up money, transition money, equipment, etc. What's important is not just the money but being quantitative about planning, setting priorities, focusing resources."

Very different from the traditional reliance on state capital funding, this was just the kind of out-of-the-box thinking that Kirwan wanted to encourage.

Building a Top-Flight Academic Medical Center

While progress had been made during the 1990s in bringing together the many elements that constituted Ohio State's large hospital and health operation, considerable separation remained. President Gee had separated management of health services and the College of Medicine and Public Health, and individual physicians operated under their own practice plans rather than as part of an overall university orientation—a behavior reformers had been unable to change despite two decades of effort.

Managing health services when Kirwan arrived was Manuel Tzagournis, widely loved and admired and considered a healer not only of bodies but also of organizations. Dean of the College of Medicine was Bernadine Healy, a graduate of Harvard Medical School who began her career at Johns Hopkins, chaired the Cleveland Clinic's Research Foundation, and was deputy director of the White House Office of Science and Technology under President Ronald Reagan and director of the National Institutes of Health during the administration of President George H. W. Bush.

In October 1997 McKinsey & Company proposed to the Board of Trustees a comprehensive strategy for the medical center that reflected varying needs and coordinated efforts of the center's individual units. Given that President Gee was leaving the university later that year, however, it was decided to postpone these actions until a new president was on board. One year later, when Frank Rhodes and his colleagues reported to President Kirwan in the fall of 1998, their recommendations reinforced the McKinsey study. "The administrative structure in the health sciences needs further and urgent review by the president," the report said. "The president probably faces no more important challenge than the rationalization of this structure, so that pressing issues can be addressed in a timely manner."

As Kirwan attended various medical board meetings, it struck him also that the lines of responsibility were very confused. "The head of the cancer center believed he reported to the president," Kirwan recalls. "Hospitals reported to the vice president for Health Services. The dean did not report to the vice president, and there was no control over the cancer center. There was no influence on the hospital. In other words, in this big key area, no one was in charge, and no way existed to bring coherence and focus. And the personal chemistry among leaders was not good. It was the worst possible situation, plus the medical school was underperforming."

Then, Bernadine Healy announced in July 1999 that she would leave Ohio State in September to become president and chief executive officer of the American Red Cross, succeeding Elizabeth Dole. Interestingly, the Red Cross search committee had been chaired by Dimon McFerson, a member of the national board and a future trustee at Ohio State. Daniel Sedmak, chair of Ohio State's Department of Pathology, was named interim dean.

Reorganization and New Leadership

On September 1, 1999, the Board of Trustees approved a restructuring of the university's academic medical center that included the creation of a unified senior vice president for Health Sciences and dean of the College of Medicine and Public Health. They also created the new position of vice president for Health Services, which Reed Fraley would later assume. In December, Manny Tzagournis turned sixty-five and retired as vice president for Health Sciences, and the trustees named the Medical Research Facility at 420 West 12th Avenue in his honor. Sedmak's title became interim senior vice president.

"Manny was ready to retire, which created the opportunity for a coherent organization," Kirwan explains. "I began to talk to national leaders in academic medicine and got their advice and their organization charts, from which I concluded that there was no one perfect structure." At the request of President Kirwan and the Board of Trustees, community advisers with significant prior university and hospital board experience undertook a review that included consultation with all academic and hospital leadership. Their reorganization plan not only created the senior vice president's position, but also proposed an oversight board that was approved by the Board of Trustees but never implemented.

"The reorganization plan was not universally well received, especially by the cancer center," Kirwan notes, "but the trustees approved it."

But who would assume this powerful new position? "Bernadine was the logical person," Kirwan says, "but she had left. Now what? I felt hugely exposed. I had created a structure, allowed Manny to retire, and had no one to run it. Then, I was told about Dan Sedmak, whom we appointed interim senior vice president and dean with the understanding he would not be a candidate. He did such a good job that he was recruited to be the vice president and dean at Georgetown."

On September 15, 1999, the president and provost named a ten-member search committee chaired by Pascal Goldschmidt, director of the Heart and Lung Institute and professor of internal medicine, cell biology, neurobiology and anatomy, and medical biochemistry, and charged it with finding a permanent senior vice president. Nine months later, with the process still under way, the Board of Trustees unanimously "directed the President to bring appropriate closure to this search process . . . and bring the appointment to the Board for acceptance and ratification at the August 30 meeting."

"It was a very difficult search that took a long time," Kirwan explained. In the midst of the search, Goldschmidt decided to leave Ohio State for Duke, but

President Kirwan with Provost Ray and change agent Fred Sanfilippo in 2000.

not before persuading Fred Sanfilippo, who after twenty-two years at Duke was chief of the Department of Pathology at Johns Hopkins, to meet with the search committee. He quickly became Kirwan's candidate and was subjected to the president's full-court press.

Sanfilippo did not have high interest in the position and met with the search committee only as a favor to Goldschmidt, with whom he had worked in the past. Sanfilippo was familiar with Kirwan's reputation at Maryland and as Kirwan continued to call, he became impressed with his persistence and his sense of "how Ohio State was ready to move from a nonacademic medical center to an academic medical center." Eventually, he succumbed to the siren's call. Why?

"Why come?" Sanfilippo asks rhetorically. "The gap between actual and potential was larger here than anywhere I knew about in the U.S. I got here and found it was even wider than I thought, on both the upside and downside. People needed to recognize the potential. They hadn't seen top-tier. They didn't know what it looked like. I also came because of the opportunity here for collaborative multidisciplinary research. Also, Pascal [Goldschmidt] said one reason to come here was that there was a lot I could learn from Brit Kirwan. And I did learn a lot."

Sanfilippo also saw two great assets at Ohio State: opportunities created by the breadth and depth of the disciplines, programs, faculty, and students, and Kirwan's "well-deserved reputation as one of the foremost leaders of higher education in the United States."

On August 8, Kirwan introduced Sanfilippo, "the latest academic superstar" to join the leadership team at Ohio State. "Just listen to some of his accomplishments . . . at Johns Hopkins," Kirwan told the Board of Trustees on August 30. "He recruited seventy-two new faculty members, doubling the size of the department. The number of funded research projects increased from 30 to over 120. And research funding increased from less than $6 million to more than $20 million, and that's just in the Department of Pathology. Also, the department's net revenue grew from a deficit budget to one which this year led all clinical departments at Johns Hopkins."

"We were looking for someone to take the bit and get things done," says trustee George Skestos, "and he has been going at 120 miles per hour [ever] since." Trustee Dan Slane calls it President Kirwan's "best appointment."

"There were questions," Kirwan recalls. "For example, he had never run an operation of this magnitude. And we had a very difficult negotiation. I called some folks I knew at Hopkins, who said Fred was driven and would make a place better but that he would also make you pay every day of your life; that he would be in your office every day. He was obviously a change agent, and change was what was needed."

"It required an enormous cultural adjustment for Fred," Kirwan continues. "He had never been at a public university and was appalled by the bureaucracy and frustrated. Many people did not share his burning ambition. He had always been at the very best places and knew what it takes to build quality. He was relentless, brought new ideas."

Sanfilippo hopes Ohio State will join the top quartile of academic medical centers by 2008 and generate a $50 million annual fund for mission development. To that end, he has battled compartmentalization, monitored the organization's culture, and encouraged teamwork, high expectations, and performance-driven rewards. He has also benchmarked nationally rather than locally or regionally.

Physician practice plans had been a contentious issue since the mid-1970s, when Tzagournis served on a committee that developed a departmental, rather than individual, approach. Over the years, attempts to establish one central

David Schuller, M.D.; Clara Bloomfield, M.D.; Dick Solove; Millie James; Bernadine Healy, M.D., dean, College of Medicine and Public Health; President Kirwan; and Manuel Tzagournis, M.D., vice president for Health Sciences. Solove gave $20 million to the James Cancer Hospital.

approach failed, and the new senior vice president was eager to install such a plan, transforming what he considered a private practice environment into an academic practice environment. He brought in chairpersons from departments at other universities to assess Ohio State's situation and encouraged them to comment on how "ludicrous" the situation was.

"During my first week, I appointed a group of key chairs to develop a plan," Sanfilippo says. "They learned we were probably near the bottom in terms of worst practices." It was agreed to begin implementing a central plan.

Asked about his success in extending the probationary period for clinical faculty, Sanfilippo replies: "You need to make your case and show benchmark data. When people know you will not take 'no' for an answer, and you present data, they do not want to head into inevitable conflict, and . . . they do it. I was told, 'Don't waste your time; it will never happen.' If that's your expectation, of course it will never happen. Then it happens, and the world doesn't end."

To strengthen the administrative side of the medical center, Sanfilippo sought out someone "not wed to the status quo or stifling, nonentrepreneurial attitudes," hiring Peter Geier to the new position of senior associate vice president for Health Sciences Business and Administration. Sanfilippo had met Geier, then president and chief operating officer of Huntington Bancshares, Inc., at Children's Hospital, where Geier chaired the board and had mentioned his interest in business development. The appointment was not without its tender moments since Geier and Zuheir Sofia, a member of the Ohio State Board of Trustees, were competitors at the Huntington, where both had been executives.

First Things First: Fixing the Deficit

Since the University of Maryland–College Park had no hospital or medical school, Kirwan arrived at Ohio State with no prior experience in an area that represents about 40 percent of the overall university budget. However, immediately realizing that the medical center had unique problems and challenges, he spent a lot of time there. Community hospitals were consolidating and were very competitive, Tzagournis told him. HMOs and other organizations were looking for lower costs, and the best bargain was not always at an academic health center. "We talked frequently about the problems we faced," the doctor recalls, "formally, and since I was privileged to be his physician and his wife's physician, we talked informally also."

It wasn't long before President Kirwan had the opportunity to benefit from such discussions. By February 2000, the health system was running an operating deficit of roughly $45 million out of a $600-million-plus total budget. The deficit was attributed to several factors, including declines in governmental and private reimbursements, a tight labor market that had forced up wages, and longer hospital stays. While reserves would cover one year's loss and possibly two, quick action was necessary. Thus, March saw the launch of a financial recovery plan developed by a task force of thirty hospital board members, physicians, medical center administrators, practice plan representatives, and academic leaders in the health sciences, who met weekly for four to five months.

The recovery plan included higher rates, renegotiation of payment schedules from managed care providers, consolidation of duplicate services, closure of some services, and investments in additional revenue sources. In addition, the health system underwent an aggressive cost-reduction initiative to examine supplies and services to include everything from prosthetics to pharmaceuticals.

The plan worked, and the deficit was eliminated in two years. And while the savings strategies noted above were vital, they were only part of the story. The strategy that Kirwan and Sanfilippo devised, with strong support and implementation from Reed Fraley, was to grow their way out of the deficit. "We could not save our way out," Fraley said later. "Our costs were generally in line with competition. We were among the most productive in the country. The typical approach would have been to close facilities and lay off people. In fact, [when it was all over] we actually added people."

For the three years following FY2000 (adjusted to include General Administrative Support in FY2003), total health system revenue was up by 48 percent while expenses rose by just 36 percent.

"The push for research excellence in the biosciences depended on finances being handled well," Kirwan says. "Reed Fraley did a terrific job on the deficit."

Bricks and Mortar

Today, the College of Medicine and Public Health includes about 650 full-time faculty, more than 800 students pursuing medical degrees, and 570 students enrolled in undergraduate and graduate programs in the college's School of Allied Medical Professions. The medical center provides care for more than three thousand patients each day.

When current and approved construction is completed, the medical center's investment in a physical plant authorized during the Kirwan years will approximate more than a quarter of a billion dollars. It will include the College of Medicine and Public Health, University Hospitals, University Hospitals East, the James Cancer Hospital and Solove Research Institute, OSU & Harding Behavioral Healthcare and Medicine, The Dorothy M. Davis Heart and Lung Research Institute, The Richard M. Ross Heart Hospital, the Biomedical Research Tower, a network of community care sites, and two new ramps connecting State Route 315 from Cannon Drive, designed to speed traffic in and out of the medical center complex.

Jerry May and his development staff worked hard not only to raise private funds for these facilities but especially to identify naming gifts. These included

A $20 million pledge from Richard Solove to the James Cancer Hospital for human cancer genetics research. Subsequently, the facility was renamed The Arthur G. James Cancer Hospital and Richard J. Solove Research Institute.

$6.5 million from John F. Wolfe and his family—via the Edgar T. Wolfe Foundation—to the James Cancer Hospital's "Threshold of Discovery" campaign, with $5 million earmarked to build The John W. Wolfe Cancer Genetics Research Laboratories in Wiseman Hall.

$10 million from Bill and Jackie Wells through the William H. Davis, Dorothy M. Davis, and William C. Davis Foundation to the Heart and Lung Institute, which opened in June 2000.

$10 million from Elizabeth "Libby" Ross for the new Richard M. Ross Heart Hospital.

Also, in April 1999, Ohio State purchased the 404-bed Park Medical Center on East Broad Street from an affiliate of Quorum Health Group, Inc., of Brentwood, Tennessee, for $12.7 million. It renamed the facility, which it planned to use primarily for the development of orthopedic and family medicine programs, and increased opportunities for medical education, The Ohio State University Hospitals East.

While more could have been done, Fred Sanfilippo feels that Ohio State made good progress during the Kirwan years in becoming a true academic medical center. He cited the return to financial health, slowdown in disinvestment (i.e., fewer medical center funds going to other parts of the university), a

The Dorothy M. Davis Heart and Lung Research Institute opened in June 2000.

more engaged and accountable faculty, development of an integrated health system, more strategic investment, dramatic improvements in infrastructure, and progress in allocating resources on a "rational versus ad hoc basis."

In addition, there was an "enormous" increase in research funding—over four fiscal years, awards rose from $54 to $91 million while expenditures increased from $45 to $72 million—and significant accomplishments in focused research areas. Finally, the medical center continues to appear in the national rankings. In summer 2003, *U.S. News & World Report* included the medical center on its list of America's best hospitals for the twelfth consecutive year.

8

Enhancing the Teaching and Learning Environment

In addition to world-class faculty and academic programs, excellence requires the best possible teaching and learning environment. Here the plan's drafters focused on three obvious needs: renovation of the Main Library, higher-quality laboratories and classrooms and more attractive grounds, and the latest technological tools for teaching, learning, research, and career development.

Signature Initiative: Library Renovation

The William Oxley Thompson Memorial Library, named for Ohio State's fifth president but more often referred to as the "Main Library," sits at the center of the campus on the Oval's western boundary—a position befitting this symbolic landmark and center of campus learning. "It affects the entire face of the campus," says senior vice president Bill Shkurti. "It dominates the Oval and is a counter to the stadium." Architectural consultants called it "[g]eographically, symbolically, and functionally . . . the intellectual center of the university."

However, this symbolic and intellectual center—constructed in 1913 and added onto in ways that compromised its visual and functional integrity—has been in need of restoration for at least two decades. Continuing appeals did not fall on deaf ears, but neither did the project reach the top of the pile. A library task force appointed by the provost and chaired by English professor Sebastian Knowles reported on the eve of Kirwan's arrival. It concluded that "[t]he Main Library has fallen into a horrible, gut-wrenching state of disrepair. All the several visions of decades of well-meaning architects have wrought

President Kirwan was determined to start the ball rolling for a major renovation of the Main Library, which provides an anchor to the Oval.

such havoc on the original building that what was once the university's greatest pride is now the university's greatest humiliation." The group proposed "a newly imagined Main Library refashioned from the original Main Library building that would provide the university a center for its academic mission."

"Every single building around the Oval in need of renovation has had a major remodeling in the last 10 years, or is scheduled to have one," the June 30, 1998, report said, "except the building in the center that provides the resources for the university's research." Four years later, *U.S. News & World Report* contrasted Ohio State's spending on athletic facilities with the library, quoting the task force report's colorful description of the Main Library's reading room, which they said "had the equivalent of quadruple bypass surgery performed by unqualified baboons."

In January 2000 the library welcomed a new director to succeed William Studer, who after twenty-two years returned to a faculty position. Joseph Branin came from the State University of New York at Stony Brook, where he had served as dean and director of University Libraries. He welcomed the opportunity to direct a larger research library and was impressed by OhioLINK, a unique statewide academic library consortium Branin calls the best in the world. He was also attracted by the presence nearby of OCLC, the Ohio College Library Center, a worldwide library cooperative.

Branin inherited a good library system. In 2001 the *Chronicle of Higher Education* ranked it as the eighteenth-strongest research library in North America and the eleventh-strongest among publicly supported research libraries. It houses more than 5 million volumes in the Main Library building and seventeen library units, operates with an annual budget of well over $20 million, and has a staff of about 250 people, including more than 80 librarians with full faculty status. But there was a problem with the centerpiece building, and with the arrival of a new millennium, the time had come to transform this vital resource into a twenty-first-century facility. Thus, the library restoration became the only building project specifically mentioned in the Academic Plan.

"When I arrived at Ohio State, I saw an impressive library structure and visited it," Kirwan says. "I was positively stunned by how depressing and dilapidated and unimpressive a place it was, so incompatible with our aspirations. You can stand at the library and look at the renovated football stadium and new basketball arena. I asked myself, How can I be part of a university where this happens? For substantive and symbolic reasons, we had to act, and I told the senate that I would consider it a failure if when I leave, we haven't developed the funding for the library renovation."

With $500,000 in state planning money, Branin hired two architectural firms—URS Corporation of Columbus and Shepley Bulfinch Richardson and Abbott (SBRA) of Boston—to conduct an architectural feasibility study. Not surprisingly, the study recommended total replacement of its systems infrastructure, inclusion of new technologies consistent with the information age, and compliance with a variety of requirements and codes, including the Americans with Disabilities Act. The report presented four distinct conceptual planning options costing between $75 and $125 million, all of which included restoration of the original 1913 portion of the building, including the grand reading room overlooking the Oval, and redesign of the building's western facade. The chosen option removes alternate floors of the book tower and adds new wings to the north and south.

The cost is just under $100 million, with $70 million expected from the state of Ohio and $30 million from private gifts. George Acock Associates of Columbus and Graham Gund Architects of Cambridge, Massachusetts, were hired to do the detailed project design. Turner Construction Co.–Smoot Construction Co. of Columbus was named as the construction manager. Renovation was expected to begin in 2005 and be completed in 2008.

While the feasibility study was under way, fund-raising began. For Branin, this meant dinners at the president's house with supporters and prospects as well as a stream of visitors to tour the current facility as he went about the important task of building relationships with potential givers. Raising money started to consume 30 to 40 percent of Branin's time, and the university gave him a second full-time professional fund-raiser. "I've told this story over and over again," Branin says, "about how impressed people are with the front of the library viewed from the Oval and how their jaws drop when they tour the inside."

In June 2002, just before Kirwan left, the university announced a $5 million gift from Thomas E. and Patricia A. Duke Robinson of Troy, Ohio, to support the library renovation to be complemented by a $2 million gift from the Paul G. Duke Foundation.

"The library project would not have happened without Brit," Jerry May says. "Ed Ray was also enormously supportive. Libraries tend to lack a constituency, and fewer than half a dozen university libraries have been built with major fund-raising. Brit and Ed gave us authority to approach the deans, asking them to share their prospects with the library drive. Thus, it is a matter of will; if you really want to do it, you can."

Aesthetics Matter: Buildings and Grounds

The Academic Plan also reflected the reality that too many classrooms were outdated and in various stages of disrepair and that too large a portion of the campus grounds required attention. When President Kirwan addressed students on campus for the Scholar Maximus Competition, at which Ohio State seeks to lure the best and brightest students, he was embarrassed. "We were competing for these kids with the University of Michigan, Miami of Ohio, and the Ivy League schools," he says. "How we look is important."

"Brit cared about how the campus looked," remembers Alayne Parson. "If you walked with him, he would say, 'This courtyard looks terrible.'"

"I was interested in aesthetics," Kirwan confirms. "That included a landscaping initiative and an Oval master plan, which I blessed. The Oval is potentially one of the really grand academic sites in America. The campus grew like rings of a tree. The inner core was built with care, but as you moved out in later years, the growth of the sixties and seventies showed less concern. And those towers! Now, more attention is being paid to such things."

What to do with the Oval, apart from renovation of the Main Library, prompted considerable discussion, especially over the kinds of activities that were appropriate for that prime location. The decision was to limit Oval frontage to student-based core academic facilities, and two current projects made powerful symbolic statements on behalf of the humanities. One is the $24 million renovation of Hagerty Hall—formerly home to the School of Business—into a World Media and Culture Center. The other is a $16 million renovation of Page Hall to house the John Glenn Institute for Public Service and Public Policy and the School of Public Policy and Management. "We made a huge commitment to Page Hall," Kirwan recalls, "moving it up in the capital queue."

As to the Oval itself, the university approved a phased project to replace walkways and restore turf and tree plantings. There was a facelift of Mirror Lake, another focal point of the campus, and plans for new bridges over the Olentangy River on Lane Avenue and Woody Hayes Drive—with the former bridge already completed.

The Academic Plan called for building additional state-of-the-art classrooms while enhancing classroom cleanliness and providing modern equipment and, on the maintenance side, adding project cleaning teams to augment custodial staff along with high-intensity grounds maintenance on seven highly visible areas of the campus. It also called for funding to fully equip approximately 250,000 assigned square feet of new research space, including a multidisciplinary

Students enjoy lunch outdoors on the Oval.

building. Likewise, several new and renovated classroom and general-purpose academic structures were approved, begun, or completed during the Kirwan era. The most striking of these, for which ground was broken in 2002, is the new Austin E. Knowlton School of Architecture at the corner of West Woodruff Avenue and Tuttle Park Place—the former site of Ives Hall, across the street from the Fisher College of Business and Ohio Stadium. It offers a good example of what presidents do.

"Dutch" Knowlton was an architect and successful builder with an affinity for university presidents. He knew eight presidents at Ohio State and got along especially well with Gee and Kirwan. Knowlton liked to kid people, and when Rob Livesey, director of the Austin E. Knowlton School of Architecture, introduced him to Kirwan, Knowlton pretended not to understand Kirwan's name. "It's Brit," Livesey finally said to Knowlton, "you know, like Dutch."

Under Gee, Knowlton had donated $10 million—matched by the state of Ohio—to renovate the existing architecture building and build an addition. Knowlton also commissioned the construction of five twenty-three-foot-high marble columns representing the classical orders of architecture: Tuscan, Doric, Ionic, Corinthian, and Composite. "He wanted a marble building, but

An executive education facility at the Fisher College of Business exemplifies the latest in classroom design and technology.

they don't build marble buildings anymore," Kirwan said. "Rob Livesey and I tried to talk him out of it. I probably spent more time with him [Knowlton] than any other donor [trying to change his mind]. Meanwhile, the cost kept rising, and we kept seeking more money."

In the spring of 2000 Kirwan asked Knowlton for an additional $15 million to build a completely new Knowlton School building. It was what Knowlton had wanted all along, and he agreed to give $6 million. The result was a memorable Saturday morning of shuttle diplomacy at which Kirwan, the only person Knowlton would deal with on the matter, went back and forth with Knowlton on the wording of an agreement—checking by phone along the way with Jerry May, Ed Ray, Ginny Trethewey, and others until the irrevocable gift language was finally approved by everyone. "I went to his house four times that day," Kirwan recalls.

Knowlton died in 2003. The $33 million structure was completed in 2004.

In sum, as many remarked, a lot of building was going on. "We're seeing the largesse of the nineties building boom on campus now," university architect Jill Morelli explains. "I hear comments downtown about all the money. But much

The new Austin E. Knowlton Architecture Building was begun during the Kirwan years.

of it is coming from a different pot than state support, what we call 'different colors of money.' At the same time, it pales in comparison with the fifties and early sixties, the extended postwar period. Based on square footage, the seventies and eighties were light, which made the nineties seem big."

Technology

The consolidation of various information technology organizations began under President Gee and reached its logical conclusion under President Kirwan. By 1994 academic computing (ACS or Academic Computing Services) and instructional technology (CTE or the Center for Teaching Excellence) had been combined into Academic Technology Services (ATS), which in turn was combined with administrative computing support (US or University Systems) to form University Technology Services (UTS). In July 2000, with the end of the Administrative Resource Management Systems (ARMS) project, the trustees combined ARMS and UTS with UNITS, the campus telecommunications utility, to form an Office of Information Technology (OIT). With that move, all central information technology organizations were integrated under a single management.

With these consolidations also came more sustained management attention. As senior vice provost, Ed Ray had also been the university's first chief information officer beginning in 1993. When Ray became provost in late 1998, he named UTS director Jim Davis interim chief information officer and launched a national search for a permanent CIO. Before the position was filled, Davis departed to become associate vice chancellor of Information Technology at UCLA, and Eileen Strider—and later, Mike Veres—assumed the reins on a temporary basis. On November 15, 2000, Ilee Rhimes became the university's first full-time chief information officer, coming to Columbus from the City Colleges of Chicago, where he had been vice chancellor for Information Technology and chief information officer.

When the trustees approved formation of the Office of Information Technology, Dimon McFerson, former CEO of Nationwide and a new trustee, amended the resolution to include strategic planning for future technology needs. Under Rhimes's leadership, the university embarked upon its first comprehensive campuswide information technology strategic planning initiative in late 2001, at the same time moving forward on a host of other projects.

To cover new technology expenses, a number of colleges assessed student fees, and in the spring of 2000 the Board of Trustees voted to implement a university-wide $50-per-quarter Learning Technology Fee. This required the Ohio Board of Regents and Ohio Controlling Board to grant Ohio State an exemption from the state's resident undergraduate fee cap, a request which, in a portent of problems to come, was denied.

Nonetheless, progress continued. By spring 2002, thirteen new central classrooms had been technology-enabled, for a total of seventy-six; thirteen existing technology-enabled classrooms were upgraded; and 228 computers were upgraded in student labs. In addition, a Pew Foundation grant was obtained to support the redesign of Statistics 135, a course that enrolls 3,250 students annually while turning many students away. The methodology employed offered the potential to help redesign other large courses.

The university also moved to enhance its work in distance education, also known as distributed learning. A distance education committee led by Bobby Moser, vice president for Agricultural Administration and University Outreach, found that Ohio State's effort was distinguished mostly by its intent to blend technology with the university's traditional missions, rather than treat it as an add-on activity. Examples include a family nurse practitioner M.S. degree delivered online by the College of Nursing and a doctorate in pharmacy offered online by the College of Pharmacy.

The committee recommended creation of a Distributive Education Support Unit to include technology support, instructional support, student services, business services, and an advisory body chaired by Moser. Susan Metros, a nationally recognized leader in this field, was hired as deputy CIO and executive director of Educational Technology and Distributive Learning to provide vision, leadership, and expertise for this initiative. Another outcome was a digital Knowledge Bank to generate, collect, index, and preserve the university's intellectual content. Helping the university think through and develop such a resource were nearby Chemical Abstracts and OCLC.

When the Kirwan years came to a close, Ohio State was making steady progress in the application of information technology. While not a leader in the field, it no longer used the term "fast follower" and had set its sights on a leadership position one day. Today, as at many other schools, students can apply for admission, register, check grades, and reserve library books on the World Wide Web. Starting in 2001, graduate students could submit dissertations electronically on the Web if they chose.

Information technology is a key part of education today.

By 2002 more than 97 percent of Ohio State students had computers in their local residences and 95 percent were connected to the Internet. A centrally supported standard campuswide course management system based in the WebCT product and industrial-strength server hardware was serving more than thirty-five thousand students enrolled in over seven hundred course selections. Graduate students trained student interns who in turn helped faculty members integrate technology into their teaching activities. Once a course is established online, students can go to the Internet and read the syllabus, get homework assignments, e-mail instructors, and link to Web sites. For their part, faculty can monitor student work, post grades, create chat groups, and automatically update the student information system.

Robert Robinson, a graduate student in history who assisted with this book, tells of a history class in which students entered to music from the time period under study, heard a PowerPoint-augmented lecture during which the professor utilized a live Internet connection to access audio/video files of Franklin Roosevelt. In classes where Robinson served as a teaching assistant, 90 percent of his one-on-one discussions with students took place via e-mail. Frequently, students received electronic copies of each other's work products.

In sum, it's a long way from the Little Red Schoolhouse.

9

Serving the Student Body

Since the presidency of Ed Jennings, Ohio State has worked hard to increase the academic quality of the undergraduate student body. Jennings oversaw a change from open to selective admissions and strengthened the Honors Program. Additional money for merit scholarships and programs such as the University Scholar Maximus Competition in the early 1990s encouraged better-prepared students to attend Ohio State. "We went from twenty-seven National Merit Scholars to one hundred overnight," recalls Mabel Freeman, assistant vice president for Undergraduate Admissions and First Year Experience. "It changed the perception of Ohio State."

As the years went by, the momentum increased. From autumn 1995 through the autumn of 2001, ACT score averages rose from 22.8 to 25.2, while the percentage of fall freshmen in the top 10 percent of their high school class rose from 21 to 32 percent.

A related priority was to improve undergraduate retention and graduation rates. Assigned to tackle this task, as well as to enhance a sense of undergraduate community, was the 1994–95 Committee on the Undergraduate Experience. Its recommendations formed a road map that the university follows to this day, and first-year retention grew from almost 78 percent among 1994 fall freshmen to 87.5 percent for freshmen in the fall of 2002.

Himself a National Merit Scholar, Gee strongly embraced such moves. During his tenure, an enrollment management steering committee chaired by Kermit Hall monitored progress and recommended further improvements. The strategy seemed to be working, but now Ohio State was getting a new president.

"Brit embraced and then embodied and articulated a vision which had been developing—a weaving together of Ed Jennings's views and Gordon's views,"

Martha Garland makes the rounds at a dinner reception in 2000.

says Martha Garland, vice provost and dean of Undergraduate Studies. "Instead of veering off, we consolidated all that in a very good way and right in the heart of it was excellence for students."

Once again, therefore, there was solid historical underpinning for the Academic Plan goal to enhance and better serve the student body. "More talented and better-prepared students," the plan said, "require less remediation, face fewer academic difficulties, and graduate in higher numbers and in a shorter time span. Better-prepared students," it continued, "also help attract better faculty, grants and awards, and enhance the university's academic reputation."

With this in mind, the plan advocated the extension of "selective" admissions—later called "competitive" admissions—to further strengthen the undergraduate student body and the creation of "a rich educational environment for undergraduates," including greater course accessibility, reduced class sizes, more Scholars programs, and more need-based and merit-based aid. For graduate and professional students, the plan called for a competitive financial aid and fellowship support package to improve graduate and professional matriculation rates.

When it became necessary to raise undergraduate tuition sharply, the impact on economically disadvantaged students was softened with attempts to hold them harmless. During the last two academic years of the Kirwan era, approximately 20 percent of such new fee revenue was earmarked for additional undergraduate student financial aid, allowing Ohio State to provide more need-based aid than other Ohio public colleges and universities. In addition, as explained in chapter 12, tuition receipts above the former 6 percent cap were earmarked for undergraduate programs. And when it came time to select a very few initial plan priorities, enhancing the undergraduate experience easily made the list.

There were other major student-related changes as well, including increasingly effective programs from Student Affairs and a major rethinking and revitalization of the regional campuses.

Signature Initiative: Excellence for All

Success in attracting the very best students brought with it the unintended consequence of losing some students at a level immediately below honors, the A-minus/B-plus student that Ohio State also wanted to attract. "High school guidance counselors were telling their kids to apply to Ohio State if they were honors students but otherwise not," says Mabel Freeman, who then worked with the Honors Program. "We were losing good kids." Looking around the country for model programs to help attract these kids, administrators kept hearing about Maryland's College Park Scholars Program, then in its second or third year.

Thus, in April 1998, Martha Garland, Mabel Freeman, Kathy Cleveland-Bull, and Steve Kremer were part of a group that traveled to College Park to see this program firsthand. At Dulles Airport, they ran into Kirwan, who was returning from a transition visit to Columbus. "He was thrilled we had been there," Freeman remembers. "The Scholars Program had [Brit's] handprints all over it."

From Honors to Scholars

Believing that research universities give too little attention to undergraduates, Kirwan wanted to extend the honors concept to as many students as possible. One way to do that was with a Maryland-type Scholars Program, a component of which was already present: living-learning programs in which students with similar interests live in the same residence hall. In addition, the CUE report

Like other presidents, Kirwan always enjoyed spending time with students—in this case, honors students.

proposed finding ways to make the university seem smaller and more welcoming for freshmen—another feature of Maryland's initiative.

The university's Honors Program is typically open to freshmen who rank in the top 10 percent of their high school class, with ACT composite scores of at least 29 or SAT combined scores of 1300 or above. Eligible for merit scholarships ranging from $750 Trustees Scholarships to full-ride Presidential Scholarships, these students choose from over 240 Honors classes that average fewer than twenty-five students and are taught by select faculty.

The Scholars Program, in contrast, is open to those graduating in the top 20 percent of their high school class, with ACT composite scores of 25 to 28 or SAT combined scores of 1140 to 1290. Beyond living and studying with other students who share their academic interest and career goals, Scholars receive individual advising, mentoring, and support and participate in special social events and student activities, including extensive program-specific cocurricular activities. They also receive priority course scheduling and the opportunity to participate in special research seminars designed for Scholars Program students.

In Garland's words, Scholars programs "blurred the bottom edges of Honors so that it was not Honors and Others but a continuum of good students."

President Kirwan greets parents and students at the Ruth Mount Scholar reception in 2000.

And they came along, she added, at a time when Student Affairs was eager to help build living-learning residence programs across the campus.

The Academic Plan called for establishing at least ten Scholars programs within five years. Starting in 1999 with the Mount Leadership Society, nine such living-learning programs were created by autumn 2002 with a tenth added a year later. Today, approximately two thousand students participate in the Scholars Program. More broadly, there are some forty-five living-learning communities at Ohio State, and by spring 2002, four in five incoming freshmen participated in such programs. The goal was to have 20 percent of the undergraduates in the Honors Program and another 20 percent in Scholars.

But while the Scholars initiative succeeded, it did not come easily. "The Scholars Program proved an incredibly difficult sell," Kirwan says. "They bought into it [only] because I wanted it. It reflects tension in the role of a university. Is it too elitist? But you can only go so far with Honors, and Scholars adds a diversity component." Dan Farrell, a former chair of Philosophy who directed the Honors and Scholars programs for two years after Scholars had been created, explains that Scholars was established without faculty consultation and that some faculty feared that Scholars would dilute Honors. In any event, he believes the Scholars Program is "working really well."

Enhancing the Student Experience

Driven by the Academic Plan and the CUE report, and determined to progress from better-prepared students to improved retention to more advanced academic achievement and accelerated graduation timetables, the university continued its efforts to enhance the undergraduate experience in a variety of ways.

"Brit was a champion for freshmen," Freeman says. "[In assessing his presidency], you have got to start there." Thus, in March 2000 Brit Kirwan and Ed Ray asked that the honors approach be extended to all freshmen, meaning that every incoming student received the same advantages in the hope it would increase retention and graduation rates.

The result was the First Year Experience Program, engaging the university community in the development of small seminar courses and other programs to ease the transition of first-year freshmen and transfer students into the university community—in effect, to make a big university seem small. "New students need more than a two-day orientation to make an effective transition into college and beyond their first year," says Freeman. "We provide ongoing networks of resources and programs to help them manage their time, their finances, and their new independence, while they pursue the academic opportunities that Ohio State offers."

Mabel Freeman's contributions included the First Year Experience Program.

Jim Mager helped develop strategies to raise the preparation level of entering students.

Garland credits Jim Mager, associate vice president for Enrollment Management, for enrollment management planning and for strategies that raised ACT scores. "Jim also developed the idea of linking the First Year Experience Program with the Admissions Office and persuaded Mabel Freeman to take on the job," Garland adds.

Such programs were noticed nationally. In 2002 *U.S. News & World Report* ranked Ohio State's living-learning programs as the nation's eighteenth-best program to assure student success; it ranked the First Year Experience Program seventh best.

Other initiatives included smaller classes, more openings in high-demand courses that could create bottlenecks to timely graduation, more and better classroom teaching development programs for faculty and graduate associates, and curricular enhancements that respond to student needs, such as a new minor in Business and a proposed general Health Sciences major. In addition, student financial services were centralized, registration was simplified, and a computerized course-monitoring program was created, along with a program to prepare students for postbaccalaureate fellowships. There are also increasing opportunities for undergraduates to incorporate research experiences into their learning, including the Denman Undergraduate Research Forum.

Historically, University College served as an "intake" college for new students, who typically began their association with their "major" colleges in their junior year. A 1998 study found that admitting freshmen directly into the college that would become their field of study, rather than beginning them in the all-purpose University College program, offered several benefits. It identified them more quickly with their major, built better relationships with faculty, and improved the effectiveness of advising services. University leaders were also aware that academic advising was a key element of academic success.

Thus, the university emphasized direct enrollment, and in May 2001, with board approval, created an Office of Undergraduate Studies under the supervision of the vice provost and dean for Undergraduate Studies. At the same time, the university combined the advising resources of University College and the Colleges of the Arts and Sciences administration into an Office of Undergraduate Student Academic Services (USAS).

"With this new structure," Martha Garland said, "we will be able to place new students close to their academic area—and the advisers who specialize in those areas—as early as possible." Garland added that students would have two advisors, a full-time professional to offer advice on general topics and a faculty member to advise them in their specific major field. In addition, an "Exploration" unit within USAS helps "undecided" students select a major and consider various career options.

One outgrowth of such changes has been a surge in the number of students who pursue more than one major or degree at a time. At the four commencements in the 2000–2001 academic year, for example, 540 undergraduates graduated with either a double major or a dual degree—one combining Chinese with molecular genetics.

In the spring of 2000, the university opened its $8.6 million Younkin Success Center at 1640 Neil Avenue, consolidating several student and some faculty services under one roof. Conceived in the mid- to late 1990s by Andy Geiger, David Williams and Nancy Zimpher, then dean of Education and now president of the University of Cincinnati, it houses a new Academic Learning Lab, Student Athlete Support Services, Counseling and Consultation Service, the Career Connection Office, Faculty and TA Development, and a resource library. The facility recognizes the family of the late Floyd Younkin of Columbus, which contributed $2 million to the project.

"It's like a supermarket open to everyone on campus," says Kate Riffee, director of Student Athletic Support Services. "Students can type a paper, hang out between classes, see a tutor or a counselor and not leave the building." First-floor occupancy made the facility pedestrian-friendly.

"We're focusing on acceleration, not remediation," says Louise A. Douce, director of Counseling and Consultation Service. "We're really contributing to the success of all students and faculty." "The center is not just for undergraduate students or student athletes," adds Chris Rideout, director of Career Connection and staff psychologist in Counseling and Consultation Service. "We want faculty, teaching assistants, and graduate and professional students to feel comfortable coming to the Success Center."

Many of the programs were made possible by higher tuition and other special sources of funding. For example, $1 million of a $5 million gift from the Longaberger family was earmarked for undergraduate activities. And President Kirwan offered Martha Garland and Bill Hall $1 million per year for three years from his Strategic Investment Fund to enhance the undergraduate experience.

"I met with Martha and Bill and requested a proposal," Kirwan recalls. "They were used to getting crumbs and submitted a modest plan. 'No,' I said, 'think more boldly.'" "You can't ask for a better president than that," Garland concludes.

What's more, Kirwan loved being with students. "Gordon was very effective at connecting with students," Kirwan said later. "I wanted to be visible and available, too."

Finally, there was closure in selective admissions. The policy adopted in 1987 had been limited to the autumn quarter, with open admissions continuing in the spring quarter and less competitive admissions in the summer and winter quarters and for transfer students.

Not surprisingly, the university was facing a growing divide between the better-prepared students entering in the autumn quarter and those admitted during other times of the academic year. Just as in the 1980s, when many admitted students failed to make the grade and soon dropped out of school, the less well-prepared students were much more likely to depart the university without a diploma than their better-prepared counterparts. In fact, 31 percent of the freshmen entering in winter quarter and just 17 percent of those entering in the spring graduated within six years—compared with 62 percent of entering fall freshmen. And not only were the less well-prepared students less likely to succeed academically, many were leaving school unhappy with their experience and carrying substantial debt. These students, it was thought, might fare better at another university or community college.

Admitting students who are unlikely to succeed helps neither the university nor the students, says Garland. She served on the Enrollment Management Committee, which at the time was chaired by Mike Hogan and resourced principally by Jim Mager and which planned the final stage of selective admissions.

The Academic Plan proposed to make admission to Ohio State selective throughout the year for new freshmen and for all transfer students within three years. In October 2002, just over three months after Kirwan's departure, the Board of Trustees extended competitive admissions year-round for freshmen, effective the summer of 2003. (Criteria for transfer students were not changed.) Interestingly, this almost happened under the interim presidency of Ed Jennings, who had started the ball rolling fifteen years earlier, but was delayed a month so the administration could assure the minority community that there would be no major impact on minority student representation.

Strong Support from Student Affairs

Creating and maintaining the services to support almost fifty thousand students, especially on the second-largest campus in the nation, requires a significant organization. With thirty-six hundred employees and a broad mission, Student Affairs is a pervasive force in the university community. It operates

Ohio State's student housing and campus dining services and manages the Schottenstein Center, Ohio Union, Blackwell Inn, Fawcett Center, and Stone Lab, among other facilities. Greek life, Service Learning, student health services, nonacademic student counseling, recreational sports, disability services, the Younkin Success Center, the Multicultural Center, Living-Learning Centers, and the Student Housing Legal Clinic are among its many responsibilities.

When Brit Kirwan arrived on campus, Student Affairs was led by David Williams II, who joined Ohio State in 1986 as an assistant professor of Law. After serving as vice provost for Minority Affairs and director of the University of Oxford–Ohio State summer law program, Williams was promoted to full professor and vice president for Student Affairs. Athletics and Campus Partners reported to him as well, and his ultimate title was vice president for Student and Urban/Community Affairs. An African American, Williams was a strong advocate for diversity and a key contributor to the development of the Academic and Diversity Action Plans.

In June 2000 Williams accepted an offer from Gordon Gee to become the vice chancellor, general counsel, and secretary at Vanderbilt University, where Gee had become president after a brief tenure at Brown. When Williams departed, Bill Hall was named interim vice president for Student Affairs, with the understanding that he would not be a candidate for the permanent position. While Kirwan was impressed by Hall, he was concerned about losing the only minority among senior university officials and hoped the best candidate would be another minority—a realistic possibility since the recruiting pool for this position was fairly deep. What's more, he wanted the search to be completely open so as not to turn off potential candidates. Hall understood, conscious not only of the minority issue but also that he lacked the Ph.D. that a majority of student affairs leaders at larger universities today possess.

"During the search," Kirwan recounted later, "everybody was so impressed with Bill and his leadership, his compassion, and the fact he was a very outspoken and strong advocate for diversity. More and more, people urged me to pick him. Bill came and asked that he be considered. Now that the pool was already formed, I said yes. There were four finalists, the other three minorities. Eddie Pauline and other students lobbied for Hall. Then a group of minority students came to meet with me, leaders of the Black Student Union."

"'We hope you will select Bill Hall,' they said. "I was very moved. It was a demonstration that while diversity is a very important goal, we go with the very best people."

Hall had joined Ohio State in 1977 as director of administration and operations of residence and dining halls, and was made an assistant vice president

Bill Hall speaking at the dedication of the Multicultural Center.

in 1994. Coming from the University of Southern Illinois, where he earned bachelor's and master's degrees and later directed the housing program, he also had a distinguished military career, retiring in 1998 as a brigadier general with the Ohio Army National Guard and graduating from the U.S. Army War College. He knew the operation and the strengths of its people, and through reorganization and leadership added more central delivery of support services and increased cooperation within Student Affairs and elsewhere.

"I aligned the associate and assistant vice presidents with their strengths [and] redirected resources from some of the larger units toward priorities of the Academic Plan," Hall says. What about his commitment to diversity? "I think that came from my parents initially," he said. "In high school, I recall seeing on television the images from the South . . . fire hoses and clubs; that had a tremendous impact on me. I come from a very lower-income family to begin with, a large family. And the military certainly encouraged diversity."

Over the four Kirwan years, Student Affairs played an active role on many fronts. None was more significant than its increasing collaboration with the Office of Academic Affairs, a combination that addressed the total development of Ohio State students and the Academic Plan's commitment to student success. These collaborations included the Younkin Success Center, which Student Affairs runs; the Living-Learning Centers, where they provide programming as well as manage the housing component; new student orientation; and service learning. Another example of partnerships is a student-run restaurant managed jointly with the College of Human Ecology.

Student Affairs also adopted a serious diversity agenda, exemplified by its key role in creating the Multicultural Center described in chapter 10.

The Kirwan years also saw progress in Greek life, where Williams and Hall—strongly backed by President Kirwan—wanted to more closely align the values of sororities and fraternities with those of the university and its academic mission. As an undergraduate at the University of Kentucky, Kirwan had been a member of Delta Tau Delta—Patty had joined Delta Delta Delta—and he remained a Greek supporter. At the same time, while at Maryland Kirwan sought to reform fraternities and sororities by limiting their social functions, maintaining academic standards, involving Greeks in community service, and reforming the rush/pledge process.

At Ohio State, Kirwan found a Greek system in decline, with just 5 percent of the student body participating in Greek activities—compared to 22 percent at Illinois, 17 percent at Michigan, 16 percent at Purdue, and 11 percent at Penn State. It did not help that *Rolling Stone* magazine featured Ohio State sororities in an exposé portraying examples of alcohol and drug abuse.

In 1999 David Williams created a Greek life task force to reinvigorate fraternities and sororities by raising academic and behavioral standards. The task force established stretch goals for academic achievement, member and organizational growth, and chapter environment—with chapters required to submit plans delineating their progress. A Greek progress review board was established to ensure that progress was being made. All of this led to action.

"There's a new sheriff in town at Student Affairs, and his name is Bill Hall," wrote a *Lantern* columnist in September 2000, and several houses were disciplined over the next few years. For the first time in many years, the fraternity grade point average exceeded the university average for all male students.

Other Student Affairs highlights included

- the signing in 1998 of a ten-year contract giving Coca-Cola exclusive on-campus "pouring rights" in exchange for approximately $30 million in cash, services, and products used in a wide range of academic and student activities;
- planning for a $26 million renovation of the Ohio Union;

a planned $140 million restoration of and addition to Larkins Hall into a more than six-hundred-thousand-square-foot Recreation and Physical Activity Center;

Service Learning courses that combine academic learning with related hands-on community involvement; and

generally constructive relations between the administration and student government leaders. Bill Hall, President Kirwan, and others worked closely with Undergraduate Student Government (USG) presidents Josh Mandel, Robert "B.J." Schuerger, Ryan Robinson, and Eddie Pauline. Kirwan "brought them into the inner circle," Hall says. "It was one reason they supported the [two-tier] tuition increase." At the same time, several USG officers were sanctioned by the university and removed from their positions in February 2001 for misuse of funds, dishonest conduct, and interference with distribution of *The Lantern.*

Graduate/Professional Students

Three studies of graduate and/or professional education were initiated in the 1990s and influenced activity during the Kirwan years. One was the research commission, which found that, "[e]ven in some strong departments, OSU appears less able to attract graduate students from highly-ranked programs than some leading peers." The other two studies were the G-QUE and I-QUE reports, both inspired by the 1995 CUE report on the undergraduate experience.

G-QUE, the Graduate Quality of University Experience, was a joint project of the Graduate School and the Council of Graduate Students. Launched in the fall of 1997, it was based largely on information from censuses and survey instruments. While almost all graduate students said they had had a positive experience at Ohio State, there were concerns, including the fact that almost half of the university's graduate teaching associates (GTAs) had not participated in university-wide training. Other complaints focused on such areas as residence halls and inadequate compensation and benefits. Those who had been admitted but elected to go elsewhere explained their decisions in terms of better financial assistance and several factors relating to the admissions process.

Susan Huntington, dean of the Graduate School, vice provost for Graduate Studies, and cofounder of the John C. and Susan L. Huntington Archive on Buddhist and Related Art, presented preliminary findings to the Board of Trustees in May 2000—with a final report appearing the following year.

Among the report's recommendations were to improve professional development and training for graduate students, including the aggressive enhancement of GTA training provided to graduate students; enhance career advising and placement services; and offer more generous fellowships, stipends, and financial aid along with health care assistance.

Again, these needs were incorporated into the Academic Plan. Taking early G-QUE and research commission recommendations into account, the plan called for attracting the best graduate students and providing a more competitive financial aid and fellowship support package for graduate and professional students.

Designed by the Inter-Professional Council, I-QUE was a joint student-administrative effort based conceptually on the CUE and G-QUE projects, with professional students taking the lead at each stage. Like G-QUE, I-QUE also began with a survey whose recommendations were to increase central administration's awareness of, and restructure administrative links to, professional students; improve the structure and appearance of facilities; improve access, safety and security; increase clinical experiences; support the growth of professional students; and improve diversity within IPC colleges.

"They wanted a central administration advocate," says Vice Provost Carole Anderson, who assumed that role, adding that many of their needs are handled within individual colleges. Now, associate deans of the professional schools meet regularly and are included in some relevant G-QUE subcommittee discussions.

Although the financial climate limited the university's ability to implement G-QUE and I-QUE recommendations, some progress was made. Graduate student stipends were increased beginning in August 2001, and graduate associates were included in benchmarking and the competitive compensation initiative. The university also phased in the subsidization of health care insurance costs for graduate students, and training became mandatory for all GTAs in 2003. Also, for the first time since Jones Tower was opened in 1969, the university began work in 2002 on new student housing—this time for more than five hundred graduate, professional, and upper-division undergraduate students. Located on Neil Avenue between West 9th and 10th Avenues, the four-story building houses students in 203 apartments and 48 double rooms. A shortage of such housing has forced many graduate and professional students to live off campus, isolating them from university activities. Student Affairs issued bonds to finance the $32 million project, with rent used to pay off the bonds.

Finally, when the university launched its benchmarking and compensation initiative, it began to include graduate associates while also raising their minimum stipend and beginning to phase in a partial health care subsidy.

Regional Campuses: Part of a University System

Unlike Ohio State's main campus in Columbus, its four regional campuses at Lima, Mansfield, Marion, and Newark maintain an open-admissions policy—an alternate way to access the university and earn a degree from The Ohio State University. Depending upon majors, students can earn their degree at a regional campus or finish in Columbus. The regionals also provide a safety valve against criticism that competitive admissions contradict the university's land-grant mission. Experience shows that less well-prepared students who spend a year or two at a regional campus—or at one of seven community colleges with which Ohio State has formal articulation agreements—generally do well when they transfer to Columbus.

"Access was always an issue with the General Assembly and others because of the land-grant mission," says Judge Robert Duncan, former secretary of the university's Board of Trustees and a trustee today. "What Brit did was bring people together and reach consensus on that and sell the idea that access can be gained through the regionals and two-years. That was a quantum leap in philosophy and attitude about how people felt about Ohio State. That was the legacy—the blueprint or the map for the future of the university, and that's huge."

Further, the regional campuses extend Ohio State's reach and offer convenient geographical access to many students. They also enhance the university's economic development effectiveness and through outreach and engagement strengthen learning opportunities within those communities.

The Kirwan years were pivotal for the regional campuses, primarily because of a commission named in June 2001 to chart their future. Chairing the Presidential Commission on Regional Campuses was Bobby Moser, vice president for Agricultural Administration and University Outreach who also chaired groups on Outreach and Engagement and Technology during the Kirwan years. The seventeen-member group included university trustees Jim Patterson and Karen Hendricks and Newark board member Tom Brannon and was led day-to-day by Randy Smith, vice provost for Curriculum and Institutional Relations. Their report was summarized at Kirwan's final Board of Trustees meeting on June 7, 2002, and issued just before he left.

Students in a math class at the Marion campus.

"We're not closing anybody out of this land-grant institution," Moser told the trustees, "and we need to communicate effectively with our applicants that there are many ways to access the university. The most important thing is to get a degree from Ohio State, and helping our students find their place in the system will be key to making sure they're successful."

The threshold question for the commission was whether Ohio State is a one-university system or a federation of campuses. "We are not a federation of universities," Moser told the trustees. "We are The Ohio State University with many locations." Among the major recommendations from four subcommittees were the following:

Mission/Governance focused on the "one university" issue and its affect on the university's vision as well as the need to modify regional campus bylaws and find ways to think more systemically and improve coordination.

Admissions/Enrollment suggested that, beginning in 2003, entering students be asked to indicate on their application a first and alternate choice for campus location and that students be required to complete forty-five credit hours, rather than thirty, before moving to the Columbus campus.

Students/Student Services recommended that Ohio State adopt the OSU-owned and managed approach to student housing on the regional campuses and that these campuses collaborate with Student Affairs in Columbus in developing student activities and services.

Faculty/Curriculum suggested looking in more detail at other institutions with regional campuses for creative solutions to curriculum issues and proposed some modest expansion of undergraduate major programs at regional campuses.

This period was also marked by enrollment growth at all four campuses, especially Newark and Marion, and by leadership stability under Violet Meek at Lima, John Riedl at Mansfield, Dominic Dottavio at Marion, and Anne Cairns Federlein at Newark. (All have since retired or left the university.) Internal planning was intense during these years, and there was significant expansion of physical facilities. All four campuses today have some form of student housing. Another trend at these "branches" is the creation of "twigs," such as the rented Bellefontaine Center at Lima and the Delaware Center at which Marion students can take courses without driving to Marion.

Regional campuses have come a long way over recent years. Gordon Gee gave them their own boards of trustees; Brit Kirwan outlined a big picture of what the regionals could become, a picture that Ed Ray and Randy Smith made happen. Contact between the campuses and Columbus accelerated, with Kirwan and Ray visiting each campus—and meeting with campus constituencies—at least once per year. The one-system approach is well launched. What's more, gift receipts to regional campuses rose from $1.8 million in 1998–99 to $3.4 million in 2001–2002 and $5.3 million in 2002–2003.

Commencements

With four per year, one for each academic quarter, commencements at Ohio State consume significant time. There are four ceremonies, four commencement speakers, four logistical challenges, and four opportunities for student protests. Thus, while serving "only" four years as president, Kirwan participated in sixteen commencement ceremonies. Ohio State is unique among major universities in having one university-wide commencement each quarter in which each graduate receives his or her actual diploma. Summer, autumn, and winter commencements are held indoors, usually in St. John Arena or the

Jerome Schottenstein Center. The spring ceremony is outdoors, with well over 6,000 graduates, 30,000 guests, and 250 volunteers.

For years, spring commencements were held on the Oval, but since 1927, most took place in Ohio Stadium. During the three-year renovation of the "Horseshoe," however, it was necessary to find another venue. Kirwan was a strong proponent of returning to the Oval, which he saw as a more appropriate site for this capstone academic event.

"Commencement on the Oval was everything I had hoped for," Kirwan says of the 1999 event, the first there since 1918 and held during a blazing heat wave. It was so remarkable to him that he felt compelled to take a picture—producing a camera and pointing it at the crowd. In 2000 a small group of graduates stood in protest and blocked spectators' view during remarks by Republican Congressman J. C. Watts. They were warned, evicted from the Oval, and arrested. Also at that event, the university's five-hundred-thousandth diploma was presented to Ebony Bonner, who received a Master of Social Work degree. Calm returned the next year when Bill Cosby charmed the audience.

When Bill Hall reported that students wished to return to Ohio Stadium in June 2002, after three years on the Oval, Kirwan relented. Planners considered the stadium, with its holding rooms, more practical, especially in case of inclement weather.[5]

The last time a sitting U.S. president addressed an OSU commencement was Gerald Ford in August 1974, and several trustees wanted to bring President George W. Bush to Columbus in 2002. A number of factors combined to make that happen, among them that alumnus Bryan Besanceney worked in the White House and that Ohio was a vital electoral battleground.

As Carol Ries, director of the Office of Commencement and Special Events, knows better than anyone, hosting a president, especially during the first commencement season after 9/11, is not without its challenges. Security, of course, was a major consideration. Further, Bush had been booed at Yale the year before, and the White House was understandably nervous. Attendees were asked to arrive at 6:30 AM for the 9:30 AM ceremony, and everyone was supposed to have a (free) ticket. Many students were unhappy, not liking Bush and/or worrying that his presence would overshadow their event. White House advance people wanted some students seated on the field, rather than in the stands where they usually sit, so they would be visible to television cameras, which had the effect of separating students one from another.

There was one other problem. Prior to commencement, Richard Hollingsworth, associate vice president for Student Affairs, advised graduates

Bill Cosby charmed the crowd on the Oval at the spring 2001 commencement.

that peaceful protest was allowed but that disruptions—including obstructing the view or hearing of others—would result in removal from the stadium and possible arrest. It is a spiel he always delivers, but this time an Associated Press reporter overheard Hollingsworth's remarks and filed a story even before the ceremony began. Some students had been promoting a "turn your back on Bush" protest, and, by OSU's count, two students and six visitors stood up and turned their backs.

"They were politely approached [and told] not to obstruct the view of others, and they complied," OSU spokeswoman Amy Murray-Goedde told reporters. There were no arrests, and few people took notice.

"We left the event happy that it had gone so well," Lee Tashjian says. "When I arrived back in Bricker [Hall], there was a flood of e-mails from all over the

When President George W. Bush spoke at the spring 2002 commencement, it was the first such presidential appearance since Gerald Ford in 1974.

world with accusations of Gestapo tactics, violations of academic freedom, a police state, etc. I sent out a statement with the facts, but that did not work. Most wrote me back calling my response a bunch of lies."

Despite this mini-flap, the event was attended by at least fifty-thousand people, Bush urged graduates to serve their country, and the day worked well. "It was a huge success and a wonderful memory," Kirwan recalls. "I will probably never go to a commencement as moving and exciting. President Bush was there at the height of his popularity in the new Ohio Stadium. It was my last [OSU] commencement."

In fact, it was not Kirwan's last OSU commencement. The following June he was back in Ohio Stadium to receive an honorary degree. "That was so typical of the classy way Ohio State conducts its business," Kirwan says. "It was so touching, and it didn't have to occur. I was enormously gratified. It was another moment of suspended animation."

Following the ceremony, Kirwan's presidential portrait was unveiled at a luncheon in the Faculty Club. A number of his former colleagues, several from out of town, were on hand to witness the event. "I have a sense of joy and fulfillment to know that this will be hung at a university I care so much about," he told the audience. "OSU has a rare, almost unique quality that is not reflected in the ratings, a sense of societal responsibility greater than almost any other university." Noting that he still wears an Ohio State ring, Kirwan said he had wanted to make certain it showed in the portrait. In reference to the honorary degree earlier in the day, he added that he had "turned the ring from the date 'out' to the date 'in'—now that I'm a graduate."

10

Creating a Diverse Environment

Raised in Kentucky by parents who instilled in him a commitment to equal treatment, Kirwan's earliest memories include the discrimination and prejudice that forced blacks to sit in the third-tier balcony at the movies and use separate drinking fountains in public parks. He had almost completed high school before coming into contact with African American peers, making friends with a black high school senior during a summer job at a rock quarry. The pair arranged to get together one evening, and since his friend was not welcome in a white establishment, they met in a black setting at which Kirwan was the only white present.

"It was a very intimidating experience," Kirwan recalls. "I knew then what blacks must feel every day."

As he rose through the ranks of higher education, Kirwan became a passionate proponent of affirmative action, which he felt was necessary to correct past and present inequities as well as to develop a high-quality workforce and add value to the education of all students. Increasingly, he came to believe that excellence and diversity, which some critics considered incompatible, were in fact linked, and that you could not have one without the other. Eventually, he became a national leader in diversity, and in 2002 President George W. Bush named him to the President's Advisory Board of Advisors on Historically Black Colleges and Universities.

He also taught his children the lessons he had learned from his parents. "I remember one time that Dad's secretary in the Math Department was invited to our house for Thanksgiving dinner," his daughter, Ann Elizabeth, recalls. "'She's white, her son is black,' Dad told us, 'and there's nothing wrong with that.'"

Thus, at his introductory news conference in January 1998, the president-elect included diversity among the four core values that would guide his administration. While no shock to those who knew him, others were surprised by Kirwan's intense personal commitment to diversity and the prominence he accorded the topic. Many also found Kirwan's emphasis on excellence through diversity a new way of thinking about the subject. Such reactions reinforced the new president's impression that Ohio State was investing far too little energy in becoming a more welcoming and diverse institution. He saw a stark contrast with Maryland, a once-segregated system where diversity had become part of the university's fabric and where the Black Faculty and Staff Association had sent him off to Columbus with expensive matching tennis rackets as a token of their affection and respect.

"I am deeply troubled by the division, the prejudice, and the bias that exists in society, and I want Ohio State to be a leader in creating a more inclusive community," Kirwan told *Black Issues in Higher Education*, which in November 1998 pictured him on its cover.

Historically, Ohio State had a relatively good record on issues related to diversity. The university had its first African American trustee in 1884, its first male African American graduate in 1892, and its first female African American graduate in 1905. Upon receiving a Doctor of Humane Letters degree from Ohio State in 1996, the Reverend Leon Sullivan—best known for his opposition to apartheid—said he was pleased to accept the honor because of Ohio State's outstanding history of educating African Americans at the graduate level during the 1950s. In the early 1970s, Mac Stewart says, Ohio State made a concerted effort to increase its participation of students and faculty of color and has been among the nation's leaders in producing African American Ph.D.s. But clearly there was more work to do.

Signature Initiative: Diversity Action Plan

In his first six months on the job, President Kirwan learned that Ohio State had conducted various studies on diversity and issued numerous reports. All concluded that the university's progress was unsatisfactory; none resulted in significant action. There was some slow and steady progress in recruiting minority students and minority and female faculty, but not enough. Further, the graduation rate for African Americans and Hispanics was well below that of whites, and it was difficult to retain female and minority faculty once they were recruited.

In January 1999 a small committee was charged with developing a plan with concrete action steps that would become the President and Provost's

Randall Robinson, well-known author, speaking at one of many Diversity Lecture Series events.

Diversity Agenda. Ed Ray appointed the members and, at Kirwan's suggestion, named David Williams and Carole Anderson, then dean of Nursing and assistant vice president for Health Sciences, as cochairs. Featuring an African American man and a white woman, the leaders also reflected two key parts of the university: Student Affairs and Academic Affairs. The group's other members were David Ashley, dean of Engineering; David Ferguson, associate vice president in the Office of University Relations and the chief writer of the Diversity Action Plan; Susan Fisher, senate secretary and entomology professor; Deborah Gill, director, Reprographics and Printing Services; Stephanie Shaw, associate professor of history; and Dara Cooper, an undergraduate student.

The committee's work took place in parallel with the creation of the Academic Plan, with a first draft circulated to the campus community for reaction in late 1999 and the final plan issued informally in July 2000 and formally in October. To make Ohio State a diversity leader in higher education, the plan set six broad objectives:

1. Create a supportive environment that is welcoming for all individuals.
2. Recruit and retain greater numbers of women and minorities into faculty, staff, and administrative positions (including deans, chairs, and vice presidents).
3. Recruit, retain, and graduate greater numbers of ethnic minority students.
4. Provide incentives to academic and academic support units for developing models of excellence for increasing diversity.
5. Collect and organize data to systematically and effectively assess progress and to align/realign programs intended to enhance diversity.
6. Assign accountability to achieve the progress envisioned in this action plan.

Each objective included specific action items, many of which have been implemented. The committee members were all diversity proponents, and discussion included such issues as how prescriptive the plan should be. David Williams recalls battles over whether faculty and administrators should be subject to incentives and disincentives and whether recruiting pools with few minorities or women were an acceptable excuse for lackluster hiring results. Some campus advocates wanted the plan to include other areas, for example, international and intellectual diversity and disability, which the committee rejected. The plan preface reaffirmed that the focus would "remain on increasing the number of women and racial/ethnic minorities and improving the campus climate for all, including persons with different sexual orientation," the final phrase added after the committee heard horror stories from gay, lesbian, bisexual, and transgender (GLBT) students.

With the president's strong encouragement, the plan included numerical targets—for example, five-year goals to increase minority and female faculty—and a strong section on accountability, including creation of a council on diversity to monitor progress and accountability and to continually redefine the plan. Anderson, who chaired the council until moving to the Office of Academic Affairs in 2001–2002, considers the formation of this council the plan's most important recommendation.

As noted, the Academic and Diversity Action plans were linked, with the Academic Plan referencing the Diversity Action Plan and including diversity among its six strategies. Two of the Academic Plan's fourteen initiatives related to diversity. One initiative was to "[h]ire at least five to ten women and five to ten minority faculty at a senior level each year for five years through the Faculty Hiring Assistance Program (FHAP) and other initiatives." Initial results were encouraging in that this goal was met or exceeded during each of the first two years. The other initiative was to "[r]ecruit, support, and retain to graduation larger numbers of academically able minority students." In 1999 about 18 percent of the entering fall freshmen were minorities; by fall 2002 the rate had risen to almost 20 percent. The African American six-year graduation rate rose from 36 to 44 percent.

When the council asked the colleges and vice presidential units for a report on first-year progress (2000–2001), the result was a hodgepodge of "apples and oranges" information, so the council developed a template to make subsequent reports more meaningful. Armed with that information, the 2001–2002 report listed university-wide concerns—for example, colleges should identify specific steps to overcome restraints posed by recruitment pools with few minorities or women—along with candid reactions to the reports from individual colleges. Gradually it became apparent that the university's approach to diversity was changing. Progress was measured, and individual colleges and other units named diversity coordinators, surveying their people and creating their own diversity plans and initiatives.

Other Diversity Accomplishments

When Brit Kirwan became provost at Maryland, he set out to increase the number of African American graduate students (they were already doing well with undergraduates). Who, he asked, is doing the best job in the nation of attracting blacks to their graduate study programs? The answer kept coming back: Ohio State and Frank Hale. So in 1983 Kirwan and a few others from Maryland spent a day with Hale in Columbus, returning with the secrets of his success.

In 1985 Hale, then vice provost for Minority Affairs, recognized the need for a cultural center for minority students on campus and took his idea to President Jennings. The Black Cultural Center, later named for Hale, was established in 1989 and is part of the Office of Minority Affairs. In April 2001 a ceremony commemorated the twelfth anniversary of the Hale Center, which had been expanded in size, programming, and equipment.

By the time Kirwan became president of Ohio State, Hale had retired as vice provost and professor emeritus for Minority Affairs and Department of Communication and moved on to Kenyon College. In May 1999 Kirwan enticed

Hale back to Columbus, as a distinguished university representative and consultant to Kirwan and Ed Ray. At Kirwan's request, Hale organized the president and provost's Diversity Lecture Series, which, starting in fall 2000, has brought scores of well-known and sometimes controversial speakers to the campus, addressing a wide array of diversity issues.

Six months after the Hale Center ceremony, Ohio State dedicated a Multicultural Center located in the Ohio Union and directed by Christine Ballengee-Morris, formerly an associate professor of art education at the Newark campus. It was the university's second attempt to create such a center, a prior planning exercise having failed to reach closure in 1993. The Multicultural Center was formed to promote greater cultural awareness and understanding. As a venue for discussion, networking, and relationship building, it offers a clearinghouse of information for Ohio State students, faculty, staff, and the public.

Another diversity initiative followed a conversation between Barbara Pinchuk, an Ohio State alumna in music, and Judith Koroscik, dean of the College of the Arts. The result was a collaboration between Arts and Sciences, the College of Humanities, the Fisher College of Business, and principals of Lifetime Television Network's award-winning cable series *Any Day Now*, produced by Pinchuk's husband. Entitled "Can We Talk?" the campus/community summit featured a discussion on diversity with about seven hundred people, including President Kirwan and Columbus mayor Michael Coleman, in Weigel Auditorium.

"I took the idea to Brit," says Koroscik, "suggesting that he should be the one on stage, not me. He was delighted to do it after we covered the issue of stage fright."

Office of Minority Affairs

In the spring of 1998, shortly before Brit Kirwan's arrival as president, supporters of the Afrikan Student Union staged a sit-in in Bricker Hall. As described in a memo to the Board of Trustees from Dick Sisson, the protestors' demands included delaying the proposed reorganization of the university's Office of Minority Affairs and denying reappointment to interim vice provost Barbara Rich, who had taken over from Frank Hale. Ready to resign, Rich agreed to remain in her post when Sisson and Ray assured her of their support.

The new president wanted the matter settled before he arrived. To do so, Sisson agreed to suspend implementation of the restructuring pending open discussions that fall and provided assurances that all constituencies would

Mayor Michael Coleman comments at the "Can We Talk?" symposium in Weigel Hall. Others mentioned in this book are seated on the far right of each row—Mac Stewart (bottom row), Carole Anderson (middle row), and Valerie Lee (top row). Seated at top row middle is J. Briggs Cormier, onetime president of the Council of Graduate Students.

have meaningful input into the selection of a new vice provost. After eight days of protest, the sit-in was over.

Following a national search, Ray nominated Tim Knowles, vice president for Student and Campus Support at Meharry Medical College in Nashville, Tennessee—the nation's largest private historically black institution dedicated to educating health care professionals and biomedical scientists—as the new vice provost for Minority Affairs. Knowles had devoted his career to helping minority students and believed strongly that institutions had an obligation not just to admit minority students but to see that they graduated.

Knowles took office on August 1, 1999. One year later, Ed Ray announced that he had terminated Knowles, following an investigation prompted by concerns from OMA faculty and the Afrikan Student Union. The office needed new leadership, Ray said, adding that Knowles had declined the opportunity to resign. In fact, Knowles later sued the university over his termination, with his attorney telling the *Dispatch* that Knowles's attempt to make needed changes in the Office of Minority Affairs had gotten him fired. The case remained in litigation as of the writing of this book.

After Knowles's departure, Ray again turned to Mac Stewart, who had led OMA on a temporary basis in the month between Barbara Rich's departure and Tim Knowles's arrival. Stewart, who joined Ohio State in 1970 and was dean of University College, was again named interim vice provost pending another nationwide search. Applying his knowledge and expertise as a licensed psychologist and administrator, Stewart spent a lot of time listening and, with funds from the provost, hired a consultant to help. A year later, things had quieted down, with some voluntary (and other, less voluntary) departures.

Stewart believes that the Diversity Action Plan—with the leadership it represented and the accountability inherent in its report cards—had a huge impact on a campus that had struggled for years to actually implement diversity strategies. "The deans knew the day was coming when they would be measured," Stewart says. He proudly recounts the progress made on the Academic Plan's diversity initiatives and adds that for the first time, *Black Enterprise* rated Ohio State among the nation's top fifty schools for African Americans. The university is also among national leaders in graduating African American

In 1998, administration officials competed in basketball with the Young Scholars, participants in a program run by the Office of Minority Affairs.

Ph.Ds, he noted, and moved from number thirty-seven to seventeen in producing Hispanic Ph.Ds.

Women's Issues

In 1995, two years from her retirement, Judy Fountain left her job in Human Resources to pursue an opportunity in the community—not intending to return. While she was gone, a grassroots movement created the Women's Place, a clearinghouse for resources and services for women students, staff and faculty, and Fountain was asked to come back and help make the concept a reality.

The Women's Place idea began during the Gee presidency, and Gee created a task force on the subject before leaving office. When President Kirwan arrived, the women met with him and found him receptive. "The idea was grounded in a core value of his presidency," Fountain says, "and he trusted that it was an approach that would work." Also important was the President's Council on Women's Issues, whose twenty diverse members advise the president and provost on "best practice" strategies to improve the institutional climate for women and on establishing the direction and priorities for the Women's Place.

In addition, Brit and Patty Kirwan became sponsors of the Critical Difference for Women, a fund-raising endeavor for three women's initiatives: scholarships for women over twenty-five who were reentering school; professional development grants; and research on women. The Kirwans were particularly interested in helping reentry scholarship students, not only financially but by getting to know them personally. One student was among the graduates at Brit's last commencement ceremony.

The president also personally painted a tile to appear in a newly established Spirit of Women Park adjacent to the University Medical Center. "The park will serve as a tribute to women and a symbol of the University Medical Center's commitment to the health and well-being of women in central Ohio," says Kam Sigafoos, executive director of University Hospitals. Patty Kirwan is a breast cancer survivor.

"I think Kirwan's legacy," Fountain says, "is that he has demonstrated a different kind of leadership style that can enable constituency groups to shape policy and practice going forward, and you don't have to be afraid as an administrator."

Sexual Orientation.

If, awakening after decades of sleep, a modern-day Rip Van Winkle wandered onto the campus of a university like Ohio State, he or she might be most surprised at the prominence of gay, lesbian, bisexual, and transgender issues. Given his interest in diversity and his failure to get domestic partner benefits enacted at Maryland, President Kirwan was hardly surprised by efforts to form a Gay, Lesbian, Bisexual, and Transgender Alumni Society or that Ohio State's GLBT students and faculty also wanted the university to provide so-called hard benefits like health care to unmarried domestic partners. Like Gordon Gee, President Kirwan supported the proposal, but the Board of Trustees did not, preferring to let the state of Ohio take the lead. Given the antipathy toward gays and lesbians in the General Assembly, such approval was not forthcoming.

Nonetheless, Kirwan fought the good fight, arguing that Big Ten schools Iowa, Michigan, Michigan State, Minnesota, Northwestern, and Indiana offered domestic partner benefits. He staked out his ground with the trustees as a matter of principle on which he could not retreat. In return, the trustees indicated that while they respected his position, there was nothing they could usefully do. Privately, some people speculated that should Ohio State approve domestic partner benefits, the legislature would mete out some form of penalty.

With hard benefits stalled, Kirwan agreed to explore the granting of "soft benefits" like group life insurance, family medical leave, and child care. A number of such benefits were approved for domestic partner use by the time of his departure for Maryland.

"Personal attitudes on homosexuality are changing," Kirwan told *The Lantern.* "There is no question that many more companies are providing domestic partner benefits than there were 10 years ago. It is important for those of us who support domestic partner benefits to recognize that those who do not support domestic partner benefits feel that there are very important principles at stake."

So how did Kirwan do with his emphasis on diversity?

"At first, there was some skepticism, but Brit got the whole community focused on diversity as one of the top three or four things to be done," reflects Ginny Trethewey. "It probably took three years or more for people to realize that something had changed." And while the climate definitely improved, she added, there were some areas—like minorities and women in senior-level appointments—where no major improvement took place.

"Brit came at a time when diversity was under question," Dick Stoddard adds. "It was being challenged. He put that challenge to rest."

"A lot of people sort of pay tribute to diversity," says trustee Robert Duncan, "but Brit lived it and believed it and was after it all the time. And that really came through because he was such a credible human being."

"We were more visibly, tangibly, credibly committed to diversity under his leadership than we ever were before, by miles," adds Martha Garland.

And what did Kirwan himself think? At the May 2002 Board of Trustees meeting, at which Carole Anderson reported on diversity, the outgoing president said he had been "very pleased with the way the university community has responded to this challenge."

11

Helping Build Ohio's Future

Since its founding in 1870 as a land-grant college, Ohio State has contributed substantially to Ohio's economy and civic well-being. It helped make Ohio's agricultural and manufacturing sectors among the most successful in the nation, producing graduates and creating knowledge to meet the evolving needs of the nineteenth and twentieth centuries. In its sixth and final strategy, the Academic Plan suggests ways to help Ohio flourish in the twenty-first century. Specifically, Ohio State would become the catalyst for development of Ohio's technology-based economy and significantly strengthen the scope and effectiveness of the university's commitment to public education, with a special focus on the education of underserved children and youth. These two initiatives were part of a more centralized approach to the university's overall Outreach and Engagement strategy, which included Campus Partners.

Signature Initiative: Catalyzing a Twenty-first-Century Economy

In the years following World War II, research universities played growing roles in major collaborations with government and industry, a development exemplified by North Carolina's Research Triangle on the East Coast and Silicon Valley on the West Coast. As recounted in *The Jennings Years*, the early 1980s saw stirrings at Ohio State to create a research park, with the West Campus becoming the eventual focus of this endeavor. Various factors slowed the progress of this initiative, however, including competing visions of what a research park should be.

In 1996 President Gee named a Research Park Corporation board that in 1998 became the Science and Technology Campus Corporation, or SciTech, a nonprofit entity affiliated with but not part of Ohio State. The next year Ed Hayes hired David Allen—a graduate of Penn State and Indiana University who was then at Ohio University—as director of technology transfer. Board leadership came primarily from Ted Celeste, whose service on the Research Foundation Board had stimulated his interest in university-related economic development.

Then, in January 1998, Kirwan was named president and, as Celeste puts it, "jumped in with both feet." "Brit not only had the experience but brought examples from Maryland, and he told the story well. He was the right man for the right time," Celeste says.

SciTech was an immediate priority for the new president, even before taking office. He soon joined in the process to choose a president of SciTech and was impressed by Ora Smith, who got the job. Then CEO of Illinois Superconductor, Smith had degrees from MIT and Harvard Law School and experience in Silicon Valley. Then, in his second month on the job, Kirwan appointed a university technology partnerships task force to build upon the work of Mayor Greg Lashutka's Task Force on Technology and the Future of the City.

Political consultants speak about the necessity to remain "on message," and no one could accuse the university's new president of not following such advice. Noting that Ohio's per capita income had been declining for decades, Kirwan cited national studies showing Ohio as an Old Economy state in a New Economy world, ranking thirty-second in high-tech jobs and twenty-ninth in venture capital placements. Over and over again, he quoted the *New York Times*, which in an October 1999 article on successful states and regions wrote: "If there is one never-absent factor at work, it is the proximity of a research university shifting from ivory tower to revving economic engine."

To meet the challenges of technology and globalization, Kirwan said, Ohio needed to transform its economy from one based largely on brawn to one based on brains. This could not happen without close linkages among Ohio's flagship university, state and local government, and business. Absolutely vital to success, he argued, was for Ohio State to become a top-tier research and teaching institution, turning out highly qualified graduates and generating research discoveries. To do so required additional state support.

Kirwan hammered home this thesis in a series of presentations that continued throughout his presidency and extended to a bicentennial lecture one year after his departure. In the process, he used current success stories to demonstrate the university's progress and potential. He recounted the university's success in luring Brad Moore and Fred Sanfilippo. He repeatedly spoke of

Mauro Ferrari, whom Engineering dean David Ashley had recruited from the University of California–Berkeley shortly after Kirwan's arrival and who had cofounded iMEDD, Inc., which later moved to Columbus, to commercialize his therapeutic devices.

"What [Mauro] was doing was so compatible [and] perfectly aligned with a major part of my agenda," Kirwan says. "He was a master communicator, witty and substantive, and moving his company from Silicon Valley to Columbus was a classic 'man bites dog' story. The Engineering College made very heavy commitments to get him to come. He became the darling of the economic development and business communities, and Mauro was responsible for our biomedical engineering program."

As time went by, however, others questioned how much was being accomplished. Feeling guilty for stretching him so thin, Kirwan counseled Ferrari to back off and reinvest in his academic and research responsibilities. When Jim Williams arrived as dean of Engineering and was less invested in the original commitments, Ferrari—in Kirwan's words—"became disenchanted and began attending medical school." To this day he considers Kirwan a mentor and credits him with being among the first university administrators to identify the interface between medicine and engineering.

Meanwhile, the university's economic development initiatives accelerated, on campus and off.

On Campus: SciTech and More

In September 1998 Ora Smith assumed his new job as president of SciTech. Its mission was to promote on-campus research alliances between businesses and the university and to provide facilities to house companies that collaborate with Ohio State researchers, including university spin-off enterprises.

"I showed up for what I thought was a get-acquainted visit at the chamber and found myself at a press conference downtown with Sally Jackson," Smith says. "Dave Lore, from the *Dispatch*, noted that he had heard talk for seventeen years about such projects and asked what was different now." "What's different," Smith replied, "is that they've hired someone and put up the money."

SciTech was given exclusive development rights to fifty-three acres on West Campus, including thirty-five acres of vacant space and three existing buildings. The development agreement with the university provided for $300,000 a year from the Office of Research and the Ohio State University Research Foundation (OSURF) to be matched by contributions from the state of Ohio and

The MicroMD Laboratory, located on Kinnear Road near North Star, was part of the Science Village extension.

city of Columbus. It also included up to $21 million in loans to develop the site.

Science Village I was SciTech's first totally new building. Situated near the corner of Kinnear and North Star Roads, this fifty-thousand-square-foot structure was intended for potential high-growth companies that need higher-quality, better-configured facilities. The anchor tenant, occupying about twenty thousand square feet, is the MicroMD Laboratory, an unofficial joint venture between Ohio State and SciTech that was part of the university's commitment to Mauro Ferrari.

The MicroMD Laboratory is a microfabrication facility for the development of Biomedical Micro ElectroMechanical Systems (BioMEMS) that is used for a fee by academic and industrial researchers. To complete the interior space, the Board of Trustees authorized up to $9 million in tenant improvements, with contributions of $1.5 million each from the College of Engineering, the College of Medicine and Public Health, and the Office of Research, along with $4.5 million from the President's Strategic Investment Fund.

On January 31, 2002, Governor Bob Taft, Mayor Michael Coleman, and other dignitaries joined President Kirwan and lab director Jon Gray in officially opening the futuristic facility—among the nation's first technologically integrated facilities dedicated to developing micro- and nanotechnology devices for use in medical applications.

"This is a great day for science, for engineering, for medicine, and for the state of Ohio," said Brad Moore. Kirwan called the lab a key investment in helping Ohio transition to a knowledge economy, reflecting the Academic Plan strategy to "build Ohio's future." "I see MicroMD as a microcosm of what can happen across the state of Ohio," he noted.

But even some of Kirwan's strongest supporters question this project. "It's an idea whose time appears not yet to have come," says Jim Williams, who also labels it "a financial albatross." Ora Smith, who left the university in 2004 but consults with iMEDD, counters by saying that the MicroMD lab could have moved more quickly with better management and that academic research facilities are not normally measured on a profit-and-loss basis.

While conceding that the investment was risky, Kirwan argues that it could make Columbus and Ohio State major players in nanotechnology. "The jury is still out," he adds, "but I have no regrets, however it pans out. You can only change the paradigm by taking risks."

Kirwan and Smith also remain positive about SciTech generally. "Ora proved to be an excellent choice," Kirwan reflects. "SciTech is on a very good trajectory."

"We are very different from other university research parks," Ora Smith explains. "We are much more physically integrated. We are one of the few to combine physical development of a park with an incubator and venture capital operation. We are one of the few really connected to a university. It's more about forming businesses and helping them grow than about real estate. Most growth comes from start-up companies. Commercialization ties are more intense with start-ups than with big licensees. And we hire students more frequently. We're now known as the Ohio State Model."

Other important entities and initiatives, which, along with SciTech, were covered under the university's umbrella label of Tech Partners, included

- the Business Technology Center, an incubator for emerging companies whose space more than doubled during the Kirwan years, thanks to $2 million from the state of Ohio and $3 million from the private sector (Some 80 percent of the incubated companies have been successful.);
- the Technology Commercialization Corporation, designed to encourage formation of technology companies, which was soon absorbed into

Ora Smith was president of SciTech.

- SciTech itself (During the Kirwan years, it housed sixteen companies.); and
- the Office for Technology Licensing, the Office for Technology Partnerships, and the Office of Business and Industry Contracts, which pursue, protect, package, and license to industry the intellectual property developed by Ohio State and serves faculty, staff, and students in all aspects of intellectual property. By 2001 the office reported 109 invention disclosures, fifty-three patent applications, twenty-three patents awarded, forty-one license/options executed, seven start-up companies assisted, $1.5 million in revenue from income-generating licenses, and research awards up almost 58 percent over three years, totaling almost $400 million.

President Kirwan initially worked on these endeavors with Ora Smith and Dave Allen, who then carried the title of assistant vice president for Technology Partnerships. When Brad Moore arrived as vice president for Research, Allen's direct access to the president was curbed. Allen became discouraged at what he felt was a lack of progress and decision making and accepted a similar position at the University of Colorado system.

"David Allen was incredibly helpful to me," Kirwan notes. "He was extremely knowledgeable and very supportive. He recognized my interest and helped prepare me. He suggested a best-practice study from Battelle regarding where we were versus other universities. He created an agenda."

Off Campus: A Different Kind of TLC

In July 1997 Columbus mayor Greg Lashutka had convened the Mayor's Task Force on Technology. In May 1998 the task force recommended formation of a private-sector technology and business council composed of top executives to focus high-level attention on the issue. In response, the Columbus Technology Leadership Council (TLC) was formed in June, just before Brit Kirwan assumed the presidency of Ohio State.

At first, Allen recalls, the council was going nowhere. The university had a reputation for not meeting its commitments, and the business leaders did not want the university to take the organization over. Kirwan himself, who badly wanted a significant connection between the university and the private-sector technology community, believed that the group should be corporate-driven. Unless we can build synergy, he thought, we will never realize our full potential. So he hosted a dinner at his residence with members of the technology community, importing the charismatic Mario Marino, founder of Potomac Knowledge Way, to explain why such partnerships were important and how they could be fashioned.

"This catalyzed their understanding," Allen said, "and got it going. Brit had showed what the university role was and could be and why such a role was important. [Business leaders] no longer feared what OSU might do. There was more confidence and trust. And we did deliver and push things forward." Kirwan became the group's chairman, and the corporate leaders became increasingly enthusiastic. "We were then able to get people to pass the hat and get a headhunter," Allen added, and in September 1999 the TLC hired Todd Ritterbusch, who had held positions at McKinsey & Company and IBM, as its first president. He was, Kirwan says today, "exactly the right person."

The TLC became an effective community mechanism, establishing the $20 million Battelle Fund, central Ohio's first publicly financed venture capital fund geared toward developing high-tech companies. Battelle itself put up $10 million, and the fund will invest between $100,000 and $1.5 million in promising companies. The Ohio State University invested $2.6 million. (Today it is known as Reservoir Venture Partners.)

Another key accomplishment was the passage and gubernatorial approval in June 2000 of Senate Bill 286, designed to encourage faculty, staff, and student participation in entrepreneurial activities. Among other provisions, the law clarified the equity that faculty or research scientists at public institutions could own in a technology start-up and increased it to a maximum of 25 percent of the total equity outstanding. It also gave boards of trustees at Ohio universities the right to devise guidelines that govern such transactions. In April 2001 Ohio State's trustees approved a set of guidelines (*Rules of the University Faculty*, chapter 13) prepared by the Office of Legal Affairs in collaboration with the Inter-University Council, Ohio Ethics Commission, and others.

Finally, Kirwan actively participated in other community endeavors. He strongly backed economic development activities of the Greater Columbus Chamber of Commerce, encouraging a visit to Austin, Texas, where a university town of similar size to Columbus had been transformed into an economic powerhouse, and promoting a chamber-led biotechnology initiative. Along with people like John F. Wolfe, Alex Shumate, and Jack Kessler, he was among the community leaders convened by Les Wexner to discuss major issues of importance to central Ohio, such as building the new Center of Science and Industry (COSI) downtown redevelopment. The group was later expanded and formalized as Columbus Tomorrow and, still later, the Columbus Partnership.

Kirwan's inclusion in this group, as well as dinner invitations from Wexner and his wife, Abigail—dinners where Kirwan was often called upon to speak—helped establish the new president as a key community player. Kirwan likewise benefited from Wexner's strategic thinking and advice offered in quarterly one-on-one meetings. Finally, Wexner was particularly helpful during the creation of the Academic Plan (for example, loaning Len Schlesinger, a Harvard Business School professor who became COO of Wexner's Limited Brands, to lead a retreat, making Harvard architect Jerry McCue available for consultation on the Gateway Project, and discussing communications and marketing strategies with Kirwan and Tashjian).

In sum, a great deal was accomplished in economic development during the Kirwan years. Those achievements illustrated what Joe Alutto, dean of Fisher College, meant when he spoke of Kirwan's contributions to Ohio State.

"Gordon came on campus . . . with a lot of flash and a lot of sizzle and a lot of Gordon," Alutto says. "I think Gordon did a lot to build the institution and change aspirations, and there was a tremendous sense of energy. But at some point that energy had to be converted into a stabilizing force that provides a foundation for growth. When Brit came, we all had a sense that this is the perfect next stage in the evolution of Ohio State University; the sense that here is a very stable, focused individual, with a great sense of values, just as Gordon had, but who really knew how to build and to reach out to the corporate community as well as the business community. You can talk about all the other things he did. What he lent us, I think, was a sense that 'yes, we're in this for the long run.'"

Filling the Pipeline: P–12 Education

As in other states, the improvement of Ohio's public elementary and secondary education was a high priority, and President Kirwan was among those who believed that helping make this happen was an appropriate part of Ohio State's contemporary land-grant mission. The Academic Plan, reflecting a desire to establish visible university-wide outreach initiatives addressing twenty-first-century needs, included among its fourteen initiatives a commitment to P–12 education, the public school system that begins in prekindergarten and proceeds through twelfth grade. In fact, Kirwan looked at education in even broader terms, as a system that extended at least through college (P–16) if not throughout life.

The P–12 initiative was led by Daryl Siedentop, who served as senior associate dean of the College of Education and then interim dean after Nancy Zimpher left in 1998 to become chancellor of the University of Wisconsin–Milwaukee. While interim dean, he was asked to begin conceptualizing the university's new P–12 project, and when a new dean came on board, he became the first P–12 director although the Academic Plan officially assigned the lead college role to the College of Education.

As outlined in the Academic Plan, the goal of this initiative was to significantly strengthen the university's effectiveness, scope, and commitment to P–12 education in Ohio, with a special focus on the education of underserved children and youth. During the last two years of the Kirwan presidency, the initiative worked with many campus units already involved in P–12 activities, including Engineering, International Studies, the College of Mathematical and Physical Sciences (MAPS), Ecology, Humanities, and the College of Food, Agricultural, and Environmental Sciences (FAES). In those two years, the initiative also

> conceived an institutional presence for the university in state-level education research and policy (Later, working through the newly formed Ohio Collaborative Research and Policy for Schools, Children and

Families, work was built around teams of faculty from various Ohio institutions of higher learning.);

participated in the Columbus Higher Education Partnership, an attempt by Gene Harris, Columbus superintendent of schools, to make Ohio State, Otterbein and Columbus State—and later, Capital University and Ohio Dominican—more strategic in their interactions with the Columbus Public Schools;

formed "Community Connection" in collaboration with the Service Learning Roundtable and Office of Student Affairs (This Web-based volunteer interface system connects school needs with willing Ohio State students while helping students create a record of their volunteer activity.); and

established "The Learning Bridge," which serves boys and girls who attend Columbus Public Schools and live within the boundaries of Campus Partners, the university's neighborhood initiative. A sample project: Through the leadership of Dean David Andrews of the College of Human Ecology, "The Learning Bridge" set out to build an early education center for 150 young children in the Weinland Park area, with core funding from Betty Schoenbaum.

Meanwhile, Kirwan convinced Donna Browder Evans—a Columbus native, holder of three degrees from Ohio State, and an expert in urban public education—to leave her position as dean of the Darden College of Education at Old Dominion University in Virginia to assume a similar position at Ohio State. Kirwan and Evans shared a desire to revisit the university's teacher education programs, with the president hoping this would include a return to teacher licensure at the undergraduate level.

Evans proposed rethinking teacher preparation in collaboration with the arts and sciences in a major university initiative to strengthen public education. The University Teacher Education Council (UTEC) was formed in March 2001 to better prepare public school teachers in an era of more formal content standards and greater teacher accountability. Headed jointly by Evans and vice provost Randy Smith, UTEC included a policy board and a dozen advisory working groups representing teacher education specialties. Among other things, these groups were charged with reconnecting with the Colleges of the Arts and Sciences and undergraduate education in some significant way that could include initial licensure at the undergraduate level.

As Evans explained to the Board of Trustees, her faculty worked with the Office of Academic Affairs; the colleges of Humanities, Arts and Sciences,

Mathematical and Physical Sciences, and Human Ecology; regional campus colleagues; the Ohio Department of Education; and local school districts to redesign and reinvigorate the university's preservice and advanced education preparation programs. The task included provision of a seamless transition from undergraduate to graduate teacher education and identifying the effectiveness of teacher education programs.

Updating a Signal Strength: Outreach and Engagement

Outreach and engagement, of course, was among the four goals that Kirwan brought from Maryland. He had spent his life at land-grant universities, growing up at the University of Kentucky and attending graduate school at Rutgers before moving on to Maryland and now Ohio State. Outreach and engagement were as important to him as they were a part of Ohio State history. He mentioned it during his initial Fawcett Center press conference with sufficient enthusiasm that Bobby Moser was accused of writing his speech.

Kirwan also oversaw a major report on the subject for the Kellogg Commission that appeared in March 2000, entitled *Renewing the Covenant: Learning, Discovery, and Engagement in a New Age and Different World.* An earlier Kellogg report, *Returning to Our Roots: The Engaged Institution,* singled out Ohio State for its collaborative work with businesses and public and social service agencies.

"Ohio State was America's leader," Kirwan says, "the leading example of a land-grant university in a traditional sense. Its commitment and connections across the state exceed anything I'm aware of. I thought we could use the Kellogg report as a springboard to enable Ohio State to refocus its great strength to reflect the new world, to become a land-grant institution for the twenty-first century. We were well suited to lead the way."

So the question was never whether outreach and engagement would be a major university initiative, but what form that initiative would take. Seeking to call attention to this change, Kirwan created a central structure and encouraged a few campuswide initiatives, such as P–12 education, economic development, and health and safety—the latter headed by Ron St. Pierre.

The logical person to lead this charge, once again, was Mr. Outreach and Engagement himself, Bobby Moser. First, Moser had chaired the President's Council on Outreach and Engagement and had influenced that portion of the Academic Plan. Second, as vice president and executive dean for the College of Food, Agricultural and Environmental Sciences (FAES), Moser was a force behind OSU Extension, a highly valued university outreach and engagement department with offices in each of the state's eighty-eight counties and which Kirwan considered the nation's best extension service model, and other FAES outreach activities. What's more, he brought a passion for O&E and definite ideas of how it should be managed, believing strongly that in true partnership all parties benefit mutually. And finally, Kirwan was impressed not only by his organizational skills but by the way he was reinventing FAES.

Thus, in early 2001 the Board of Trustees gave Moser the added title of vice president, Outreach and Engagement. At the same time, the university established an Office of Outreach and Engagement, staffed by Karen Bruns, leader of OSU CARES, and Janet Sanfilippo (wife of Fred), newly hired director of University Outreach. In addition, two new committees were formed, a dean's advocacy committee chaired by Nancy Harden Rogers, then vice provost for Academic Administration, and the Outreach and Engagement Leadership Action Committee, chaired by Moser. The new office also created databases, one listing the hundreds of existing campus outreach projects, the other listing resources available to support such initiatives.

A storyteller entertains students at Hubbard Elementary School as part of the 2002 African American Heritage Festival.

Ohio State's Outreach and Engagement projects ran the gamut from economic development and elementary/secondary education to health literacy for residents of Appalachian Ohio counties. Efforts extended even beyond the United States, and, as described later in the book, Kirwan participated in two major international trips to strengthen connections between Ohio State and other nations as well as to build alumni relations.

Also during the Kirwan years, the trustees created an Office of International Affairs under the leadership of an associate provost for International Affairs, Jerry Ladman, professor of agricultural, environmental, and development economics. And finally, in September 1999, the trustees established the Wolfe Study Abroad Scholarships Endowed Fund with a $1 million gift from the Dispatch Printing Company to foster undergraduate involvement in foreign study experiences.

Campus Partners

Each New Year's Day, Brit Kirwan lists five or six major things he wants to accomplish during the coming year. On January 1, 1999, that list included Campus Partners and its Gateway Project—among the university's largest current outreach initiatives. Formed in the mid-1990s to revitalize portions of the university neighborhood east of High Street, Campus Partners' nonprofit activities included community assistance in such areas as code enforcement, housing, education, and urban redevelopment. The university's Board of Trustees had authorized $25 million for Campus Partners to buy property, then find a developer to improve it. Terry Foegler, former director of development for Dublin, Ohio, had succeeded Barry Humphries in 1996 as the Campus Partners president. Kirwan considers Foegler "a remarkably talented individual."

It was a terrific vision with lots of work needed to make it a reality. "It was clear that we had to focus on it or it would not happen," Kirwan explains. "It was not part of the academic mission but was so very important. If the neighborhood near the campus continued to decline, that would compromise the university's future." Kirwan was aware that when he was being recruited, officials never brought him up High Street; instead driving north on Neil Avenue.

Students writing in *The Lantern* found the Gateway Project a target of opportunity, arguing that driving bars from the area contributed to student disturbances, that the university was stomping on small neighborhood businesses in favor of large outside corporations, and that low-cost student housing would be replaced by gentrified apartments beyond their means.

Much more important was the fact that relations between the university and the city of Columbus were, in Kirwan's words, "absolutely awful," the mayor feeling that the university had double-crossed him on the arena project by going around him in the General Assembly. The new president and the trustees agreed that relations needed to be rebuilt. Fortunately, Mayor Greg Lashutka was an Ohio State grad—a football star (he and Kirwan had both played tight end)—and also wanted good relations. Early on, Kirwan breakfasted with the mayor and his family.

"We immediately hit it off," Kirwan says. "He could not have been more supportive. Herb Asher also helped. We built a collaborative team effort." Eventually, the city agreed to do the infrastructure for the Gateway Project, while the state of Ohio agreed to help support a parking garage.

As already noted, Kirwan attended regular meetings with Jerry McCue, former dean of Harvard's Graduate School of Design and a consultant to Les Wexner at his New Albany development, to discuss neighborhood and High Street planning issues. In addition, a forty-person steering committee of campus and community leaders—funded by Ohio State and the city of Columbus—worked with a Boston urban planner, Goody Clancy & Associates, to develop "A Plan for High Street: Creating a 21st Century Main Street," published in August 2000. The plan, later adopted by Columbus City Council, outlined a four-point mission to

1. restore High Street as the symbolic heart of the university district, providing a variety of public places for people from all walks of life to gather;
2. reestablish it as the district's vital main street, providing a dynamic mix of retail, entertainment and services;
3. create a place for new economic opportunities, providing jobs and other public benefits to adjacent neighborhoods; and
4. reinforce High Street as an environment that supports learning, providing settings and activities that draw Ohio State students, faculty, and staff to the district.

Specific suggestions included forming a parking management entity to create approximately fifteen hundred to twenty-one hundred new spaces; establishing a Special Improvement District to organize property owners and businesses; and supporting strategic redevelopment opportunities to energize High Street, starting with a lively University Gateway Center to transform the street's most troubled area into a regional destination that would draw students, residents, visitors, and others back to High Street.

In 1999, while the plan was still in draft form, Campus Partners chose the Druker Company of Boston as master developer of the Gateway Project. And in December of that year, the Columbus City Council approved an important agreement with the Gateway Area Revitalization Initiative, a subsidiary of Campus Partners. The city agreed to use eminent domain in acquiring properties and created a tax increment financing district to capture new nonschool property tax revenues generated by Gateway to help finance a needed parking structure. Columbus put up $5 million in infrastructure support, and the state of Ohio later provided $4.5 million for the parking garage. The following year, the U.S. Department of Housing and Urban Development gave Campus Partners one of five national Front Door Awards for Best Practices in Public-Private Partnerships.

In March 2000 David Williams, chair of the Campus Partners board, told the trustees that Campus Partners was "working on a lot of fronts." He mentioned a successful Homeownership Incentive Program and work in social services and K–12 (later P–12) education. Progress on Gateway had been slow, Williams explained, due to a desire to achieve buy-in from the community and the difficult task of acquiring thirty-one properties and relocating or buying out twenty-five businesses. He credits Kirwan with allowing the project to go forward while he was under pressure to let it die. Trustee Dan Slane, whose board portfolio included significant involvement with Campus Partners, concedes that the Gateway Project was bogged down at one time and praises Kirwan for rebuilding momentum and improving relationships with city hall.

"Both mayors were very helpful," Kirwan said. "I had tried to talk Greg into running again and was very sad when he did not. However, I built a similar relationship with Mike Coleman, with whom I became very good friends. I called him 'my mayor,' and he called me 'my president.'" Kirwan also arranged a part-time community relations job for the mayor's wife, Frankie, who had served as executive director and CEO at the local Private Industry Council.

Following the death of its longtime owner, Long's Book Store was put up for sale and purchased by Campus Partners. At the same time, Campus Partners and Ohio State contracted with Barnes and Noble College Bookstores to operate both Long's and the University Bookstore. The two bookstore operations eventually will be combined as a major anchor store in the new Gateway Project.

By spring 2002 the final six properties were acquired for the Gateway site, and demolition was scheduled for the existing buildings. On May 1 President

Finally, in the spring of 2002, buildings began to come down in preparation for construction of the Gateway Center, a project of Campus Partners.

Kirwan and Mayor Coleman released a wrecking ball to begin the demolition process along two blocks of North High Street. That in turn set the stage for public infrastructure improvements such as reconstruction of the roadway, water and sewer line relocation, and the burial of overhead power lines. And as Campus Partners moved into the construction and marketing aspects of the project, it modified the name from University Gateway Center to South Campus Gateway.

"Another great day in my tenure was swinging the wrecking ball with Mike Coleman," Kirwan says. "I felt it was going to happen now."

"Gateway Project's time has come," announced *onCampus*, describing a mixed-use development of approximately 210,000 square feet of retail, restaurant, and entertainment space; 70,000 square feet of office space; 150 to 200 apartments; and a parking garage for twelve hundred vehicles. The redevelopment area extends between West 11th and West 10th Avenues on the west side of High Street and between Chittenden and East Ninth Avenues on the east side of High Street. The site totals 7.4 acres.

Another major Campus Partners initiative was the acquisition of the nation's largest portfolio of project-based, scattered-site Section 8 housing.

Concerned that a 1997 change in federal housing law would undermine efforts to improve the University District's Weinland Park neighborhood, President Kirwan and Mayor Coleman asked the U.S. Department of Housing and Urban Development in September 2000 to postpone implementation until Campus Partners could study alternatives. The result was an innovative alternate restructuring plan under which ownership changed in April 2003 from the Broad Street Portfolio, a group of private investors, to Ohio Capital Corporation for Housing (OCCH), a nonprofit group. The plan also includes a two- to three-year significant renovation of housing units that began in spring 2004. Thanks to federal funding for this national model for Section 8 housing, this work required only a modest investment from Campus Partners and no investment from the university.

Ohio State's size and philanthropic success allow it to do a lot of things, Kirwan said when asked about creative approaches to financing. The innovative use of future faculty grants to pay off bonds and thus build the Biomedical Research Tower was unique among public institutions, he believes. And he calls SciTech and Campus Partners "two of the most creative initiatives I know of in higher education, both of which were basically self-funded."

Managing the University

12

Paying for It All

University funding comes primarily from five sources: the state of Ohio, especially through its instructional subsidy; student tuition and fees; grants from the federal government and industry; private contributions; and user charges for medical care, football tickets, and so forth. As with other public universities, the proportion of total funds coming from these sources has changed significantly over the years. Once providing a dominant portion of total funding, state support has steadily declined as a percentage of the total. In the mid-1980s, Ohio State's share of instructional support was nearly double its student fee income; by 2002 the trend lines had crossed, with tuition providing more money than state subsidy.

In response to this trend, universities like Ohio State are becoming more self-reliant, aggressively raising money from private donors and seeking more and larger grants from the federal government and industry. These funds help enlarge the total pie, making the other pieces look even smaller by comparison. What's more, many university resources are not fungible, which is to say that they are earmarked for certain uses and not transportable. Thus, money donated or granted for construction, for example, is not available for faculty salaries or academic programs.

The story of financing Ohio State during the Kirwan years includes declining state support, rising tuition, highly successful private fund-raising, solid progress in federal and industry grants, and changes in how the university budgets its money. So far as the Academic Plan was concerned, the administration found creative ways to move it forward despite disappointments downtown.

This chapter covers state support and tuition. Development is covered in chapter 13.

CHAPTER 12

Lower State Support, Higher Tuition

Brit Kirwan was recruited to help make Ohio State a top-tier public university. The trustees and search committee had hammered home that goal, one reason Kirwan was intrigued by the offer. Not surprisingly, those courting candidate Kirwan were upbeat, and, while no promises were made, a meeting with Governor George Voinovich left him feeling encouraged.

Initially, his optimism seemed justified. Four months after Kirwan took office, the Board of Regents requested a 7 percent annual rise in funding for higher education over the biennium beginning July 1, 1999—4 percent for the base budget and 3 percent for performance-based activities like the Research Challenge. The Regents were newly led by Chancellor Rod Chu, who at thirty-four had been the youngest tax commissioner in New York State history and who had come to Ohio at the beginning of 1998 from the consulting firm Accenture. Chu and his staff were particularly effective at compiling statistical arguments that the Regents and others—Kirwan included—used to seek additional funding.

As usual, the Regents' request was the high-water mark in the budget process. Nonetheless, by the time Governor Bob Taft signed a $17.2 billion education budget, Kirwan was still able to say that while it didn't provide the university with everything it wanted, it "expressed a clear commitment to quality education at all levels." Combined with a 6 percent increase in tuition, the budget allowed for an overall 4 percent increase in faculty and staff compensation.

At the same time, two challenges hovered over the Ohio landscape. One was a historic reluctance within state government to fund higher education generously. By the end of the twentieth century, census data ranked Ohio thirty-ninth in the nation in the percentage of residents with a four-year degree, and Ohio's support for higher education as a percentage of total tax revenue lagged below the national average.

How did this affect Ohio State? In March 1999 Bill Shkurti—whom Kirwan considered "a superb CFO"—compared Ohio State's revenues to its nine benchmark universities. He found that state appropriations on average were about 8 percent below that of benchmark institutions, while tuition and fees were off by about 7 percent. Compared with other Ohio public universities, Ohio State was ninth out of thirteen for undergraduate tuition and fees. Leading the list in resources per student, Michigan came in at $39,999—about $15,000 more than Ohio State. "Multiply that over forty or fifty thousand

President Kirwan called Bill Shkurti "a superb CFO."

students," Shkurti told the trustees in a bit of understatement, "and that is a lot of money."

Like Rod Chu and others, Kirwan argued that an inadequate investment in higher education was shortsighted in a "knowledge economy" in which education was a key competitive factor. In a May 2001 editorial, *The Columbus Dispatch* agreed, writing that a strategy of starving higher education "will save a nickel now at the cost of not earning a dollar later." But despite support among many editorial boards and some thought leaders, the General Assembly received few constituent requests to spend more on higher education. At the same time, members were besieged by PTA groups, hundreds of school district superintendents and parents, and the business community to put more money into elementary and secondary schools, a need that became urgent as the century wound to a close.

The second challenge was a legal action to force greater support of K–12 public schools. In 1991 Dale R. DeRolph filed a lawsuit in Perry County, Ohio, on behalf of his son Nathan, alleging that Ohio's funding of public schools—with its heavy dependence upon property taxes—resulted in wide and unfair disparities among schools. DeRolph prevailed in a decision that in 1997 was upheld 4–3 by the Ohio Supreme Court. Kirwan says he was either unaware of this action or had not focused upon it, arriving in Ohio optimistic that additional state resources would be available. But the historical lack of support for higher education was destined to continue. Throughout the Kirwan years, and beyond, *DeRolph v. State of Ohio* consumed state dollars and, combined with a declining economy, adversely affected funding for higher education—especially during Kirwan's final two fiscal years. Because this subject is so central to the Kirwan years, it is covered below in some detail.

FY2002

Preparation of the budget that took effect in July 2001 began positively. In the fall of 2000, the Regents recommended a double-digit budget increase as well as significant growth for the Research Challenge, added funding for the Success Challenge, and implementation of the Ohio Plan, a proposal to invest an additional $150 million per year for five to seven years to build a university research infrastructure that would benefit the lagging state economy.

"Then," as Kirwan told the trustees in June 2001, "in an unrelenting series of setbacks over the intervening months, we have watched the 16 percent increase evaporate; the Ohio Plan—gone; increments to the Research Challenge and Success Challenge—gone; additional support for the state's share of instruction—gone. We now face a budget for the upcoming biennium with essentially no increase, meaning that, when inflation is taken into account, our purchasing power is actually reduced."

"At each step along the way," Kirwan continued, "there has been an explanation: the DeRolph mandate, the declining economy, a shortfall in the Medicaid budget. The net effect, however, is that in terms of state priorities, higher education has become the source for our other fiscal needs and shortfalls in the state budget." To illustrate his point, Kirwan noted that 45 percent of the most recent cuts to the governor's budget request were assigned to higher education, which represents just 13 percent of the total state budget. Six months earlier, he added, about half the $150 million in state agency cuts came from higher education.

"This has been the most difficult budget year since 1995," Bill Shkurti added, "and reflects the smallest increase in state support in nine years. That, combined with the largest increase in health care costs in a decade and the largest increase in energy costs in two decades, leaves us making only limited progress on many of our goals outlined in the Academic Plan."

"Quite frankly," Kirwan told the University Senate, "Ohio State has reached a level of quality that the state doesn't deserve, given its dismal support of higher education." The senators applauded.

One strength of the Academic Plan—and one reason it was taken so seriously—was its specificity. Each of the fourteen initiatives included specific implementation costs over the first five years. Overall, the Academic Plan was estimated to require an investment of approximately $750 million in new and reallocated resources over that period of time, compared to $3.3 billion in total university spending for education and general functions (excluding such auxiliaries as the hospitals and athletics) over the prior five years. Academic Plan funding was divided into two categories: continuing funds that would reappear annually and onetime expenditures. Beyond revenue available from existing (baseline) funding, money was expected to come from new state programs (e.g., tobacco funds), more creative internal approaches, relief from the state's 6 percent cap on tuition increases, and private fund-raising. Continuing funds appeared to present a greater challenge than did onetime resources.

Without question, budget cuts sharply limited the extent to which Ohio State could implement its brand-new Academic Plan. "We cannot proceed at anything close to the pace that we believe would best serve the university and the people of Ohio," the president said. But "disappointed as we are with the budget," he added, "we will do the best we can with what we have."

In responding to these negative budgetary circumstances, the university administration enacted a number of austerity measures—chief among them the flat $395 salary increase described in chapter 5. In addition, when a $28 million cut in state support surfaced in the middle of FY2002—the second reduction in state support that year—the university dipped into its Rainy Day Fund for just over $5 million, which it repaid the following year. It redirected $6 million from central budgets and identified another $8.4 million from support units and colleges. Other steps included the

limitation of strategic hiring of senior, national academy–caliber faculty to those cases already in progress;
imposition of a selective freeze on hiring for most noninstructional personnel;
postponement of new commitments to Academic Enrichment funding; and
delayed implementation of a transition to competitive admissions.

On the plus side, higher-than-expected summer and autumn 2001 enrollment provided additional tuition and (formula-based) state support at a time when they were badly needed. And the creation by the trustees of a President's Strategic Investment Fund provided some discretionary funding for new projects. In addition, the governor and General Assembly lifted the 6 percent cap on tuition. Ohio State and other Ohio public colleges and universities had long sought that objective, arguing that a cap violated free-market principles and that if the state was not going to adequately fund higher education, it should at least permit the institutions to raise more money on their own.

When it came to tuition, Ohio State was trying to dig itself out of a hole. During the 1980s, the university agreed to keep its tuition rates down in exchange for increased state support. Most other public universities, which also received additional state support, raised tuition anyway and later, when tuition was capped at 6 percent, Ohio State was locked into these lower rates. Unsuccessful in the past in eliminating tuition caps, Ohio State now sought special dispensation to exceed 6 percent.

When the dust cleared in 2002, however, the General Assembly had eliminated the cap entirely, giving all of Ohio's public universities the ability to raise tuition at will. Ohio State raised tuition by 9.3 percent, warning that similar increases were likely over the next few years. The university also committed to using tuition revenues above the former 6 percent cap to directly benefit improvements in undergraduate education and to affect a corresponding increase in financial aid so that students otherwise qualified academically to enter Ohio State were not penalized. With the increase, tuition and fees totaled $4,761 for the 2001–2002 academic year. That money was important. Of the projected $35 million increase in the FY2002 budget, 80 percent would come from tuition and fees.

"Although the 9.3 percent increase is larger than recent years," the university said in a news release, "Ohio State continues to be a bargain. Assuming that other institutions raise their fees at least six percent, Ohio State tuition will [now] rank seventh out of 13 public [Ohio] universities."

FY2003

No sooner had these decisions been made than the university began working on its FY2003 budget, which would take effect on July 1, 2002. This time, the news was even more somber, with the economy continuing to worsen, the State Supreme Court ruling that the state needed to appropriate yet more money to K–12 education, the events of September 11, 2001, and declining state revenues. As things developed, Governor Bob Taft ordered a 6 percent rescission on all state agency funds—totaling over $27 million university-wide and more than $19 million from instructional subsidy at the Columbus campus. Clearly, stronger measures would be required than in the prior year, especially since the Kirwan administration had committed itself to pay raises that would start to close the gap with competition.

Available options, the president said, were to "hunker down, put our vision on hold, and muddle through the next few years as best we can" or to "develop an active response built on self-reliance and prioritization." Not surprisingly, he chose the latter course. Recognizing that the key to progress in the current environment was to focus on a small number of critical objectives, and that the Academic Plan was helpful in forging such a focus, President Kirwan proposed a list of items that became four focus areas. These items were tweaked to comprise what he called "a respectable and meaningful agenda" for the coming year.

In addition to compensation, which was the top priority, the university proposed to advance the Academic Plan through initiatives (discussed earlier) to continue enhancing undergraduate programs using "over-the-cap" tuition funds; begin a major biomedical research initiative, drawing in part upon tobacco settlement funds; and establish an Institute for the Study of Race and Ethnicity in the Americas, using funds earmarked the prior year. As the president told the senate in October, these items were selected "not only for their intrinsic merit and their effect on various Plan strategies but also because funding for them has been identified."

How would Ohio State fund the compensation initiative, make progress toward Academic Plan goals, and otherwise operate with an anticipated $19 million cut in state General Funds? The administration presented a four-point plan to generate between $35 and $45 million in FY2003:

1. Aggressively pursue increased revenues from sources other than General Fund appropriations, e.g., tuition, private fundraising, and government/industry grants.
2. Reduce centrally funded initiatives by 10 percent to free up funds at the college and unit level, including a cut in the Strategic Investment Fund from $4 million to $2 million.
3. Ask academic support units to reprogram up to 7 percent of the next year's budget.
4. Ask colleges to reprogram up to 5 percent of the next year's budget.

"Difficult though it will be," Kirwan told the senate, "it is important to keep our challenge in perspective." He noted that during the early 1990s, the university cut budgets for support units by 20 percent and colleges by 15 percent, leading to the elimination of some eleven hundred positions—but fewer than one hundred actual layoffs. Moreover, those earlier cuts were primarily intended to reduce expenditures. In contrast, Kirwan said, the later cuts were intended to free up money that could be redirected to higher priority items.

At the February 2001 trustees meeting, by which time university units had formulated their plans, Kirwan outlined a $73 million funding package for the fiscal year beginning July 1, 2002. It included budget reductions and reallocations as well as revenue-generating actions that included increased tuition for new students. The money would go to attract and retain high-quality faculty ($30–$34 million), student scholarships and financial aid ($11–$12 million), programs such as Selective Investment and enhanced recruiting ($8–$11 million), and absorption of state budget cuts ($20 million). Of the $73 million, budget savings and reprogramming would provide $36 million (and eliminate almost six hundred jobs in 2002), which, combined with $24 million in previously planned undergraduate, graduate, and professional tuition increases, would produce $60 million. The remaining $13 million needed, Kirwan said, must come from additional tuition funds.

Despite the changing circumstances, Kirwan and his colleagues were mindful of an implied commitment to charge current students no more than 9 percent for the next four or five years. So Kirwan proposed maintaining that rate for current students but raising tuition for *new* students by $1,200, which amounted to a 34 percent increase. This ingenious two-tier approach had been implemented successfully at the University of Illinois and offered the advantage that new students still had the option to enroll elsewhere. It also played better with current students, who would not have to pay the higher amount and who eventually endorsed the proposal.

As he had done the year before, Kirwan emphasized that the equivalent of 30 to 40 percent of the differential tuition money from new students would be placed into financial aid, on which Ohio State was already spending $32 million a year. He also emphasized that the university would continue to reduce costs and reprogram existing resources, reallocating funds to high-enrollment areas and otherwise continuing to enhance the undergraduate experience.

"It all comes down to this," Kirwan wrote in a *Dispatch* op-ed article. "Like the state, we are obliged to balance our budget. If we can't do it with state funds, we must reluctantly turn to tuition or compromise the excellence that Ohio needs. Given this reality, we have proposed an approach that is necessary, reasonable and fair."

The tuition plan was "our ace in the hole," Kirwan states, "and our only hope of moving the university forward toward the goals of the plan."

In February and March a battle raged, largely behind the scenes, over the two-tier tuition proposal. In January Kirwan had outlined the proposal to Governor Taft, the legislative leadership, and the Board of Trustees—receiving

President Kirwan with Governor Taft.

what he considered a green light to proceed. Taft, Kirwan recalls, "said he hated to see it but that he understood [the need] and would not object publicly." On the day before the February board meeting, Kirwan ran into the governor, who "said he could not support the 34 percent increase for new students because the fallout would be too severe."

"I was flabbergasted," Kirwan says. "I told the governor that we were set to make the proposal public the next day, and we would probably have to move forward with it. I reported all of this to the board, and they agreed that we should proceed with the presentation—with the understanding that they would not vote until the next meeting in March."

Kirwan remained confident. He felt that the trustees, who had long complained about tuition levels that were among the lowest in Ohio, had committed to the plan. What's more, he considered their comments at the February meeting supportive, with one trustee citing the need "to put a stake in the ground." Thus, he and representatives of the Inter-University Council began to negotiate with Brian Hicks, Taft's chief of staff. Ultimately, the universities agreed to spread the large increase over two years, although the governor's office did not commit to support the second installment.

In fact, some trustees were uncomfortable about a confrontation with the governor and hoped for a compromise. "As we approached the meeting to vote on the plan," Kirwan says, "board members began feeling squeamish about it. I suspect many had talked to the governor. During the week of the board meeting, support for the plan fell apart. Some board members even said they had never really been for it. No one spoke up in its defense. I felt betrayed."

"I wanted to say [publicly] that we intended to accomplish both steps," Kirwan says, referencing the two-year approach. "To me, it was a matter of principle. The board wanted us to be silent on the second year. I asked that they at least let me inform the governor's office of the board's intention to proceed in year two. They said 'no,' at which point David Brennan objected, saying, 'You have to let him do that.' So I called, telling them [the governor's office] I wanted to say it was our intention to complete the second step the next year but not committing the governor. Taft said, 'Okay,' and when I informed the board, there was stunned silence. I believe several, if not all board members were somewhat embarrassed that they had not been more supportive. It turns out the governor was more supportive than they were."

These discussions constituted a low point in Kirwan's relations with the Board of Trustees and a factor in his decision to return to Maryland. Among those with grave concerns about the tuition proposal was former Speaker of the House Jo Ann Davidson, who was very close to the governor and Republican legislators.

"It was a tough position, particularly for me," Davidson recalls. "I had six years as Speaker of the House, two of these years with Governor Taft's administration. I just had to be very up-front with the board members and say, 'Look, these are my experiences, this is where I've come from, and consequently I want to be very sensitive to where the governor's office and the legislature are on these things,' and I think that didn't please Brit a lot. But you know you have to deal with the situation you find yourself in at the time, and that is where I was. It was not pleasant for me, particularly as the new board member, the new kid on the block, so to speak. And yet my background was my background, and everybody reflects their background."

How did Speaker Davidson think all this affected Kirwan? "I think he was discouraged," she says. "I think there was a period of time when he felt the board was not giving as strong a support as he would have liked. . . . I think he felt he went down the road thinking the board was there, and when it came to the final decision, there was a little bit of resistance and a little bit of backing off—do you take the governor on or not? I think that at some particular point there was a honest feeling on the part of some of the board members that perhaps he [Kirwan] got too far out on the limb."

"Unfortunately," says Ginny Trethewey, "Brit had no confidant on the Board of Trustees. In contrast, Gordon worked the board all the time." While there had been a board of visitors and a system board in Maryland, Kirwan's job did not include managing a board relationship. At Ohio State, he had a board that met ten times a year, which, in Kirwan's words, "encourages a level of involvement and micromanagement." "The board realized that and commissioned the McKinsey Report in 1997," he says. "It is fair to say I could have worked the Board of Trustees more." With few exceptions, however, Kirwan adds, the board was very supportive.

Those who served with Kirwan on the Board of Trustees likewise considered relations generally good. Members of the board loved Ohio State, felt honored to be appointed, relished the opportunity to give back, enjoyed the collegiality that mostly characterizes board relations, and liked watching the Buckeyes from the University Suite in Ohio Stadium. Presidents of universities like Ohio State work very hard, and even hard-nosed businesspeople like David Brennan are impressed. "Gordon and Brit each taught me that being a university president is the hardest job I've ever seen," Brennan says. "Twenty-four seven. So my number-one job was to serve as cheerleader for the president." In response, Kirwan says that Brennan "was extraordinarily supportive as chair."

In any event, the Inter-University Council and Governor Taft reached agreement on a set of tuition principles at IUC schools. (There was also an informal understanding that the governor would not further cut higher education that year.) Ohio State scaled back its new-student supplement from $1,200 to $474, an increase of 18.9 percent. "Regarding future years," Kirwan said, "we remain committed to our original plan." Interestingly, when the process ended, Ohio State still ranked ninth in tuition for continuing students and eighth for new students among Ohio's thirteen public universities, since the others had raised their rates also. Then, in 2003, the governor and General Assembly imposed a 9 percent tuition cap, with a special 12 percent cap for Ohio State.

But the story wasn't over. In late June 2002, the General Assembly passed and the governor signed a budget with even less money than had been anticipated in May. When the trustees met on July 11, shortly after Kirwan had left for Maryland, they were forced to raise tuition even more. The two-tier system became a three-tier system: increases of 9 percent for continuing students and 19 percent for new students in FY2003, and increases of 15 to 16 percent for all resident undergraduates in FY2004. At the time, Provost Ed Ray pointed out that the state's share of instruction—the mainstay of state support—was "lower now than it was four years ago."

Pondering the trend of falling state support, at least as a percentage of total university revenue, different people react in different ways.

"The economic future of the university is in very serious jeopardy," warns David Brennan. "Tuition cannot keep going up, and the state does not have the money. I would make a deal with the state in which OSU would gradually work its way out of state support in exchange for lifting the shackles [of state regulations and requirements]. Unfortunately, it will take a crisis to do that, which is too bad since planning ahead could soften the blow."

Others disagree. Ted Celeste, another former board chair, notes that "other states have committed the money and bought into the economic engine theory." Kirwan believes the state's claim of poverty is a "cop-out," noting that many other states support higher education more generously.

"One of the mysteries that I hope one day to figure out and write about," Kirwan has said, "is how is it that people in Ohio can care so much about Ohio State and give to it, and yet the state ranks forty-first per capita in support of higher education. This needs to change."

Budget Restructuring

Beginning July 1, 2002, Ohio State began to change the way it distributes money to academic units, hoping to foster increased entrepreneurship and accountability. The university had been designing and preparing for this change since the mid-1990s under such rubrics as "incentive-based budgeting" and "responsibility-centered management," but adoption of the Academic Plan helped make it a reality. Quoted in *onCampus*, CFO Bill Shkurti explained that "[a]s early discussions of possible changes in the budget process took place, it became clear that any budget driven by academic goals required a plan that reflected exactly what those goals would be." The Academic Plan identified those goals.

Budget restructuring sought to replace the incremental, across-the-board increases that have long characterized the allocation process with incentives for academic units to generate revenues or reduce costs. The first step, initiated in FY2002, began a five-year process to "rebase" budgets for the eighteen degree-granting colleges, utilizing such factors as a college's role in advancing the Academic Plan, its ability to generate revenues, and the cost structure of its academic programs. This rebasing will result in the redirection among colleges of between $9.5 and $13 million.

The extent to which funds have been used for focused purposes was reflected in the fact that during FY2002, five of the eighteen colleges received 73 percent of Strategic Investment Funds.

As noted in a university news release, the budget restructuring process will encourage colleges and departments to provide new programs, create new courses, reduce course access problems, collaborate with industry partners, expand federally funded research, and undertake other initiatives. Revenue generated by such activities as offering more sections of high-demand courses to students closed out of courses and creating new majors that meet student career plans will be used to provide direct financial support for the programs that create them.

"We are . . . decentralizing decisions regarding both revenues and expenses to the colleges," Ray added. "We think that this activity will make the flow of revenues and expenses more transparent to all of us and, in the process, make it possible for us to increase accountability at every level in the use of those resources."

"It is not my goal to make every college a 'tub on its own bottom' by driving every college to a break-even position under some formulaic procedure," Ray said. "Instead, the goal is to give every college a clear understanding of what we

Ed Ray (center), shown here with Bobby Moser (left), President Kirwan, and Thomas Payne, then director of OARDC and now dean at the University of Missouri.

expect from them academically, what resources they can expect to generate themselves, and what resources they can expect from the university."

Senior vice provost Alayne Parson emphasized that budget restructuring "is simply a tool. People make the decisions. We have to continue to rely on our leadership to make decisions in alignment with the mission of the university." But this tool did not come easily.

"I know of no other university that did it," says Ray. "I was told by outside consultants that to do it would be like holding the Nuremburg trials and trying to win the peace. We did it because there was strong internal support for it. [But] everyone who did not get new money, and even some who did, gave me a hard time and made it a tough policy to implement."

13

Strength in Numbers

Recognizing that times were changing, the Board of Trustees and administration have become increasingly proactive in seeking to control Ohio State's own financial destiny. In the process, the university built one of the nation's leading academic fund-raising operations and, as described earlier, has been ever more successful in winning grants from the federal government and private industry. While state support continues to slip as a proportion of its revenues, the university has become more aggressive in making its case to the governor and General Assembly. It also works hard to maintain, enhance, and build upon its extraordinary level of alumni support and has strengthened its communications capabilities.

"Affirm Thy Friendship"

Between 1985 and 1990, under the leadership of Ed Jennings, Ohio State raised $460 million in a capital campaign that made the university a credible player in big-time university fund-raising. In 1995, under Gordon Gee, the university launched an even more ambitious $850 million, five-year capital campaign—naming it "Affirm Thy Friendship," inspired by the words in alma mater "Carmen Ohio." The 1990s were an extraordinarily good time to raise money—donors "gave more and more again and more than they thought they would give," says Jerry May, former vice president for Development and president of the University Foundation—and the campaign was progressing well. In fact, by June 30, 1998, the eve of Kirwan's arrival, the campaign had raised 91 percent of its goal.

May had been on the Presidential Search Committee and had gone on the second trip east to meet Kirwan. "As soon as I saw and heard him, I knew this was the right person for us," he said later. Then, as they walked down the hall in the Fawcett Center on January 5, 1998, Brit put his arm around his new Development vice president and not so subtly asked, "So, can we make a billion?" May and his staff, who had been thinking in a similar fashion, could hardly wait to talk further.

"One of the neatest things you can do with a new president is give him the opportunity to increase the goal," May says. "It becomes his. We fell into it. He took a level of ownership for our success. We decided it was feasible, added some projects, and went ahead. It was the most seamless relationship I think I've ever seen. Immediately, we went on the road with him, where his warmth and affability won people over."

Kirwan and Foundation Board chair (and campaign cochair) Thekla "Teckie" Shackelford announced the new $1 billion goal on September 11, 1998, at a ceremony on the Oval—with more than fifteen hundred people raising flashlights over their heads to form an illuminated Block "O." Ohio State thus joined only six other public universities that at the time had billion-dollar campaign goals: UCLA, the University of California–Berkeley, and the Universities of Illinois, Michigan, Minnesota, and Virginia.

By year's end, campaign gifts, pledges, and planned gift totals exceeded $885 million. By January 31, 1999, the university endowment—separate from the campaign—broke the billion-dollar mark, placing it in the top ten nationally. As Kirwan told the trustees, "[I]t took 113 years to reach $50 million, 20 more years to reach $500 million, and 4 more years to reach $1 billion." The overall campaign closed on June 30, 2000, and on September 22, to pyrotechnical accompaniment, Kirwan announced to a thousand guests in Mershon Auditorium that final campaign commitments totaled more than $1.23 billion—more specifically, $1,230,910,996.

Ray Groves, chair of the University Foundation Board, and Shackelford were two of the first people Kirwan met after becoming president. Groves visited the president-designate in Maryland for a two-hour private lunch shortly after the announcement and concluded that Kirwan was "one of the most sincere people I have ever met in my life," adding that "you get 110 percent of his attention." Kirwan developed what he calls "a special relationship" with the then-managing partner at Ernst & Young and often traveled to New York for relationship-building dinners that Groves hosted, including the annual Night at the New York Philharmonic, arranged by Foundation Board member Fred Krimendahl.

Reese Medal recipient Teckie Shackelford (second from right) with (left to right) Ray Groves, Erin Moriarty, Jerry May, and President Kirwan.

Kirwan and Shackelford also bonded quickly. Daughter of the late Everett "Ev" Reese, for whom the university's highest private philanthropic honor is named and herself a recipient of the Reese Medal, Teckie Shackelford is an education consultant and a founder and chair of "I Know I Can," an organization that encourages and assists Columbus school children on their path to college. Along with her husband, Don, chair of Fifth Third Bank of Columbus, they are generous givers to OSU. She and Kirwan shared a common interest in diversity, including especially the need for all students to have the opportunity to succeed academically.

In the end, all individual campaign goals were surpassed:

Scholarship and student support: $105.9 million (106 percent of goal)
Quality learning environments: $146.4 million (122 percent of goal)
Faculty and teaching: $94.4 million (135 percent of goal)
Arts, culture, and libraries: $43.4 million (108 percent of goal)
Research and service partnerships: $242 million (121 percent of goal)
Health and wellness: $226.6 million (142 percent of goal)

Ray Groves sports the white hat normally worn by trustee David Brennan (right) in this photo with President Kirwan.

Academic learning and leadership: $111.8 million (140 percent of goal)
Annual giving: $93.7 million (117 percent of goal)
Planned giving: $166.6 million (111 percent of goal)

The numbers were indeed impressive. The campaign would fund 493 newly endowed scholarships and fellowships for Ohio State students; seventy-nine newly endowed chairs and professorships for faculty; over $146 million in new and enhanced facilities, laboratories, equipment, and technology; and more than $242 million for outreach and discovery initiatives, including 269 new endowed research and program funds. More than $35 million was contributed by faculty, staff, and students. Overall, 258,426 donors made 1,222,271 gifts, an average of one gift every forty-three seconds of every workday. Over the five-year period, the university endowment grew from a market value of $493.2 million to almost $1.3 billion. Finally, the $1.23 billion in total campaign commitments exceeded the total amount of gifts received during the previous 123 years of Ohio State's existence.

But as reported by *onCampus*, the end of "Affirm Thy Friendship" did not signal the end of fund-raising. "I don't think there will be one moment of lost momentum," Teckie Shackelford accurately predicted. "Striving toward being the best completely changes your way of thinking." Instead of taking a breather at campaign's end, Kirwan made certain that Development got the necessary resources to keep going, and in the first year following the campaign, the results continued to be good—gift receipts were actually up over the last campaign year. By the next year, in contrast, the economy was in a recession and giving tailed off.

Over the four Kirwan years, only two of which were part of the campaign but all of which benefited from the excellent work that others had done, there was more than $1 billion of fund-raising activity—almost $718 million in gift receipts, $160 million in annual pledges acquired, and $140 million in acquired planned gifts.

The Magic Touch

Why has Ohio State been so successful in its fund-raising? Jerry May, whom Kirwan calls "one of the best in his business in America," attributes that success primarily to "amazing resources," including an alumni body that "by and large has fallen in love with the university and its service mission and cares deeply about Ohio State." Another resource is the state of Ohio, which "seems to have adopted Ohio State, in part because of football, and which is filled with folks who did not attend Ohio State but are fervent supporters nonetheless." For example, approximately 55 percent of the university's donations come from individuals (as opposed to corporations or foundations), and of that number, only about 60 percent are alumni. Donors in the city of Columbus and Franklin County contributed more than $350 million to the "Affirm Thy Friendship" campaign.

It's a good thing, too. With state support continuing to decline, fund-raising is one way to fill the gap. "The pressure to raise funds today is relentless," May told *Dispatch* reporter Alice Thomas for a major article on the topic. "Fundraising at a public university 20 years ago was an extra. It was, 'Yes, it would be nice to have it.' Now, it's becoming part of the budget."

Ohio State takes full advantage of this support with a sophisticated development operation that the *Dispatch* termed a "Money Machine." May calls it a "systematic approach" to fund-raising comprised of six elements:

1. A Board of Trustees that "emotionally and financially supported the campaign enterprise and gave proportionately to their wealth quite generously."
2. A University Foundation that not only gives generously but also hosts events, identifies prospects, serves as ambassadors, and performs other vital functions. At the urging of Ray Groves, the Foundation was expanded from thirty to forty-five people, with most of the new members coming from outside Ohio.
3. A series of major gift committees around the country to help identify prospects university-wide and within individual colleges.
4. Development advisory committees within schools and colleges to perform a similar role.
5. The involvement, engagement, stimulation, and education of college deans, an effort begun under President Gee. Deans are trained in fund-raising and strongly encouraged to visit prospects all over America. They can spend a quarter of their time—or more—on fund-raising, and are evaluated in part on their fund-raising ability.
6. Finally, the recruitment, sustenance, and stimulation of a great Development staff. "It was a team unlike any I've ever seen," May says, praising their work in preparing publications and other marketing materials, arranging donor events at the president's residence and those on the road hosted by the Foundation Board.

That staff totals around 250 people campuswide, with about 160 of them (including 90 or so professional fund-raisers) paid by the Development Office. Even at this size, notes John Meyer, associate vice president for Development, OSU is lean relative to its peers while raising more money. The budget is approximately $14.5 million, and of every dollar raised, about seven to eight cents goes to support the fund-raising operation. As noted elsewhere, Development costs are now paid out of fund-raising receipts rather than from the university's General Fund. Even students are called into play, paid to staff fund-raising phone banks five nights per week.

Yet another success factor is good collaboration among various parts of the university. "The walls between units are not thick; they are porous and not too high," May says. "Good collaboration is possible there. It is a very professional group of people, of which I was proud to be a part." Clearly, no walls existed between May and Kirwan, who played tennis regularly, often at Dr. Howard Sirak's home near the president's residence. Other regulars included David Frantz and Alex Shumate and, less frequently, John Berry Jr. and Harley Rouda.

May also attributes some of their success to the Academic Plan. "People don't give to leaderless or directionless institutions," he notes. "Brit set the direction, built on OSU strengths, increased aspirations, and presented concrete steps to get there. The plan was everything. It provided clear direction, a level of assurance donors wanted."

Finally, May considers himself fortunate to have worked for two presidents who were strong leaders and superb fund-raisers. While both were effective, the two presidents offered decidedly differing styles. Gee was a master at working a room; Kirwan spoke with fewer people, but in more depth. Thus, when Kirwan replaced Gee, Development handled public events by bringing people to the president. The two presidential couples also entertained differently. "Gee preferred large groups, noisy, high-energy," says John Meyer. "The Kirwans were more subdued. It was the difference between MTV and PBS. Both were effective."

Among the highlights of the fund-raising year is Winter College, when a few hundred donors gather during February in Naples, Florida, to rub elbows and attend seminars by high-profile OSU faculty such as the husband-and-wife geologist team of Lonnie Thompson and Ellen Mosley-Thompson. Initiated during the Gee years, few universities can match the breadth and depth of OSU's Winter College program. "Faculty members clamor to participate," Jerry May says. "It's a fundraising magnet. Every dean in attendance visits five to ten donors in addition to participating in the college event itself."

Another very important method of building relationships that often lead to major gifts is football. The new stadium boxes hosted by the president, athletic director, and trustees—as well as some boxes hosted by colleges and companies—are highly coveted and used for entertainment. Kirwan and May would go from box to box, visiting prospects like George Steinbrenner. "I can barely quantify, but it's worth tens of millions of dollars a year," May estimates. "And not just for athletics. It especially facilitates academic fund-raising."

Another excellent entertainment venue was the president's residence in Bexley. The Kirwans had become friendly with developer Ron Pizzuti and his wife, Ann, and were entertained at the Pizzuti's home on North Drexel, just down the street from the presidential residence on Commonwealth Park North. The Kirwans had admired the house, and later Ron and Ann donated it to the University Foundation in exchange for the current presidential

Among the faculty presenters at Winter College in 2001 was Mauro Ferrari, shown here with President Kirwan and Michael Hermanoff (far left) and Paul Werth (second from right).

residence. The actual gift represented the difference between the Pizzuti home, appraised at $2.3 million, and the eventual sale price of the Commonwealth property.

"Patty and I were very touched and overwhelmed," Kirwan says. "We very much enjoyed living there. The kids loved it, and our grandsons were always pushing their parents to visit. One grandson said, 'This is the best house you ever lived in.'" The other grandson, later commenting about the Kirwan's current official residence in Maryland, expressed the hope to his grandparents that "[o]ne day I hope you'll have a house you can keep."

Government Relations

Like presidents before him, Kirwan spent considerable time attempting to wring more money out of the General Assembly—sometimes as a representative of Ohio State, other times representing the Inter-University Council and higher education generally. Among those helping him with this task were Bill

Napier, special assistant to the president for Government Relations; Colleen O'Brien, director of State Relations; and Ohio husband-and-wife team Curt Steiner and Jan Allen.

When Steiner and Allen were hired to help Ohio State and other institutions get a portion of the tobacco settlement money for biomedical research, they were communications and issues strategists at HMS Success Partners. They later helped found Steiner/Lesic Communications, which offers media relations and public affairs services as well as strategic counsel. Steiner was a key GOP strategist in Ohio, having served as chief of staff and communications director for Governor George Voinovich (where he first met Kirwan in 1998) and having played a major role in Voinovich's two elections as governor and his election as United States senator. He also helped Mike DeWine win election to the U.S. Senate. Allen, a life and executive coach, lawyer, and psychotherapist, was deputy chief of staff and communications director for Governor Dick Celeste—the first woman to hold a top position in the governor's office.

Kirwan relied heavily on this "power couple" for public affairs advice and legislative strategy and tactics. While Napier was downtown courting legislators, Steiner and Allen were formulating policies to build support and attract additional funds for Ohio State and other public colleges and universities. Kirwan also spent time downtown, testifying and buttonholing legislators.

Another player in the governmental arena was Herb Asher, a professor of political science who was especially close to his students and to many Democratic public officials. When Napier left Ohio State in 1982, Asher was asked to handle the university's lobbying on a short-term basis. He agreed, liked it, and remained in that position, devoting half his time to political science and the remainder to building relations downtown. He also gave broader advice to Presidents Jennings and Gee. Asher took early retirement in 1995 but continued to teach part-time while assuming the position of counselor to the president. Kirwan found Asher to be a very valuable resource and kept him in that role. As previously noted, Asher also served as interim director of the Glenn Institute during its first two years.

The university's government relations endeavors were buttressed by Lee Tashjian and University Relations professionals such as Elizabeth Conlisk and Karen Patterson. Together, these staffers honed and disseminated the president's message on campus and off and arranged for frequent meetings with newspaper editorial boards all over Ohio. These visits resulted in strong editorial support. Repeatedly, major dailies echoed the president's position and strongly encouraged Governor Taft and the General Assembly to follow Kirwan's lead. "He did as much as anyone in the twenty years I was involved in

Former House Speaker Jo Ann Davidson was named to the Ohio State Board of Trustees in 2001.

the legislature in raising awareness, in gaining editorial support," says former House Speaker and trustee Jo Ann Davidson.

"Ironically," adds Bill Shkurti, "while Gordon was considered the consummate politician and great communicator, under Brit the university made a better case for state money. If the budget crisis had not intervened, there might have been a breakthrough."

Kirwan's message was also communicated on campus, through traditional publications such as *onCampus* and new distribution media like the e-mail-delivered *OSUToday*. Further, the Alumni Association's Ohio State Advocates contacted legislators and others on behalf of the university and its needs.

Despite such efforts, the success rate downtown was not high. At the same time, most felt that Kirwan did about as well as could be expected. "It was tough sledding and still is, and it will be in the future," says Alex Shumate. "It is an extremely conservative body," adds trustee Robert Duncan. "The degree of difficulty was huge. The other thing that made it difficult was the fact that we've had such a long history of lack of support. We're almost entrenched with this notion we've got a good university, who needs to do anything to make it better?" The situation was also aggravated by the imposition of legislative term limits, under which longtime experienced legislators like Davidson were forced to retire, replaced by new members with less knowledge and experience in state government.

"We trustees probably could have done a better job of getting out in front with the president, and the friends of the university should have perhaps rallied more aggressively," says Dimon McFerson. "We allowed him to go down to the State House alone too many times. Legislators, when they have to make difficult decisions about balancing the budget, look around and say, 'Well, what are the ramifications if I cut here? Am I going to hear from anybody or not?'"

Kirwan believes that he might have done better with the General Assembly. "For a variety of reasons, not all of my making, I did not develop the kind of relationship with the General Assembly that I had in Maryland," Kirwan says. "I should have spent more time building that relationship, although I did have a good relationship with some members." He feels better about his relationship with Governor Taft, noting, "We had a good personal relationship. He was very supportive on most issues. He faced a fiscal challenge that made it impossible to invest in higher education in the way I hoped he would. Patty and I always enjoyed being with him and Hope."

Jim McCollum, who directs the IUC, notes that Brit was the key negotiator between the IUC and the governor on FY2003 tuition and budget cuts. McCollum also calls Kirwan instrumental in the passage of SB 286, which allowed academics more freedom to benefit from entrepreneurial activity. And for the first time, the General Assembly asked the IUC to prepare model rules to implement that concept.

"When he came on board [the IUC]," McCollum says, "there were the usual suspicions and fears about the nine-hundred-pound gorilla. Will OSU strike out on its own, ignoring the others? Whatever anxiety there was evaporated very quickly. Through alphabetical happenstance, Brit was thrust into a broader lead role as vice chair in his second year. He brought the same consensus-building approach as he did on campus. He also managed to set an ambitious OSU agenda in a way that didn't threaten the others. He was a warm person, concerned about how his colleagues would feel about any OSU initiative."

Kirwan also encouraged a more proactive, aggressive posture between the university and the federal government. Led by Richard Stoddard, who in 1995 transferred from the Office of Research to the Office of the President as director of Federal Affairs, the university sought not only additional funding but also to influence legislation that affected higher education's ability to do its job. After failing to get Congress to earmark funding for the Glenn Institute, the university hired the lobbying firm of Cassidy Associates to increase its effectiveness, later dropping them and returning to in-house representation.

Other resources for higher education issues generally were the several Washington-based associations to which universities like Ohio State belong. Here again Stoddard was Kirwan's point person, staffing his activities and representing him between major meetings. With his seniority and wealth of contacts, Kirwan was a national leader in higher education and played key roles within these groups. He chaired two major committees at the National Association of State Universities and Land-Grant Colleges (NASULGC) and later became that organization's chair. As noted, he also chaired the final report of the Kellogg Commission on the Future of State and Land-Grant Universities.

Kirwan was also active in the Association of American Universities (AAU), a more exclusive group of sixty-one presidents of Research I universities, and the American Council on Education (ACE), later becoming its chair. Along with KPMG CEO Stephen Butler, he cochaired a business–higher education forum report entitled, Investing in People: Developing All of America's Talent on Campus and in the Workplace.

"Enter a hotel lobby with Brit (during a NASULGC meeting), and eighteen people would cluster around," says vice provost Randy Smith. "He was known and respected."

Kirwan is highly complimentary of the support he received at Ohio State. "In general, the quality of staff and professionalism was extraordinary," he says.

Alumni Relations

Like other presidents, Kirwan spent a lot of time with alumni, many of whom are strong boosters of the university and help it in many ways. Almost four hundred thousand alumni are alive today, and many of them belong to the Alumni Association, which was founded in 1879 and features fifty societies and two hundred clubs located throughout the world. Kirwan visited a number of these clubs, including some outside the United States.

Brit and board chair Ted Celeste led a delegation to India, where in 1957 the State Department had invited Ohio State to help create three agricultural universities. As part of the first "Green Revolution," these universities were instrumental in converting India from a nation that could not feed its own people to one with a surplus of food. That prior relationship was helpful when the ten-member delegation returned in 1999. During that visit, they met not only with Indian agricultural officials—who sought help in a second-generation "Green Revolution"—but also with leaders in the humanities and engineering. "I remember on the India trip," Ted Celeste says, "that one time our bags—with OSU stickers on them—arrived on the airport carousel and some stranger yelled, 'Go Bucks!'"

The second trip took place in June 2000, when Kirwan led a twelve-member contingent to Japan, Korea, and Taiwan. Kirwan met with several government leaders, including the new president of Taiwan, Shui-Bian Chen, and Taiwan's new minister of education, C. L. Tseng. He also visited the National Chung Hsing University in Taichung, Taiwan; the National Taiwan University; Yonsei University in Seoul; and Tokyo University—lecturing on the global university at National Chung Hsing and Yonsei. Upon return, Kirwan told the trustees that "our focus at these universities was to signal our interest in recruiting outstanding students for graduate study at Ohio State, to create opportunities for our students to study abroad, and to develop stronger research collaboration possibilities for our faculty."

The delegation was particularly impressed by the enthusiastic participation of alumni, who arranged receptions in Tokyo, Taiwan, and Seoul, with well over one hundred people at each event. "In Taiwan," says Dan Heinlen, then president of The Ohio State University Alumni Association, "they met us at the airport and stayed with us the entire trip. Without any request on our part, they raised enough money to cover all ground transportation, our hotel stay, the entire alumni reception—and it was elaborate—for four days. Then they presented Brit with a check for an additional $15,000 for the university. It was absolutely astounding. They couldn't do enough for us."

"The premier [of Taiwan] at that time was not an Ohio State alumnus," Bobby Moser recalls, "but we gave him an honorary degree. So he became an honorary Buckeye, and he became one of the first contributors to the endowment we established there. We held a dinner. We sing 'Carmen Ohio' here all the time. But you know what, there's more than one verse to 'Carmen Ohio.' They sing all the verses. We had to read them off the page like everybody else." Says Kirwan, "When you hear a large group of alumni in Taiwan, about as far from Columbus as you can get, singing all three verses of 'Carmen Ohio' with passion and gusto, it just leaves an indescribable feeling of pride in the university and its impact on people all over the world."

A new alumni facility had been planned in the early 1990s as an addition to the Fawcett Center for Tomorrow. It was at the depths of a recession, when fund-raising was difficult, and by 1996 it was decided to reduce the project's scale. Then, an initial turn of bad luck brought a happy ending. "Four weeks before breaking ground," says Heinlen, "we were called into a meeting and informed that we were building on a nuclear waste site. We had to start over from scratch with a brand-new building."

Heinlen convinced President Gee that the environmental problem wasn't the association's fault and that the university should participate significantly in the project, which would now cost $11 million rather than the original $4.3 million. It took nine years, but the new building is impressive—"the best example I've seen," Heinlen says, "of making lemonade from lemons."

Meanwhile, Tami Longaberger, appointed by Governor Voinovich to the Board of Trustees in 1996 and a former vice chair of The Ohio State University Alumni Association Board of Directors, and her sister Rachel wanted to contribute in a significant way to the "Affirm Thy Friendship" campaign. Introduced to material from a dozen potential campus suitors, they identified a half dozen or so areas of potential interest. Among those with whom they spoke were Jerry May, Dan Heinlen, and Chief Justice Thomas Moyer, then a member of the Alumni Association Board of Directors. Eventually, The Longaberger Foundation, under the direction of Dave Longaberger—founder of The

Laying of the Longaberger House cornerstone in June 1999. Left to right: Dan Heinlen; Thomas J. Moyer, chair of the Alumni Association's Board of Directors; Tami Longaberger; Rachel Longaberger, president of the Longaberger Foundation; Richard Longaberger, and President Kirwan.

Longaberger Company—and his two daughters, donated $5 million to various initiatives, including $2 million for what is now known as the Longaberger Alumni House. This had all happened under President Gee, but Tami thought it would be nice to include the new president in the announcement ceremony. The completed building was dedicated in November 1999.

The building was beautiful, and on the day before the grand opening, President Kirwan was there for a tour—before the staff had moved in. When he saw Heinlen's office, he took a card from the desk holder and penned a short note: "Dan," he wrote, "I'll trade you my office, 20 parking spaces, and a box in the new stadium for your office."

"The alumni considered Brit a wonderful leader," Heinlen says in relating the story, "appropriately presidential but at the same time, approachable. He did it as a consensus builder, without a lot of flash and dash, but with substance."

Marketing the University

Upon his arrival in Columbus, Kirwan found general agreement that Ohio State was not telling its story as effectively as it could. "Ohio State is much better academically than its reputation," Kirwan says. Supported by a recommendation in the Holmes report, the consulting study he commissioned after arriving at Ohio State, the university launched a national search for a vice president for University Relations, replacing the executive director for Communications position then held by Mal Baroway.

"The quality of candidates was good," Kirwan says, "with two or three finalists who were very able with substantial records in the corporate world." Among them, responding to an ad in the *New York Times*, was Lee Tashjian, who had graduated from Ohio State with a major in journalism in 1968 and whose wife, Vicki, had earned OSU degrees in 1972 and 1975. An avid OSU alumnus and rabid football fan, Tashjian had worked at International Harvester, DuPont, Fluor Corporation, and, most recently, ARCO.

"In the end," Kirwan continues, "the decision hinged on the chemistry between Lee and me. He had a very outgoing, warm, enthusiastic, optimistic personality, and enthusiasm and optimism are elements I value a lot. I felt very good about the appointment."

"When the qualifications for the job were assembled," Tashjian remembers, "a committee led by David Milenthal emphasized not crisis communications or things like that but marketing the university—creating a brand and a marketing plan around that brand. During my first interview, the first question I was asked was to discuss branding, which was a softball question for me since I had done a lot of branding in the corporate world."

Once he was on the job, Tashjian began to define a brand, working with David Hoover of University Relations and Marc Gobe of Desgrippes Gobe Associates, an international design firm based in New York suggested by Judith Koroscik, dean of the College of the Arts. Based on research, Gobe proposed building the brand around the idea that Ohio State was "inspired to impact the world." The next step was to retain an Ohio agency to execute the brand strategy, in this case, the local firm HMS Partners led by Milenthal, himself an Ohio State graduate, and a team that also included alumnus Jan Allen. The work was funded by the President's Strategic Investment fund and the Alumni Association.

When you define a brand, Tashjian explains, you create signals that suggest the essence of the brand. An example was the tagline proposed by HMS: "Do Something Big." At Tashjian's suggestion, the agency conducted a series of focus groups to test the proposed brand and brand signals.

"Fairly early on," Tashjian recalls, "word leaked out and Alice Thomas called, wanting to do a story for the *Dispatch* on our branding efforts. I tried to tell her that she had no context, that it was a work in process with nothing ready to discuss, that no decisions had been made." He offered her an exclusive story later if she would wait until the process played itself out. She declined, Tashjian did his best to make the case, and an article appeared the next morning.

"It was not helpful at all," Tashjian continues. "We got off on the wrong foot. The story suggested that 'Do Something Big' was the direction. Every TV station picked up on it, and the debate began. A history professor alleged we were corporatizing the university. Things spun wildly out of control, and we went into a damage control mode."

While Provost Ed Ray had cautioned Tashjian early on that his corporate background would be an issue, Tashjian was surprised at the extent of negative feelings. In an effort to salvage the program, Tashjian made a series of presentations to deans, faculty leaders, and others. While he felt the meetings went well, and some faculty appeared to be persuaded as to the merits of the branding endeavor, others would not budge, arguing that marketing has no place at a university.

"The very term 'branding' was an anathema for most faculty," Kirwan adds. "It connotes superficial and nonsubstantive promotion of products and people and entities often not based on reality. The term created a real problem in terms of broad acceptance. Lee was very careful and always said it was not about unsubstantiated claims, it's about telling the story of the university and doing it over and over again." In response to the criticism, the term "branding" was replaced by "strategic communications."

At one of Tashjian's presentations, Fisher College dean Joe Alutto, who supported the branding effort, questioned the use of the word "big." "Big," he argued, reinforced the concerns of many that Ohio State's bigness was a negative factor, that the university was too big, too complex, too bureaucratic. Why not, Alutto asked, modify the tagline to read, "Do Something Great"? After all, the Academic Plan goal was to make Ohio State one of the world's truly great universities. Tashjian liked the idea, but not everyone was ready to jettison the original proposal. Eventually, however, with help and guidance from trustee Dimon McFerson, who had gone through a branding exercise at Nationwide, "Do Something Great" became the new university tagline.

Kirwan, who consistently supported the branding process, sympathized with Tashjian's problems. "He had a tremendously difficult job," Kirwan says. "First, he had to create the job, which had not existed before, and second, Ohio State was one of the largest and most decentralized universities in the country, with a culture of local autonomy. It was tough to create a coordinated, cooperative message strategy in this environment. Those were two obstacles I hadn't appreciated."

"We engaged faculty, conducted focus groups by independent people," Kirwan continued. "Despite very substantial efforts to engage a broad cross-section, we met with scorn from some faculty nevertheless. When the accurate message was presented in focus groups to people around the state, it was stunning to see their reaction. It was a good effort. Could we have done it better? Absolutely, but given the circumstances, we handled it about as well as it could have been handled."

Branding programs, and particularly taglines, seldom win immediate universal acclaim. In the longer term, however, if they are thoughtfully designed, they often meet their intended goals. In this instance, University Relations began to produce materials built around Ohio State faculty and students and their accomplishments. Most faculty found these high-quality, professionally produced public service announcements—presented during televised sporting events, on the stadium scoreboard, and in other venues—highly positive, even substantive. Faculty saw that academics and research were emphasized, and while some will never support the concept, the uproar began to quiet.

Like many other programs, however, implementation ran into the budget crunch that limited so many promising initiatives. "It was a good idea," says

Control room at WOSU-TV.

Koroscik, who argues that others will brand you if you do not brand yourself, "but the timing has to be right."

Finally, there were major changes at WOSU, the campus radio and television station. First, responsibility for WOSU was transferred from the College of Social and Behavioral Sciences to University Relations. Next, it was decided to expand the station's quarters in the Fawcett Center to meet its growing needs. Funds were also raised to meet a federal requirement that WOSU switch to digital transmission. And finally, Dale Ouzts retired as general manager after more than two decades. He was replaced by Thomas Rieland, who had been general manager for the Center for Public Television and Radio at the University of Alabama in Tuscaloosa.

14

Crises Come and Go

Even for an experienced president, academic life includes unforeseen developments beyond the predictable disagreements with students, faculty, and state government. Sometimes, and unexpectedly, things just go wrong. The Kirwan years were no exception.

Call to ARMS

In 1994, during the Gee presidency, it was decided to update and integrate the information technology systems that keep the university running—procurement, general ledger, payroll, and other human resource functions put in place during the late 1970s. Thus, the Administrative Resource Management System (ARMS) was born, with general ledger and payroll selected as initial priorities and PeopleSoft software chosen for human resource applications.

The new ARMS payroll system was introduced in the fall of 1997, and, to say the least, installation did not go smoothly. Some employees were paid incorrect amounts—one custodian got a check for a million dollars—and there were erroneous credits for vacation and sick leave. Many academic users were furious, arguing that the new system offered more work and complexity rather than the simplification they had been promised. It was bad enough that the system did not work as well as expected. More scary was a national concern bordering on paranoia about Y2K: What would happen to America's computer systems on January 1, 2000? Would the machines, programmed to read years by two decimal points, show 2000 as 1900, shutting down elevators, banks, and universities?

The issue was unresolved when Brit Kirwan arrived in Columbus in mid-1998, and by fall he was in it up to his neck. "The board was rightly upset," Kirwan recalls. "The project was bleeding money. I jumped into the issue, and Ginny Trethewey found Strider & Cline, a private consulting firm that specialized in assisting with difficult systems installations, who we employed to look into the problem and make recommendations. A disgruntled former employee was feeding information to the board, and some board members suggested that the board hire this person as their personal consultant. Ted [Celeste] asked me what I thought. I said that if you think you need a personal consultant, then what you really need is a new president. After I said that, there was silence, and they backed off."

Kirwan asked Ed Ray and Bill Shkurti to oversee the Strider & Cline study and fix whatever was broken. In February 1999 the consultants issued their report, concluding that the current plans were not achievable.

"The organization in general and the ARMS project in particular has demonstrated an inability to define a plan, stick to that plan, and execute to completion," the report said. "The scope of projects seems to change daily with no formal control mechanisms requiring written approval. Decision making authority has been unclear, leading to unmanaged user expectations and decisions made by default. The focus has been on time and cost without clear regard to scope and quality. In order to achieve your Y2K objective in 1999, you must scope the work to the bare minimum required, control that scope, and execute the plan. Do not attempt any changes not absolutely necessary to continue operating in 2000."

The Year 2000 goal could be achieved, Strider & Cline said, with the existing general ledger and with ARMS procurement and Human Resources Management System (HRMS), but only if the university followed its recommendations. Ray and Shkurti named Brad Englert as the new project director, and with his help and that of others throughout the university, the objectives were met. By fall 2000, *onCampus* reported that ARMS would "officially end its existence as a separate unit because it now is functioning as it was intended—as a comprehensive integrated system used for everything from posting job notices and processing payroll to completing purchase orders and determining departmental budget balances." The final cost: $86 million.

"Though it's been a long and painful process to implement ARMS," Shkurti said, "we have met our goals. I hope we'll eventually see that the investment has been worth it."

And as January 1, 2000, dawned, The Ohio State University computer systems were working normally. As happened elsewhere, preparations for this nonevent had been substantial. The Risk Reduction Program and Y2K Task Force formed in 1998 had done their job. But just in case, the start of winter quarter had been delayed two days, until January 5.

CWA Strike

Just as the crisis over ARMS was cooling down, another was heating up that would become, in Kirwan's view, the low point of his administration.

The issues that precipitated the CWA strike first came to Kirwan's attention at a planning cabinet meeting in February 2000. Larry Lewellen, associate vice president for Human Resources, informed the group that the university's three-year collective bargaining agreement with the Communications Workers of America (CWA) would expire on March 31. He showed the cabinet the first wage scenario discussed among the vice presidents, which was somewhat higher than the previous agreement and at the higher end of public sector bargaining unit agreements at the time.

Kirwan challenged the group, asking that OSU depart from business-as-usual collective bargaining and take bold action to improve the "living wage" status of these twenty-one hundred or so food service and maintenance workers as well as skilled trade employees and health care assistants. As a result, the university upped its proposal to 18.5 percent over three years, about double the typical labor settlement at that time and about where the final settlement ultimately came out.

While the first known (nonwage) labor agreement at Ohio State was signed in 1967, precipitating the only work stoppage prior to the 2000 CWA strike, legislation to allow Ohio's public sector employees the right to bargain collectively was signed by Governor Richard Celeste in 1983. Prior to that time, wages were set by the General Assembly. Afterwards, Personnel Services (now Human Resources) vice president Madison Scott began to bargain with the CWA and its president James Ervin, the result being a series of three-year agreements. In 1996, Ervin retired and was replaced by Gary Josephson, who had worked at the OSU Medical Center before joining the CWA staff. More aggressive than Ervin, Josephson raised expectations among the membership.

Two issues dominated the negotiations in March 2000. Historically, the union had preferred a system in which incoming workers were hired at the bottom of the pay range and progressed gradually over the years—creating a significant spread between newer and longer-term employees. Automatic across-the-board increases perpetuated this process and widened the disparity, also lowering the workers' average pay. Conversely, the university had long wanted to modify the system to benefit those at the low end of the scale. By 2000, union members also wanted to make up the discrepancy that had been created over the years, and they wanted to do it all at once.

The second issue involved the university's desire to differentiate wages between medical center and other employees. The two labor markets were different, the university argued, and that difference should be reflected in salaries. The issue was timely in that the medical center was working hard to eliminate a substantial operating deficit.

At first, the union sought an increase of $2 an hour beginning in the new contract's first year. When the university refused, they proposed $1 the first year with further increases in years two and three—a rise of more than 25 percent over three years. A tentative agreement was reached, but when Josephson took it to his membership, they erupted, torching copies and stomping on them. "I lit the fire, and I can't control them," Josephson allegedly told Lewellen.

On April 1 the union voted to strike and soon was picketing outside Bricker Hall and the medical center as well as at the Ohio Agricultural Research and Development Center in Wooster. They also staged a Unity March down High Street to a meeting of Columbus City Council, which passed a supportive resolution, and held a Unity Vigil on the Oval. On April 28 the university made its final offer, which was countered by CWA. The strike itself began at 12:01 AM on May 1. A week later, the membership rejected another tentative agreement, with protestors interrupting the meeting when Josephson attempted to speak. Meanwhile, the university, rushing to complete the renovation of Ohio Stadium, was forced to halt construction for a day as picketers marched. Many CWA members were African American, which added to the controversy.

The strikers' cause was adopted by many students and some faculty. *The Lantern* endorsed the union position, writing that "members of the OSU community can no longer sit and watch as administrators continue to take advantage of students and staff for their own financial advantage." Students camped out on the second floor of Bricker Hall for several weeks. Bricker employees faced an obstacle course of sleeping bags along with strong odors and, from time to time, chanting to the accompaniment of bongo drums. Determined not to make life too easy for the occupying students—the university had provided cots and refrigeration during a prior Bricker Hall protest—Ginny Trethewey asked safety and fire officials to preserve some access by taping open lanes on the floor.

Many people had to decide whether to cross picket lines during the CWA strike.

Some faculty members moved their classes outside, or elsewhere, to avoid crossing picket lines. Former trustee Ted Celeste, brother of the governor who had signed the collective bargaining law and now a candidate for the United States Senate, not only refused to cross the CWA picket line but joined the workers in their protest. Incoming Undergraduate Student Government

(USG) president B. J. Schuerger took his oath of office on the front steps of the Union to make a statement in support of the strikers. In response to student complaints about lost class time, the president and provost sent a letter to faculty upholding their right to support the union but reminding them of their obligation to meet their commitments to students.

Meanwhile, a group that included President Kirwan, Provost Ray, Ginny Trethewey, Bill Shkurti, Larry Lewellen, Reed Fraley, Bill Hall, and other inside and outside legal counsel met daily to devise and adjust negotiating tactics, keep the institution running, and implement some semblance of a public relations strategy. (The coverage wasn't good, but improved once Kirwan, Lewellen, and Tashjian visited the media with charts comparing university salaries with those elsewhere.)

In a decision that she herself questioned after the fact, Trethewey—concerned that the president could become trapped—advised Kirwan to avoid his office in Bricker Hall and operate instead from his home and other campus buildings. Had the president been more visible, some felt, the strike might have been shortened. Kirwan did participate in a number of public forums on the strike, during which he and other university officials were subjected to rude behavior and abusive, graphic language. "They were pretty tough sessions," Kirwan recalls. He also received hundreds of e-mails and attempted to answer them all, especially those from students.

It was Kirwan's first experience with such events—Maryland did not have collective bargaining—and the strike struck at the heart of his desire for campus consensus. Seeking agreement not only with the union but also with a variety of involved university officials was challenging, and Kirwan was eager to end the stalemate.

On May 19, 2000, another tentative agreement was struck, this time successfully. The university raised wages for campus workers by $2 an hour over three years, negotiating a separate increase for medical center employees that, while not a separate contract, established a precedent for differential pay. Workers returned to work on May 22, ratifying the agreement by May 25.

Kirwan called it a "landmark agreement"; Josephson called it a "win/win." Nonetheless, neither the university nor the union was happy about the experience, and three years later agreement was reached promptly. On June 14 CWA Local 4501 asked to be placed into receivership amid allegations that Gary Josephson had misappropriated funds. Josephson was later removed as president, replaced by Richard Murray, and the receivership was lifted.

"The strike caused dissension and complicated our initiatives," Kirwan recalled later. "It was a setback for what I had felt to be very positive

One of several pro-CWA rallies during the strike period. This one was on the steps of Bricker Hall.

momentum." At the same time, Kirwan was amazed at how quickly relations were restored after the settlement. There was some irony in the fact that such an event happened on Kirwan's watch since, in the words of Larry Lewellen, many viewed him as "a champion for staff."

"Brit related extremely well to staff," Lewellen says. "He was probably the first president who understood who they were and what they wanted. He went to town meetings with an open mind. If he heard something, he would ask about it, and if it made sense, ask, 'Why don't we do that?' Brit was constantly learning from people," Lewellen continues, "and he did not differentiate ideas by the rank of those expressing them." Kirwan also attended regular meetings of the University Staff Advisory Committee (USAC) and enjoyed working with USAC chairs Jeri Kozobarich, Jamie Mathews-Mead, Richard Wofford, and Willa Young.

Riotous Behavior and Public Safety

On December 1, 2000, President Kirwan rose to deliver his monthly report to the Board of Trustees. It was an especially important meeting at which the president would formally present the Academic Plan for final board approval. But first, he felt it necessary to report on campus disturbances that had taken place east of High Street following the Michigan football game twelve days earlier. Things had been uncharacteristically quiet until about 2 AM on that Sunday, when a twenty-five-keg party on 13th Avenue, to which students had been alerted via e-mail the week before, got out of hand. A car was overturned and police urged people to disperse. Some responded by throwing rocks and bottles at police, who then used tear gas and wooden "knee-knocker" bullets, and the battle was on.

As reported in a NCAA case study, "More than 100 fires were set, cars were overturned, storefront windows were smashed, and bottles and rocks were thrown at law enforcement officers and firefighters as they tended to the situation." One student was stabbed (and recovered) trying to usher guests from his apartment. Columbus Police arrested thirty-four people, one-third of them apparently not Ohio State students. Cost to the city of Columbus: $125,000 in overtime pay by police alone.

While excessive partying on and off campus is nothing new at American universities, alcohol-induced behavior has become increasingly violent and destructive. Crime also exists on and around most university campuses, especially those located in large, urban centers. Unfortunately, the Kirwan years included both kinds of behavior.

The student disturbances had little to do with football. Rather, they were the result of too many people—not all of them students, and those who were students representing a small portion of the student population—drinking too much alcohol. They then got caught up in crowds that swelled as friends called friends on cell phones and suggested that they join the revelry. The result was a series of misdeeds and sometimes criminal behavior that was often caught on videotape and often committed by high-grade-point students who had never been in trouble before and had never intended the kinds of outcomes that resulted.

"The next morning, when they talked to me," Bill Hall said, "it's 'Oh, my God, I have a 3.8 or a 3.6—have mercy on me.' In the past, students in those situations were not the most talented. Today, they often are."

After the Penn State game in 1998, liquor control agents made more than sixty arrests and seized forty-two kegs of beer. Then there was the November 2000 post-Michigan event, followed by other serious disruptions—or, as many viewed them, riots—in the spring of 2001 and 2002. Each time, as with the post-Michigan events, the university issued strong statements, with forceful backing from the trustees and, generally speaking, the Columbus community.

"We have to face the fact," the president told the trustees, "that as a university community, we are at risk of developing an image that is antithetical to our goals and aspirations for academic excellence."

University leadership did everything it could think of to ameliorate the situation. Law enforcement was beefed up as public safety officers from the university and the city of Columbus better coordinated their efforts and experimented with joint patrols in the "East of High" area. There were crackdowns on the sale of alcohol, especially in large quantities and in glass bottles, as liquor agents combed the neighborhoods for violations.

Most important was extending the *Code of Student Conduct* to cover serious offenses such as "riotous behavior" that occurred off campus. The proposal had languished for years, in part because of faculty who worried that the change would threaten or chill peaceful protest. Thus, the code revisions included a provision protecting peaceful demonstrations and similarly constitutionally sanctioned behavior. Both the Undergraduate Student Government and the Council of Graduate Students supported the change, and this time the University Senate followed suit. The trustees approved the change, which also more clearly defined procedures for handling allegations of academic misconduct, on March 2, 2001.

David Lieberman, a prelaw student who was active in student government and was a writer for *The Lantern*, was among those making an effective case during senate debate. "He is a remarkable young man," Kirwan says. "He helped get the *Code of Student Conduct* through the senate through his rhetorical skills, analysis, and courage."

Besides beefing up law enforcement and sanctioning students—suspending or dismissing them—there were surveys to find out what students thought about these disturbances. (Relatively few participated and most were opposed and embarrassed.) The university provided alcohol-free parties and free food late at night, and a collection of university alcohol policies were consolidated into a single, easier-to-understand document.

Those hosting large parties were warned that they would be charged if their parties got out of hand. Landlords were asked to crack down on unruly tenants. Hall contacted nearby high schools and colleges to discourage their students from visiting OSU on these occasions. A Party Smart program was created. In addition, a task force was named to study the situation. Kirwan joined Mayor Coleman and City Council president Matt Habash in writing parents of undergraduate students, urging them to talk with their sons and daughters, and Kirwan apologized to the people of Columbus "for what has become a far-too-frequent occurrence."

"It was one of the most frustrating and challenging times," Kirwan said later. "We put forth so much effort to prevent these acts and met with very little success. The silver lining was that we improved our relations with the city. There were dynamics at work that we weren't able to adequately control." As to the assertion that the riots were caused by a shortage of bars, some having been torn down to make way for the Gateway Project, Kirwan countered: "The student response that there is no place to go doesn't ring true. In the heyday of High Street, bars accommodated only hundreds of people, and students were carded. The riots involve thousands. Also, there was a longtime tradition of keg parties."

Ohio State is in effect a "city" of some seventy thousand people within the city of Columbus. As with any population center of this size, there are ongoing public safety issues, including occasional assaults, rapes, and murders involving Ohio State students. Compounding the problem is the condition of the "East of High" area where student disturbances and much of the crime takes place.

For years, Bill Hall says, "[w]e ignored what was happening around our university." Like other universities, Ohio State backed away from providing new student housing, encouraging many students to live off campus. Little attention was paid to zoning codes and ordinances or to the fact that permanent residents were fleeing the neighborhood. Those remaining lived in crowded conditions, with little diversity, poor lighting as well as trash and parking problems, all of which contributed to crime and panhandling. Campus Partners was created during the Gee administration to address many of these problems, but it will be a long-term battle.

Looking beyond the High Street corridor, the university has faced increasing demands upon its public safety resources. Until 2000 John Kleberg was an assistant vice president in Business and Finance, with 20 percent of his time devoted to public safety. That was possible, he says, because historically, the campus itself has been safe, with most serious crime occurring off campus and the most frequent on-campus crime being theft. Off-campus crime became a priority during the Gee presidency, and when Kleberg retired after twenty-seven years (taking a part-time position in Student Affairs), it was decided to create a full-time public safety position. The new AVP post went to Vernon Baisden, then at Keene State College in New Hampshire, whose family was eager to return to the Midwest.

Baisden oversees a group of about 125 people who perform the same kind of tasks—patrols, investigations, crowd control, SWAT team, protecting dignitaries, etc.—that other police forces perform, but with some differences relating to the university environment, including a student population that turns over frequently. Other challenges include a diverse array of facilities, from the Don Scott Airport and animal laboratories to experimental equipment and a major medical center—all located in an urban center. The university's status as a public institution also affects how public safety does its job.

Under Baisden's leadership, the public safety operation was reorganized for greater focus and, consistent with the president's vision, began to coordinate and streamline public safety efforts at the regional campuses as well as the Columbus campus. And as already noted, outreach efforts were initiated with the city of Columbus to address problems east of High Street. One year after Baisden's arrival came 9/11, which had a big effect on how public safety deals with crowd control, executive security, and the campus' large international population.

"September 11 changed our lives, not only on a personal level but on a professional, public safety level as well," Baisden told *The Lantern*. "There was an impetus to look at everything we do."

September 11

Before their meetings, officers of the Inter-University Council typically breakfasted with Rod Chu, chancellor of the Ohio Board of Regents. On Tuesday, September 11, 2001, President Kirwan, then IUC chair, had left that breakfast and was headed for the Capital Club. He and the other officers were walking along State Street when a member of the General Assembly told them that a plane had crashed into the World Trade Center. They quickly ducked into the Hyatt Capital Square hotel to find a television and canceled their meeting.

Returning to campus, Kirwan assembled his administrative team to discuss next steps, including ways to reassure and support the student body. Kirwan and Athletic Director Andy Geiger immediately agreed to reschedule Saturday's football game against San Diego State in Ohio Stadium—a decision reached before President Bush requested such action and the first such postponement in the nation. In a brief statement, Kirwan announced that all necessary steps had been taken to put its precautionary security plans into place and that while all special events for the day were being canceled, the university was remaining open.

Two days later, Ohio State announced that the school year would begin on

Among those participating in the Show We Care post-9/11 rally were (left to right) Mayor Michael Coleman, Governor Bob Taft, John F. Wolfe, and President Kirwan.

schedule, with autumn quarter classes beginning on September 19. On Saturday, replacing the football game, a Show You Care Telethon to recognize the week's tragedies and show support for the victims was staged in Ohio Stadium, sponsored by the university, the American Red Cross, and the Dispatch Family of Companies. The three-hour event included remarks by Governor Taft, Mayor Coleman, and President Kirwan and attracted more than ten thousand Ohioans, each of whom was given an American flag. The scene was so dazzling—filling the north curve of the Horseshoe with waving flags—that it made the national news that evening. The event also raised over $800,000 for the Red Cross Disaster Relief Fund, with a student-sponsored white ribbon campaign raising about $13,000.

Jim Tressel received the biggest ovation. "A week ago we came out here in front of a hundred thousand, and I wasn't sure there could be a more glorious day in Ohio Stadium," Tressel said, referencing his first game as head football coach. "And again central Ohio has proved us wrong. There isn't a more glorious day in the history of this stadium [than today]."

The following Tuesday, one week after September 11, incoming freshmen were in St. John Arena for the 2001 convocation ceremony. While in many ways the event mirrored those of other years, it was also different. Profiling was a national concern, and Kirwan urged the students to "practice tolerance, understanding and empathy" and "not [to] make assumptions based on someone's appearance . . . not judge one based on his or her ethnicity, nationality, or religion."

The next day at sundown, more than two thousand members of the university community gathered for a candlelight vigil on the Oval to commemorate the prior week's tragic events. English professor and poet David Citino read a poem entitled "Cell Phone" he had written for the occasion. President Kirwan, USG president Eddie Pauline, director of Counseling and Consultation Service Louise Douce, Jesse David Hill, pastor of University Lutheran Chapel, and others made remarks. Friends and strangers held hands in prayer.

"Today, as we begin a new academic year," President Kirwan said, "let us dedicate ourselves to building a new sense of community here . . . one that is more inclusive, more secure, more supportive of everyone. We owe it to the memory of those we mourn—and to the spirit of unity that has brought us to this place tonight. Shalom, salaam, paz, huh ping, shanti, peace be with you."

Community was another theme that Kirwan took seriously. One of his best presidential speeches was delivered at the State University of New York's Stony Brook campus. Drafted by University Relations writer Will Kopp, the speech articulated Kirwan's views on the need to build community among students on campus and between the university and nearby neighborhoods.

On September 20 the university held a teach-in for students, faculty, staff, and the community to discuss issues associated with the attack on U.S. soil and its aftermath. Professor Margaret Mills, chair of the Near Eastern Languages and Cultures Department, moderated a session addressed by Provost Ray; Donald Sylvan, professor of political science; Ahmad al-Akhras, president of the Council on American-Islamic Relations in Ohio; Rabbi Howard Apothekar of the Temple Beth Shalom; Linda Mercadante, professor in Ohio's Methodist Theological School; and Nancy Rogers, dean of the Moritz College of Law.

Kirwan was proud of how the university had responded to this tragedy, informing trustees that just twenty-three of four thousand international students had elected to return home and that there had been very few reports of verbal harassment or threats and no reported physical harm.

One item that might have become a crisis but did not was the issue of university-licensed apparel manufactured in developing nations, allegedly under inhumane working conditions. Rather than denying that a problem existed, Ohio State joined with Harvard, Notre Dame, the University of California, and Michigan to study and report on working conditions in Mexico, China, Hong Kong, El Salvador, Thailand, Pakistan, Korea, and the United States—followed by discussions with university licensees.

Ohio State also forged a relationship with the Reverend Leon Sullivan, author of the Sullivan Principles on South Africa, who was developing a new set of economic-based principles and who died in 2001. Kirwan and Trethewey attempted to keep ahead of this issue, and OSU attorney Rick Van Brimmer became a national leader among collegiate licensing officials. Credit also went to Janet Ashe, vice president for Business and Administration, for creating a student/faculty committee to study the problems and work with other universities.

15

Hooray for the Scarlet and Gray

In the spring of 1994, Andy Geiger was in Columbus, weighing an offer to leave the University of Maryland–College Park and become athletic director at Ohio State. Geiger had held similar positions at Brown, Pennsylvania, Stanford, and Maryland. He was not looking to move but was in his fifties and recognized this as a now-or-never opportunity.

"I stood in the middle of the stadium and got a good, thirsty sip of the tradition and what was and could be in athletics," Geiger recalled. "It was an extraordinary opportunity, the largest program in the nation."

As of 2003, OSU had thirty-six varsity sports—seventeen for men, seventeen for women, and two coed—involving more than one thousand students. The budget is around $80 million a year, with football providing almost half the revenue. Athletics not only covers its costs, it pays the university for all of its scholarships (roughly $10 million) along with $1.2 million in cost containment, $3.5 million in overhead, $1.5 million to the Schottenstein Center, and $150,000 in transfers to other departments.

The job is also a pressure cooker. In March 1997 Geiger fired men's basketball coach Randy Ayers—hardly a new experience for Geiger, since the first thing Kirwan had enlisted him to do at Maryland was to clean up the basketball program. "That was a very difficult time," Geiger reflects, "but we pulled through it. We made some changes and started to rebuild that program." Part of that rebuilding included the hiring of coach Jim O'Brien from Boston College. With the help of Sandra Harbrecht, president of Columbus public relations firm Paul Werth Associates, Geiger also revisited the Athletics Department's vision and mission and set his department's sights on the Director's Cup, emblematic of the nation's best overall athletics program.

Kirwan, who had recruited Geiger from Stanford, hated to lose him at Maryland. "It was a proud day when he came and a sad day when he left," Kirwan notes, citing Geiger's presence as "a huge plus in coming to Ohio State." Before Geiger left Maryland, Kirwan quizzed him on what was different about Ohio State. Four years later, he found out for himself.

"Early in my tenure in Columbus," Kirwan recounts, "I attended an Ohio State Foundation Board dinner with forty or fifty people. I was seated between two elderly, wealthy women who talked about football the entire evening. 'Dr. Kirwan,' one said, 'we were at the first game played in Ohio Stadium [in 1922] and have not missed one since.' Then, I went to my first game. OSU was ranked number one in preseason, but they were playing Toledo, and I told Patty that there was no way the stadium would be full for a game like that so we did not have to hurry. I remember when we exited 315 onto Lane Avenue and saw the scalpers on the ramp. I knew then that we were in a different world."

It was a world that troubled the new president, who felt that athletics and academics were badly out of balance. The son of a football coach, a tight end at the University of Kentucky, and a rabid basketball fan, Kirwan nonetheless worried about "the power and pervasiveness of Ohio's football culture."

"I am happy to be quoted on this," Kirwan volunteers. "There is an upside and a downside to it. The upside is that it builds tremendous school spirit, rallying friends and alumni. And it is a spectacle. But the community and statewide fixation on football pushes the real purpose of the university into the background."

Kirwan was particularly bothered by a "lack of proportion" in campus facilities. The university had just built the Jerome Schottenstein Center for $105 million. It was preparing to renovate Ohio Stadium at an ultimate price tag of $195 million. With the $4.7 million William C. Davis Baseball Stadium, opened in 1997, and the almost $11 million Jesse Owens Memorial Stadium, opened in 2001—plus the Jack Nicklaus Museum, which opened in 2002—Ohio State almost certainly boasted the finest university athletic facilities in the world. *The Other Paper*, an irreverent weekly, labeled it "Andyland."

"Thanks in part to Geiger, almost half the university's capital budget ($316M of $635M) had gone toward building athletic facilities over the past four years," said an article in *U.S. News & World Report.*

Geiger has no problem with the program's scale. He is also pleased that Ohio State met the requirements of Title IX without diminishing men's programs. "We do not have to commit university resources to athletics," he says. "It's the other way around. Our budget is 3 percent or less of the university's

$2 billion total. If the tail wags the dog, it's a massive dog with a tiny tail. It's not out of scale. What's out of scale is the rhetoric and place of the program in our culture."

Many faculty, and some others, were concerned with scale. Why, they asked, can the university find the money for such projects while starving other building projects like the library renovation or faculty salaries? The answer—that the athletic facilities were built entirely with private funds from donations, seat licenses, luxury-box rentals, and so on, none of which was available for academic pursuits—did not satisfy the critics. Nor did it entirely satisfy Kirwan, who arrived in Columbus when the issue of athletic spending was on the front burner, and he devoted considerable time to the topic. Athletics reported to the vice president for Student and Urban/Community Affairs, and when David Williams left for Vanderbilt, Kirwan changed the reporting structure. From then on, Geiger reported to the president, with considerable day-to-day involvement by Ginny Trethewey, the president's executive assistant and general counsel, and CFO Bill Shkurti.

But could the new president do anything about Ohio Stadium?

"The train had left the station on design of the stadium when Brit got here," Geiger says. "He was not happy but recognized there was no alternative to going ahead. If he had had his druthers, he probably would have stopped it. But delay would have cost a tremendous amount of money, so he agreed to get it done. 'We're the poster child for the arm's race in athletics,' Brit would say to me," Geiger continues, "acknowledging his role as president of the NCAA board. He was embarrassed. 'You've done well . . . damn it!' he would say to me about the athletic department."

"The nine-hundred-pound gorilla dilemma was Ohio Stadium," says university architect Jill Morelli. "It was conceptualized and formed before his arrival. He was very much an academic, and at the time it seemed as though OSU was all about athletics. We were coming off the Schott issue. I recall a halftime interview, maybe in 1999. Brit was being asked about the stadium but pointed out that 'right over there is the Fisher College, a landmark project.'"

Geiger was sympathetic to Kirwan's concerns, and the pair often discussed the balancing of athletics with academics. Geiger, David Frantz, and others visited four or five universities—schools like Nebraska, Penn State, and Florida State that had big-time football programs but much higher graduation rates—seeking best practices. Academics, especially within the football and men's basketball programs, had to improve.

"I was explicit," Kirwan says of his conversations on the topic. "I expected radical change, and Andy agreed."

Exit John Cooper

The 2000 football season was not pretty. The Buckeyes' regular-season record was 8–3, (mediocre by OSU fan standards but better than the prior year's 6–6 result) with yet another loss to archrival Michigan. More distressing, discipline and morale were faltering, with one player suing another over a practice incident and another player losing his eligibility over a 0.0 GPA for the autumn quarter. Then came the Outback Bowl against South Carolina, where the team was humiliated in a lackluster performance ending in a 24–7 loss.

Kirwan was increasingly concerned about the academics. "After all of this conversation about upgrading," he later said, "if the bowl game had been played a day or two later, twenty-three players would have been [academically] ineligible."

"I will never forget the banquet at the bowl," Kirwan continued. "The two teams came into the hall. South Carolina players were in sport coat and tie. They sat at their table and listened to the program. Ohio State players were attired in sweat clothes, lounging around, some with their Walkmans on. I was embarrassed. Then the team played with no spirit."

At halftime Lee Tashjian, vice president for University Relations, escorted Kirwan to his usual radio interview. During that stroll, Kirwan shared his frustration, which Tashjian passed along to Geiger. Then, near the end of the game, unable to reach him because of the crowds, Kirwan called Geiger on his cell phone. "When we get home," I told him, "we have got to talk."

The topic, of course, was head coach John Cooper. Cooper had joined Ohio State in 1988 after three years as head coach at Arizona State University. By most standards, his record was excellent, with a .715 winning percentage in the always-tough Big Ten Conference, trips to eleven bowl games, and two teams ranked second in national wire service polls. At the same time, however, he lost eight of those eleven bowl appearances and was 2–10–1 against Michigan.

In 1998 Geiger had given Cooper a new contract worth more than $1.1 million a year. "He had won two Sugar Bowls and one Rose Bowl, had two number-two finishes and gone ten and one," Geiger says. "So we rewarded him with a new contract, feeling we will do that and try to improve the academic and social aspects. We probably made a mistake," Geiger adds. "We reinforced the athletic part and did not send a strong enough message about the other part."

"About a third of the team was doing very, very poorly academically," Geiger said later about the 2000 season. "And the body language, behavior on and off the field, was unattractive. The climate within and the aura about the program

John Cooper and his wife, Helen, at his farewell press conference.

was not consistent with our values. We concluded that fixing this would be hopeless without a change in leadership. We had talked quite a bit about our concerns. The experience in Tampa, during that week, and then the presentation of football in every aspect in that game pushed us over the top."

The decision to fire Cooper, essentially made during that cell phone conversation, was confirmed the next morning (January 2, 2001) in Columbus and quickly endorsed by the Board of Trustees. Geiger immediately informed Cooper and scheduled a press conference for 4 PM. Calling Cooper "a fine representative of this university and an outstanding citizen of our state," Geiger expressed appreciation for his service.

Cooper, who had refused an opportunity to resign, also met with the media. He expressed his disappointment and disagreement with the decision—he was seven career wins short of two hundred, and the timing made it tough for Cooper and departing assistant coaches to find work for the upcoming season. Nonetheless, Geiger says, Cooper handled the situation with class. "It is impossible to describe the disappointment I am sure he felt; I have no ill will toward him," Geiger later said. Cooper also professed his ongoing loyalty to Ohio State. "They will have no better fan than John Cooper," he said. "I can tell you that." He declared himself available for the right head-coaching opportunity and signed on to do commentary with ESPN and as a consultant with the Cincinnati Bengals.

While the firing cost him his $100,000 annual contract with Kroger, he left with the $1.8 million buyout provided in his contract.

"It is often said that the reason Cooper was fired was that he did not beat Michigan often enough and lost the Outback Bowl," Kirwan says. "I can't speak for others, but I can say for myself that that was not the reason. On balance, he was a very successful coach and produced some outstanding teams. But he lost the ability to motivate players on the field, in the classroom, and in the community."

Enter Jim Tressel

When you search for a head football coach at Ohio State, you want to do it quickly and quietly. "The search for a coach is night and day different from a presidential search," Geiger says. "For a president, the search is deliberate and thoughtful. For a football coach, the search is deliberate and thoughtful . . . and done in three days." Not quite, but almost.

"It is marked by restlessness and tumult," Geiger continues. "A dozen staff are dependent on who is chosen. You get no peace or sleep. You call everybody you know and some you don't know and ask about people. We retained a consultant, whose identity was known only to me and Brit, so he could work quietly and without being part of the formal process."

While Geiger created an advisory committee to help draft a profile of the ideal candidate and to interview the finalists, most of the work was done under the radar, with Geiger speaking many times each day to the search consultant. "When the time came," Geiger says, "I would call the schools for permission to interview a candidate, having already laid the groundwork via the consultant. We interviewed eight or ten people. Many of those names never surfaced. We brought three here: Bellotti, Mason, and Tressel."

Mike Bellotti, head coach at the University of Oregon, came for the interview, then asked to be dropped from the list. Minnesota head coach Glen Mason, on the other hand, wanted the job badly. As the head coach of another Big Ten university, he was in a difficult position, with his superiors eager to have the issue resolved. With his strong OSU ties—he was a letter winner on the 1970 Big Ten championship team and for eight years worked under Woody Hayes and Earle Bruce—Mason was something of an in-house favorite.

Tressel was a highly successful coach with strong Ohio connections but compiled his record at Youngstown State University, a Division 1-AA school. Geiger had known Tressel somewhat for years, having interviewed him at Maryland, and said he was always an "obvious candidate." But could Tressel make the leap? And what punishment awaited a president and athletic director who passed over "big-time" coaches to name a 1-AA recruit who didn't produce the championships fans expect? "I was aware that many 1-AA coaches had failed in 1-A jobs," Kirwan said later. "I had heard stories about this being a big mistake."

The rumor mill was in overdrive. Candidates, real or imagined, included Bob Stoops, whose Oklahoma Sooners had just finished number one; Jon Gruden, then with the Oakland Raiders of the NFL and a Sandusky, Ohio, native; Baltimore Ravens defensive coordinator Marvin Lewis; Ohio State's assistant head coach, Fred Pagac; Walt Harris of Pittsburgh; and former all-American Buckeye linebacker Chris Spielman, a popular personality in Columbus and among listeners of Radio 1460–The Fan.

On January 14, just twelve days after Cooper's firing, a *Dispatch* headline read, "NFL Names Pop Up as Rumors Fly; Search Drags." Geiger loved the final two words. Only in Columbus could such an important search "drag" after a dozen days. But four days later it was over.

Naively, Kirwan concedes, he suggested that Geiger bring candidates to Bexley to avoid the media. To call the tactic unsuccessful would be an understatement. When Geiger drove up to the president's house, media were lying on the floor of parked cars, ready to spring up when his car approached. A helicopter followed Geiger's car to the airport, trying to see who was inside.

"I told Andy that I wanted to interview the finalists and be part of the decision," Kirwan recollects. "I talked with all three and was absolutely captivated by Jim Tressel. It had nothing to do with his record. It had to do with his values and commitment to academic success and to character and development of young people."

Academics was "all I talked to them [the three finalists] about," Kirwan says. "First of all, I went to the Web and found out what all their graduation rates were. And then I asked them for specifics: How does it work? What are the mechanisms that you employ to have the kind of success you are having? Do you have study halls? What are the incentives or disincentives you employ to ensure that students do the right thing in the classroom?"

Checking the academic records of the three finalists, Kirwan learned that Tressel's graduation rate of 59 percent was the highest of the three; what's more, Youngstown State's *overall* student graduation rate of 32 percent was well below that of Minnesota and Oregon, making Tressel's achievement even more dramatic. During his final two years at Youngstown State, a total of sixty-seven players earned a grade point average of 3.0 or better. His 2002 recruiting class at Ohio State came with a combined high school GPA of 3.35.

"The interview I had with him at the house was one of the most impressive, in fifteen years as a university president looking for senior people, that I've ever had," Kirwan says.

For his part, Geiger wanted Kirwan's approval. "I wanted his instincts," Geiger says. "If he was uncomfortable, I would be, too. We talked a lot about every aspect, including the risk of hiring Tressel. We were aware of those risks. We both did a lot of telephoning. We checked and double-checked everything. The resume had to be squeaky-clean. A lot of time was spent on discussing the search strategy and potential of the other candidates. There was no more important decision than, 'Okay, we have met three candidates. Here are some other names. Should we call it off or keep on looking? Are we at peace with the process? Have we served the university and program well?' It was nerve-wracking. We lived on cell phones."

A major but less visible presence in the search was Archie Griffin. "Archie was an unbelievable asset to this university [in the search]," Kirwan told the *Dispatch.* "He and Andy were just joined at the hip throughout."

On January 18, at 4 PM, Andy Geiger introduced Tressel to the media on the second floor of the Wolstein Football Center in the southeast tower of Ohio Stadium. Tressel's background seemed close to perfect. Born in Mentor, in northeast Ohio, he was the son of Lee Tressel, a coaching legend at Baldwin Wallace College. As a boy, he shagged balls for Lou "The Toe" Groza, the Cleveland Browns' star placekicker. He also worked at Miami of Ohio—the "Cradle of Coaches" that had produced such legends as Paul Brown, Woody Hayes, Ara Parseghian, Bo Schembechler, Weeb Ewbank, and Red Blaik—before becoming a quarterbacks and receivers coach at Ohio State under Earle Bruce. At thirty-three, he became head coach at Youngstown State, where over the next fifteen seasons his teams won four 1-AA national championships and compiled a record of 135–57–2.

More than two hundred people attended the press conference, with strong media representation from northeast Ohio. Kirwan said a few words, then Geiger introduced Ohio State's twenty-second head football coach, whose confident and polished thirty-minute presentation—given without a single note—charmed and delighted "the Buckeye nation." He touched every conceivable Ohio base and stressed the importance of the football "family" while emphasizing academics and character.

All agreed that Jim Tressel's introductory press conference was a tour de force. Behind him are President Kirwan and Andy Geiger.

"We had our first discussion about the importance of class with our team this afternoon," Tressel told the assembled media. "I explained to the team something my dad used to always explain to us. There is only one reason to miss class: A death in the family . . . your own." That explained, he went on, why his oldest son, Zak, an OSU junior, wasn't at the press conference. He was in a physics class. Clearly, Tressel "got it."

"Wow," *Dispatch* columnist Bob Hunter wrote. "This guy is good." "Tressel may or may not win enough games at OSU to be revered as he is in Youngstown," Hunter continued, "but our one-day assessment of him is that Geiger & Co. may have called this one right."

But was Tressel too good to be true? "You have to learn how to tell whether a person really believes what he tells you or whether he's just saying what you want to hear," Kirwan said. "And from the best of my ability to judge, this is one of the most sincere individuals I've ever met. When I looked him in the eye, I could just tell this man was speaking from the heart. This man truly believed in the things he said, from a deeply held sense of values, not only his personal values but in the importance of personal relations and trust. I know we have a very real and sincere person here, who, as far as I'm concerned, is the answer to my dreams."

The new coach would be paid $700,000 a year with a $100,000 signing bonus. Following the national championship, Tressel signed a new contract that, according to the *Dispatch*, starts at $1.3 million and escalates to $1.87 million in the sixth year. This is still less than several other top coaches, including some in the Big Ten.

How did Geiger feel after Tressel's press conference triumph? "It was beyond a home run," he says. "The first time Brit and I saw each other, in private, we hugged." As if to say, it's gonna be all right.

That night, as luck would have it, the Ohio State men's basketball team played Michigan at Value City Arena in the Jerome Schottenstein Center. At halftime Geiger introduced his new coach, and the fans were not disappointed. To a prolonged standing ovation, Tressel walked to midcourt, where Geiger handed him the microphone.

"I am so proud, so excited, and so humbled to be your football coach at The Ohio State University," he told the souped-up fans. "I can assure you that you'll be proud of our young people in the classroom, in the community and, most especially, in 310 days in Ann Arbor, Michigan." After losing ten of their last thirteen games to the Wolverines, this was raw meat to the faithful, just what the fans wanted to hear.

The next day, his first full day as head coach, the *Dispatch* began applying the pressure: "Clock's Ticking on Tressel, Fans Say," read the headline. "Welcome Coach: You Have Three Years."

Seven months later, Tressel asked Kirwan to address the team at practice before its first game. "I arrived early," Kirwan recalls, "and found the players in uniform seated in a lecture hall setting. They're in their quiet time, Tressel informed me, so I took a seat and leafed through the thick notebooks the players were studiously perusing. These books contained no reference to football whatsoever. It was all about values, responsibility, and so forth. After awhile, Tressel asked which team members had read something that day that really

Among the new traditions established by Coach Tressel was for players to sing "Carmen Ohio" after the game.

spoke to them, and five or six of them responded, after which the coach delivered a brief follow-up lecture on each point."

The president loved it. And fans loved it when Tressel brought his team onto the field via a scarlet carpet and under a scarlet cover, when his players were allowed to "draft" their colleagues for the spring game, and when each home game was followed by the players singing "Carmen Ohio" at the southeast corner of Ohio Stadium, with accompaniment from the Best Damn Band in the Land.

And while Tressel's initial season record of 7–5 was mediocre at best, he did in fact defeat Michigan (and without starting quarterback Steve Bellisari, whose DUI arrest had him on the sidelines). Then in 2002, in just his second year, he delivered what the fans wanted: Ohio State's first national championship since 1968, capped off by a double-overtime victory over favored Miami in the Tostitos Fiesta Bowl.

When that happened, Kirwan was back at Maryland as chancellor of the University System of Maryland. "There are many things I admire about Karen [Holbrook's] leadership capabilities," Kirwan later said about his successor at Ohio State, "not the least of which is the fact that I have been a president or chancellor for fifteen years and in all that time, my football teams never won a national championship. Karen, on the other hand, accomplished this feat three months after becoming a president."

After the national championship, Tami Longaberger wrote a note to Kirwan, recalling the meeting when the trustees discussed a new coach. "I remember Brit's optimism about Jim Tressel," she says. "There was some concern about whether he could do it, moving up to the big leagues. It was Brit's optimism and confidence, and Andy's, too, particularly in Jim Tressel's character that was so convincing. It was not the safe choice."

Three other coaching items, all basketball-related, deserve mention. First, legendary coach Fred Taylor, who coached the Buckeyes from 1959 to 1976 and was the only Ohio State men's basketball coach to win a national championship, died in 2000. Second, Geiger did not renew the contract for women's coach Beth Burns, replacing her with Jim Foster, whose teams at Vanderbilt won 72 percent of their games. And third, men's coach Jim O'Brien led his Buckeye team to the Final Four in the 1999 NCAA tournament and enjoyed strong fan support. And there was no bigger basketball fan than Brit Kirwan.

"Brit is an incredible basketball fan," Geiger notes. "I remember Brit in Knoxville for the regionals. He was out on the floor, dancing with the crowd, wearing an OSU hat. He was also very proud of the men's gymnastic champions, especially because of their academics. The men's gymnasts won the Big Ten and national titles in 2001 led by such stars as Jamie Natalie, a student from Hockessin, Delaware, who went on to OSU Medical School.

Lea Ann Parsley, a firefighter from Granville and a Ph.D. candidate in community health nursing, won the silver medal in skeleton (small sled) in the 2002 Winter Olympics in Salt Lake City. Emma Laaksonen, a sophomore women's hockey player and business major, cocaptained her native Finnish women's hockey team, which finished fourth. Finally, during Cooper's final game with Penn State, Nittany Lion cornerback Adam Taliaferro suffered a severe injury and the potential that he might never walk again. Thanks in part to the immediate assistance he received on the field and at the OSU Medical Center, Taliaferro recovered and returned to Ohio State to thank all those who played a role in his recovery.

Saturday Afternoon Shrine

By any measure, the renovation of Ohio Stadium was an extraordinary project. From the standpoint of history, one of America's great sports landmarks was updated, expanded, and restored, maintaining its horseshoe configuration. Engineering-wise, lowering the field fourteen and a half feet required construction of an underground slurry wall—a forty-five-foot-deep trench filled with concrete—to keep the Olentangy River at bay. Taking tradition into account, it involved moving the Jesse Owens track to a separate location north of Lane Avenue.

Among the stadium's many special features is a sophisticated "Prescription Athletic Turf" system that makes the grass tougher, better to play on in rainy conditions, and easier on athletes' bodies. It was designed by Joe Motz, a graduate of Ohio State's turf science program in the College of Food, Agricultural, and Environmental Sciences. Motz operates the Motz Group in Cincinnati and installed the same system for the Sydney, Australia, Olympics.

The renovation cost was $195 million, plus a $10 million scoreboard with a ninety-foot video screen paid for mostly by sponsors. (A brand-new stadium, the university said, would cost $300 to $400 million.) Included in the cost was construction of the glass-enclosed Richard L. Shelly Family Press Box, which towered 183 feet above the field, as well as the Bert and Iris Wolstein Football Center. Also included was shell space for a band room, on top of which the band raised $2.7 million—$1.5 million of which came from Joan and George Steinbrenner—to complete the interior space.

No public money was used for any of this, with almost 80 percent of the renovation cost covered by the sale of eighty-one hospitality suites and the twenty-five hundred club seats on the west side of the stadium. Naming rights gifts and revenues from increased ticket sales and concession income covered the remaining portion. The twenty-one-thousand-square-foot social focal point for suite and club seat holders and their guests was named the Huntington Club in recognition of support from Huntington National Bank. There is a similar Huntington Club in the Schottenstein Center, reflecting a partnership with Ohio State that began in 1968. In each instance—one during the Gee years, one during the Kirwan years—the bank gave $5 million for this purpose.

Not included was the temporary relocation of four academic units ($1 million) and three projects of which 60 percent was paid by stadium revenues: the Jesse Owens Memorial Stadium for soccer and track (almost $11 million), parking ($6 million), and relocation of the Stadium Scholarship Dormitory to Mack Hall on Neil Avenue ($3.9 million).

The stadium project was undertaken in three phases, with renovation beginning in December 1998 and continuing during the off-seasons until completion just prior to the September 8, 2001, home opener against Akron. The Jesse Owens project was done in two stages, with the track and temporary

The newly renovated Ohio Stadium.

bleachers completed in the summer of 1998 and permanent stands and support facilities, including a Jesse Owens Hall of Fame, completed in 2001. That same year, the university announced that the Motorists Insurance Group Foundation had donated $2 million to support the stadium project, including installation of glass art in the stadium rotunda.

Ohio Stadium was originally constructed in 1922 at a cost of $1.3 million and, with its unique double-decked horseshoe look, was added to the National Register of Historic Places in 1974. Originally holding 66,210 spectators, today's official paid seating capacity is 101,548—up from 89,841 before the renovation. Depending upon the number of media, ushers, and other workers, parkers, Boy Scouts, band members, and so forth who crowd the facility, today's crowds have exceeded 105,000—just as they regularly reached 94,000 before the renovation. This was the "Shoe's" first renovation and addressed a variety of needs, including bringing the facility into compliance with various codes, adding elevators and more modern restrooms—including those for fans with disabilities—and upgrading food concessions. These facilities are part of a shell that surrounds the original structure.

The Kirwan years also marked the first time that the jersey numbers of football greats were retired and hung in Ohio Stadium. The honored players and numbers (alphabetically) were: Howard "Hopalong" Cassidy (40), Eddie George (27), Archie Griffin (45), Les Horvath (22), and Vic Janowicz (31).

Scholar Athletes

As noted, President Kirwan had charged Geiger and others with improving the academic performance of student athletes, and when Geiger's contract was renewed effective July 1, 1999, it included new incentives relating to grades and graduation. Just over two years later, during a report on this topic to the Board of Trustees, there was better news. Comparing entering students from 1994 and 1990, six-year graduation rates for all aided student athletes rose from 49 to 62 percent, while rates for football players climbed from 29 to 50 percent. (In contrast, the 55 percent graduation rate for all OSU students—athletes and nonathletes alike—remained static over that period.) Results from 2003—the 1996 cohort—showed the graduation rate for football players at 50 percent, while the rates for all aided student athletes and all students were 60 and 59 percent, respectively.

How had these improvements come about? Frantz identified a number of initiatives, including:

1. A strong partnership between athletic and academic leaders, with strong involvement from Geiger; English professor David Frantz, who had been named liaison for Academic Affairs; and Kate Riffee, who directs the Student Athlete Support Services Organization.
2. A shift in emphasis from grades only to grades and progress toward graduation.
3. An outreach program to student athletes who did not complete their degree, urging them to return to school. Those successfully completing this program included basketball greats Clark Kellogg and Scoonie Penn. Another former student athlete who returned to complete his degree, though not part of this program, was Heisman Trophy Winner Eddie George, who received his Bachelor of Science in Landscape Architecture degree.
4. Changes in study tables and at the Younkin Success Center, with coaches checking in regularly to see what their athletes were doing.
5. A preadmissions review or screening of every student athlete to whom Ohio State planned to make an offer.

Geiger also credited the work of Kate Riffee and her organization, which included nine full-time staff, six graduate students who mentor groups of student athletes, four additional part-time mentors, a tutorial staff of more than sixty, and an operating budget of $1.2 million. The hiring and evaluation process for coaches is based as much on their off-the-field as on-the-field performance, he said. Calling the appointment of David Frantz a "godsend," Geiger also credited outstanding communications among those involved and the change under which Athletics reports directly to the president.

"We think the variety of things happening will sustain this movement in the right direction," says vice provost Martha Garland. "These initiatives, combined with Ohio State's eligibility standards—which are tougher than the NCAA's—ensure that if student athletes leave school early, they leave under conditions in which they've made genuine academic progress and are in good standing should they later decide to complete their degrees. And if they do leave, we encourage them to remain focused on earning those degrees whenever the time is right for them."

"There's no question that if you're going to compete at the highest level, you're going to get some kids who are going to come in as marginal students," David Frantz told a reporter for the *Chronicle of Higher Education.* "The challenge is to provide the appropriate support so they have an opportunity to succeed academically."

Toward the end of his presidency at Maryland and during his presidency at Ohio State, Kirwan was a key member of the NCAA Division I Board of

President Kirwan met with Ohio State's men's gymnasts in 1999.

Directors, eventually serving as board chair. In that capacity, he strongly encouraged the NCAA and its member universities to uphold academic values and address other issues relating to student athletes.

Kirwan also named a committee to review the second Knight Commission report and recommend reforms. The result were proposals that Kirwan felt would "revolutionize" NCAA academic standards and impose meaningful sanctions (including their ability to participate in NCAA tournaments) against teams that do not meet acceptable academic norms. At his last meeting—he had to give up the role as board chair when he returned to Maryland, but was named to an advisory committee—the board endorsed these recommendations in principle. Most were later adopted.

"Brit deserves the lion's share of the credit for the [NCAA] academic reform plan and the achievement of legislation," Geiger says. "There was great concern and disappointment when he left OSU and had to leave the NCAA. He was also a very important voice at OSU with the Big Ten presidents."

Geiger had set out to win the Director's Cup. In 2003 Ohio State finished third, an accomplishment so significant that President Karen Holbrook cited it in her State of the University address. The achievement, she said, came from a national championship in football, top ten ratings in men's gymnastics and lacrosse, and women's fencing, golf, lacrosse, rowing and baseball. She added that "a record 411 student athletes [48 percent] achieved GPAs of 3.0 or better" and that Ohio State "led the Big Ten Conference with 250 student athletes named to Academic All-Conference teams."

"We are much better than we were," Geiger says. "It's part of an effort to counter all the emphasis on football and have our other sports do well—not be 'football uber alles.'"

There were many successes during that period. Who would have thought that just two years later, Geiger would have to fire Jim O'Brien for an admitted violation of NCAA rules and that as he prepared to retire in 2005, the football program would have become the target of sustained national media criticism?

Changing of the Guard: The Sequel

16

Time to Change Partners Again

The Jennings era lasted nine years; the Gee era, seven. The Kirwan era, while highly productive, was considerably shorter and, most believe, ended too soon.

Maryland, My Maryland

In December 2001 the media reported that some members of the Maryland legislature wanted Kirwan back as chancellor of the University System of Maryland, where he had served as president at the flagship College Park campus before coming to Ohio State.

"David Brennan, then chair of the trustees, asked me if they had to worry about this," Kirwan said later. "'No,' I said, "looking him in the eye. I have not been contacted." Kirwan also knew that Governor Parris Glendening wanted the job himself and that some members of the Maryland Board of Regents, who would make the decision, were the governor's own appointees. So far as he was concerned, the idea was a nonstarter, but while he continued to disavow any interest, his East Coast supporters were hard at work.

"About March, I started to get calls from members of the Board of Regents," Kirwan continued. "Congressman Steny Hoyer, an old friend, wanted to talk to me about the position and called, he said, just to establish communication. He said it would not be the governor and that I was the right guy. He said he would call me from time to time and tell me where things stood. I had known him forever, and I listened but expressed no interest."

"Every couple of weeks, I would get a call," Kirwan continued. "I was told a groundswell was building. Also, during March I was in DC one night and agreed to meet with a few people. There was no offer, and I made no comment.

They said I was needed, that things were in turmoil, that some donors had said that if Glendening became chancellor, they would withdraw their donations. The Maryland papers were incensed over the idea [of Glendening becoming chancellor], calling him unqualified and conflicted since he named the board. They wrote that the credibility and integrity of the board were at stake.

"Then I was stunned one night, after returning from Chicago, when the phone rang. Eight or nine members of the board and search committee, including the university's major donor, were calling to offer me the position. They said I had to come back. I said I was not prepared to answer; I needed time to think, talk with Patty, etc. I also told them I wanted it to remain confidential, that nobody's interest would be served by going public, and I immediately began to discuss it. Unfortunately, it leaked in the *Post* or *Sun,* then the *Dispatch.* I told David [Brennan] I had an offer and would have to think about it."

It was the time of winter commencement, and Kirwan worried that a media circus would draw attention from the graduates. He decided to say nothing about the offer until after commencement and a weekend at the family retreat in western Maryland.

"It was an awfully tough week," Kirwan says. "Many expressed the hope I would not leave. When I marched into commencement, the students rose and applauded. They would not stop. They unfurled a banner: 'Please Stay Brit—We Need You!' At that moment, I would not have left."

Three days later, on March 25, 2002, Kirwan announced that indeed he would leave Ohio State to become the chancellor at Maryland. He cited family as his primary motivation, playing a card others found impossible to trump. At a press conference in Maryland, his family was seated in the second row. As Kirwan walked in, he reached out to his two young grandsons, a scene caught by a *Baltimore Sun* photographer and reprinted on the front page of the *Dispatch.* "It made my rhetoric real," Kirwan says. "Without the family consideration, perhaps there would have been some bitterness. By and large, the decision was accepted."

In a letter to the campus community, Kirwan wrote, "The decision has caused me great anguish because I feel enormously proud and privileged to serve as president of this university. Until this offer came, . . . it had been my expectation to remain at Ohio State for at least another year or two."

Looking back, a June 1998 Kirwan *onCampus* interview is revealing. "The long goodbye at College Park has been difficult," Kirwan told Jeanette Drake. "I told some people the other day [that] my father was at the University of Kentucky for thirty-four years. And I had been at the University of Maryland for

Students demonstrated their desire during the winter 2002 commencement.

And the president was deeply moved.

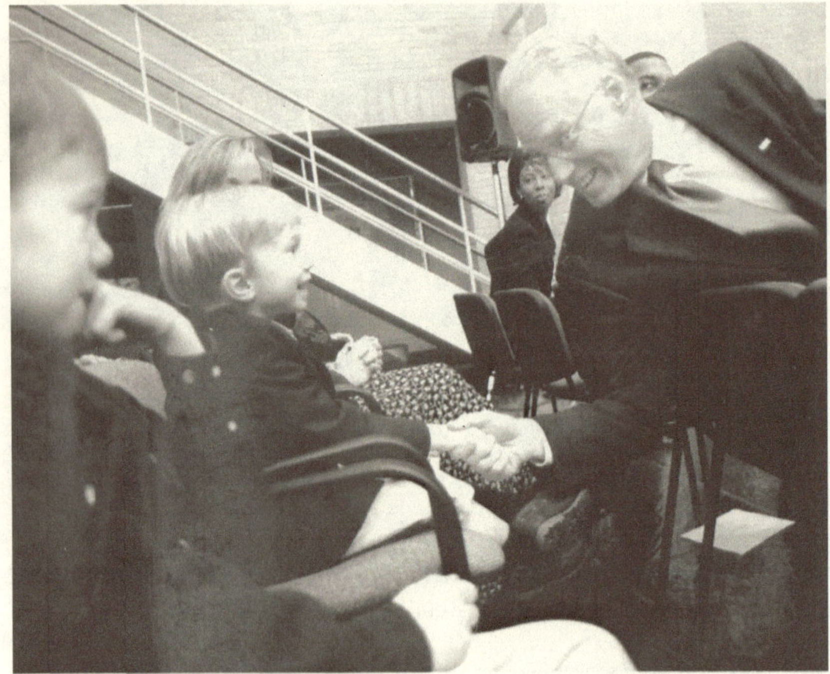

President Kirwan's young grandsons were on hand in Maryland when Kirwan announced he was returning to become chancellor of the University System of Maryland. (Photo courtesy of *Baltimore Sun*.)

thirty-four years and really not thinking about leaving. It's just not in the Kirwan genes to move around. So this has been an adjustment." Later, referring to his first two years at Ohio State, Kirwan told the *Lantern*'s Shannon Wingard that the experience "is not for the fainthearted," adding that "it's been a learning experience."

But why did he leave when he did?

"Such decisions are not made on any one factor," he says in retrospect. "There were several things. My disappointment with the way the tuition proposal was dealt with by the board and governor. I was frustrated that the state wasn't really going to make a commitment to supporting OSU."

There was also an issue over his contract. "I was in the fourth year of a five-year contract," Kirwan says, "and the Board of Trustees had begun to talk about extending it. I would be sixty-five when the contract expired in 2003, and the board initially suggested a year-to-year extension. 'No,' I said, 'I wanted something more than that.' They said they would do whatever I wanted. I was a bit put off that the board suggested a year-to-year agreement. It was a slight negative, not huge."

Kirwan contrasted that with the chancellor's job offer, where a five-year contract meshed well with his interests. "I still had a tremendous amount of energy and enthusiasm for work," he says. "I was too young to retire now or in a couple of years. Plus, Patty made this point often: We were always going to move back to Maryland, where we had a vacation home and where our kids had settled and where our three grandchildren were. Are we going to wait three, four, or five more years when our grandchildren would be that much older or do we go back now and be part of their growing up? That was probably the largest single factor, an overwhelming consideration. And the position gave a time frame that seemed right."

"I called David [Brennan] to tell him of my decision," Kirwan continues. "He was very disappointed. He said, 'Just tell me what you want and we'll do it.' He was very magnanimous, suggesting some compensation things and to do some things at the house. He then came to my office and sat with me to reinforce the desire that I stay. For David, family has deep and personal meaning. He respected the decision. We continue to have a very good relationship."

"We clearly would have loved to have had Brit stay," says Dimon McFerson. "We were very comfortable with him, but we also very much understood. You can compete on money, you can compete on perks, but you can't compete on heart and family ties."

Kirwan's new job paid a base salary of $375,000 plus $100,000 to cover lost pension revenue (federal law prohibits drawing salary and pension at the same time), versus the $275,000 at Ohio State and the $345,000 that the previous chancellor earned. He would live at Hidden Waters, a handsome Georgian mansion near the Baltimore Beltway. However, Kirwan assured the *Washington Post*, "This is not about the money."

"Maryland is where his heart is," said a University of Maryland insider. "This is where his wife wants to be. This is where he wants to end his career in higher education."

In hindsight, was it the right decision? "Being here has been an important blessing over the last year," he said in the summer of 2003, "everything I had hoped it would be and more. Although I miss Ohio State and get pangs of homesickness from time to time, it was the right decision."

Among the many who were sorry Kirwan was leaving were members of the Board of Trustees. "While the Board of Trustees is saddened by President Kirwan's decision, and will miss him greatly," said Brennan, "we appreciate his many contributions to Ohio State, particularly his leadership in developing and implementing the Academic Plan. The trustees remain fully committed to that plan."

Acknowledging the role of family in Kirwan's decision, many trustees understand that the budget battles—and especially the tuition issue—played a role also. "The fight with the governor over tuition took the wind out of Brit's sails," Brennan added later. "It became too much. When the board backed down, I could tell by the tone of his voice. It was the straw that broke the camel's back." Trustee Karen Hendricks agrees that the incident "was a source of misunderstanding and mistrust between Brit and the board."

Many did feel that Kirwan had left too soon.

"I was very disappointed Brit left when he did," says Alex Shumate, who had recruited Kirwan to Columbus. "He did good things, but his best work was yet to come. It was a solid four years, and he handed off a better university than he received." Asked if there were any disappointments in Kirwan's presidency, Fisher College dean Joe Alutto replied: "To be candid, the biggest disappointment was his leaving when he did. We were just reaching a point where I think everyone was benefiting from all the investments that had been made."

The *Washington Post* cited a special irony about the departure, noting that when Kirwan was president at College Park, he had lobbied against creation of the chancellor's job and had chafed under it. The Ohio media mourned his impending departure. "[M]ake no mistake," editorialized Cleveland's *Plain Dealer*, "this is a profound loss for OSU and for the future of public higher education in Ohio." "OSU and Ohio are losing a leader they can't afford to lose," wrote Joe Hallett in the *Dispatch*.

Clearly, the Kirwans are a very close family and the parents missed their children and grandchildren. "Whenever we came to meetings in DC," Patty says, "it would be strange to leave the kids. When we moved to Columbus, they were very supportive. They loved to visit. After visiting, Ann decided to get married there, rather than at the chapel at Maryland, and have the reception at the president's house." When she became pregnant and her water broke, Ann called her parents in Columbus at 11 PM, and they were in the hospital room early the next morning. Ann, who along with her brother loved Columbus, had hoped her dad would stay. "It was a great place," she says. "We had mixed emotions. Leaving broke his heart, but the third grandchild did it." "It was hard for him to leave Ohio State," seconds Bill. "It was earlier than he wanted, but the opportunity to return to Maryland was too good, with their eventual plans to go back and the third grandchild on the way."

Kirwan promised to be "the best lame-duck president ever," saying "it is the least I can do to demonstrate my deep and abiding affection and appreciation for The Ohio State University community." His agenda over the next ninety days, he added, would include the full implementation of the four Academic Plan initiatives—compensation, undergraduate enhancements, the Institute for the Study of Race and Ethnicity in the Americas, and biomedical research—plus moving forward with the Gateway Project.

He did all that and more, pressing to see that, to the extent humanly possible, every project then underway was completed by June 30. This included the announcement from the NSF of the Mathematical Biosciences Institute and the report on regional campuses.

John Meyer recalls that during his final weeks in office, Kirwan made two quick development trips. One was a final visit to Dutch Knowlton in Florida, an unsuccessful attempt to close a $3 million gap in funding the new architecture building. The other was to Boston for lunch with Frank Stanton, an alumnus and former president of CBS, who had earlier endowed a chair in psychology in honor of his professor, Harold E. Burtt.

Kirwan had an excellent relationship with Stanton and hoped to attract one more gift before he left for Maryland. Through active listening, Kirwan determined that Stanton's Ohio State passion was veterinary medicine and left with Stanton's commitment to endow a chair in that college. Only later did the university learn that many years earlier the Vet Med School had saved the life of the Stanton's Boston Terrier. In gratitude, Stanton named the chair in honor of his wife, Ruth, with whom he had happily roamed the banks of the Olentangy, adjacent to the College of Veterinary Medicine.

Introducing . . . The Holbrook Years

The trustees wasted no time in searching for a new president. Ten days after the announcement, at their meeting on April 3, Chairman David Brennan expressed an eagerness "to complete this process as soon as possible without sacrificing in any way quality, thoroughness or due diligence." The board named an eighteen-member search committee chaired by incoming chair Jim Patterson and including trustees Robert Duncan, Karen Hendricks, and Dimon McFerson along with five members of the faculty, two deans, three students, two administrators, an alumni representative, and a staff member. The trustees also voted to retain a search consultant and to delegate transition details to the president's planning cabinet.

"One of the first things the committee did was invite Kirwan to talk about the job," said senate secretary Susan Fisher in a June 2003 *Columbus Monthly* article. "He spent fully an hour and a half just listing—not describing but listing—the things he has to do. It was mind-boggling. How can any human being keep up with a schedule like that?" And at an exit interview with the board, Kirwan shared a list of potential candidates, just as Gee had done five years earlier.

At the May 3 Board of Trustees meeting, Patterson outlined the search committee's progress, which included a series of meetings with selected individuals and groups inside and outside the university, including leaders of national educational organizations. Besides advertising the position broadly and establishing a Web page to provide information and facilitate comments and suggestions, the committee held two public forums that month. Patterson emphasized the importance of discretion, noting that, "[a]s is true in comparable private sector searches, [attracting the best possible person] cannot be accomplished if the entire process and all of the candidates are subject to constant, intense public scrutiny."

The next report came at the June 6 meeting, at which Patterson—now chairman of the Board of Trustees as well as the search committee—made three important announcements. First was the hiring of A. T. Kearney, Inc., of Alexandria, Virginia, a firm experienced in academic searches and led in this instance by Jan Greenwood. Second was the adoption of a presidential profile representing input from many sources and featuring six key attributes: exemplary integrity, trustworthiness, and wisdom; superb interpersonal and communicative skills; a breadth and depth of intellect; a high level of energy; tenacity and judgment; and self-confidence. As noted earlier, one requirement for a new president was his or her absolute adherence to the Academic Plan. The trustees believed strongly that they had the right plan in place and were not interested in an alternate vision or different approach.

And third was the appointment of former president Ed Jennings as interim president, effective July 1. The trustees deliberately avoided choosing someone who was a candidate for president, selecting a man who not only had served as Ohio State's tenth president but also had remained active on the faculty at Fisher College and maintained strong relationships in the community.

"We are fortunate," Patterson said, "to have an ideal candidate available to us who brings great familiarity with the university and considerable experience in raising academic quality, working with faculty and addressing budget issues." His tenure, Patterson added, "could last anywhere from one week to several months."

On July 25, four months after Kirwan announced his departure, the Board of Trustees met in special session to elect Dr. Karen A. Holbrook, provost at the

Ed Jennings, Ohio State's tenth president, was recalled to duty to serve on an interim basis when Kirwan left for Maryland.

University of Georgia, as Ohio State's thirteenth president. The search committee, said Patterson, had "reviewed well over one hundred names, narrowing the list first to about fifty names, and met face-to-face with more than a dozen individuals. For the most part," he continued, "these candidates were presidents or provosts at major American universities." The committee concluded that Ohio State would be best served with someone from a public university, he added, eventually recommending "a small number of candidates to the Board of Trustees," which voted unanimously—"and I should add, enthusiastically—for . . . Dr. Karen Holbrook." "Holbrook," Patterson said, "meets or exceeds all the attributes in our Presidential Profile." He singled out three specific factors that attracted her to the search committee and board:

> Her "total, unequivocal commitment to academic excellence and the Academic Plan" and her "passionate interest . . . in Ohio State." "More than any person that we spoke to," he said, "Dr. Holbrook conveyed a

thorough understanding of our vision . . . and what it will take to achieve it."

Her broad experience at the Universities of Washington, Florida, and Georgia, three land-grant institutions "that bear many similarities to Ohio State." Patterson specifically cited her "experience with academic medical centers, medical research, and biotechnology."

Her "extraordinary set of interpersonal skills." "Her marks in developing positive relationships with faculty, staff, and students," Patterson said, "are more than high—they are stratospheric."

In expressing her delight at the board's decision, Holbrook noted that "The Ohio State University stands especially tall among land-grant research institutions because it has it all, and I do mean all. It has the people, a broad array of undergraduate and professional programs, including an outstanding medical center complex, a statewide purview of education and outreach and an unparalleled infrastructure."

The new president would be paid $325,000 a year, up from the $275,000 base salary Kirwan had received. She started work October 1.

As a relatively new trustee, Patterson had been honored to participate in the 1997 search that landed Kirwan, which served as something of a pattern for the 2002 exercise. There were differences, of course, including how the search committee members were chosen. In 1997, campus organizations were asked to submit names; in 2002 Patterson did some consulting, then made the choices himself. And while this search seemed to be conducted very quickly, Patterson notes that both searches consumed about the same four months. (The Kirwan search did not start until several months after Gee announced he was leaving, while the Holbrook search started within days; also, the Kirwan transition lasted six months, versus two months for Holbrook.)

"When the trustees met with Brit," Patterson says, in contrasting the searches of 1997 and 2002, "it was like, this is our person unless we reject him. This time, we talked to two or three. Before, it was very much Alex's pick. People now probably say Karen Holbrook is pretty much my pick. That's never the case, but the chair has a lot to do with it."

Patterson also ran names by Kirwan, who was, he says, "extremely helpful." "He talked with Karen before she was hired," Patterson adds, "and told me, 'You have found a good person.'"

McFerson, whose considerable experience on search committees was limited to business and nonprofit organizations, is complimentary about the

President Karen Holbrook at her first Board of Trustees meeting.

search process. "Chairman Patterson did an outstanding job," he says. "I think we were very thorough and that the board did a professional job."

Hail and Farewell

Kirwan's announcement was followed by a series of tributes and farewells. "As the period of time between March 25, when Brit announced he was leaving, until June when he left, the longer the time, the more goodbyes we had for him, the tougher it seemed for him to leave," Jim Patterson recalls. "I just wonder if you'd asked him in June if he wanted to change his mind, what he would have said. It was too late, of course. The decision became tougher after he made it rather than easier. There was such an outpouring of support and genuine respect and love that it was hard."

"It was a redo of what happened when I was leaving Maryland, although I was not there [Ohio State] as long," Kirwan notes. "I am a very emotional

President Kirwan and his tennis partner and friend, David Frantz, hug during a farewell reception in June 2002.

person and develop bonds of affection to institutions and people. I got very emotional on many occasions. I remember a very difficult meeting with the planning cabinet. I was sobbing. I was very touched by the outpouring of appreciation and support."

And an outpouring it was. At a farewell reception at the Blackwell Inn on June 21, Susan Fisher accorded Kirwan the ultimate faculty tribute. "Brit has shown," she said, "that it is possible to fundamentally change the way business is done even at a place as big and bureaucratic as OSU. But perhaps the most remarkable aspect of Brit's stewardship of the university is that, in every case, the changes were made not by presidential fiat or ultimatum but by reasoned discussion and consensus."

"He stood up for what he believed," said USG president Eddie Pauline, "and he compelled the rest of us to do the same thing. Through financial struggles, day-to-day dilemmas, and the plethora of problems and worries that plague any university president, he held true to his heart and as a result, we are, today, in a place that four years ago was hardly imaginable."

Perhaps the strongest words came from David Brennan at Kirwan's last Board of Trustees meeting, who called Kirwan "the finest president this university has had" and "the finest university president now sitting at any university in this country."

"Brit never created undue problems for himself," Patterson recalls. "People could agree or disagree with something, but nobody ever got out of joint with Brit."

"He was on a roll," trustee Dan Slane notes. "It was very exciting. He was right on target. We were getting better. I was extremely depressed when he left."

"The word that best describes Brit is genuine," says Judith Koroscik.

"He is a truly genuine, down-to-earth person," seconds University Relations' Sue Jones, who recalls seeing Kirwan at the Race for the Cure and waving hello. "He ran up and gave me a big hug and directed me over to Patty and his daughter," she adds. "Here I was cautious that he might not recognize me and he treated me like family."

"It feels kind of like the Kennedy presidency," says one colleague, "that it was Camelot. It was absolutely wonderful, and it was way too short. I am very sad about that."

"We had three great presidents in a row: Kirwan, Gee and Jennings," adds Mike Hogan.

Before leaving, Kirwan participated in an exit interview with the Board of Trustees conducted at the Fawcett Center. "Brit shared with us quite candidly his thoughts on Ohio State and where we are," recalls Jim Patterson. "He shared his thoughts on some individuals. The challenge he saw was the legislature and public funding. He was very much worried about that. I think he felt good about some things he had done, which he had every right to do. And he talked about the Academic Plan.

"'Don't lose it,' he implored us. 'It's too good. Keep it updated annually. Don't forget it.'"

Appendix

Members of the Kirwan Search Committee

Alex Shumate (chair), trustee
Tami Longaberger, trustee
James F. Patterson, trustee
George A. Skestos, trustee
Bruce E. Bursten, professor of chemistry
David O. Frantz, professor of English
Jane M. Fraser, associate professor of industrial, systems, and welding engineering
Alan J. Randall, professor of agricultural economics
Sally V. Rudman, associate professor of allied medical professions
Jerry A. May, vice president for Development and president of University Foundation
John Carney, president of Undergraduate Student Government
Clara Cuellar, doctoral candidate in sports management
Kermit L. Hall, dean, College of Humanities
Bernadine P. Healy, dean, College of Medicine and Public Health
Dan L. Heinlen, president and CEO, The Ohio State University Alumni Association
Jeri Kozobarich, director of Development, College of Education
Jack D. Miner, fiscal officer, Department of Physics
William J. Napier, secretary, Board of Trustees, and search committee coordinator

Members of the Kirwan Transition Team

Richard Sisson (chair), provost
Theodore S. Celeste, trustee
William Napier, secretary, Board of Trustees, and executive assistant to the president
William Shkurti, vice president, Finance
David Williams II, vice president, Student and Urban/Community Affairs

Nancy Zimpher, dean, College of Education; executive dean of professional colleges

Trustees Who Served during the Kirwan Administration

TRUSTEE (TERM)*

Theodore S. Celeste (1990–1999)
Michael F. Colley (1991–2000)
George A. Skestos (1992–2001)
David L. Brennan (1993–2002)
James F. Patterson (1994–2003)
Zuheir Sofia (1995–2004)
Tami Longaberger (1996–2005)
Daniel M. Slane (1997–2006)
Judge Robert M. Duncan (1998–2007)
Karen L. Hendricks (1999–2008)
Dimon R. McFerson (2000–2009)
Jo Ann Davidson (2001–2010)
Douglas G. Borror (2002–2011)

*All trustees chair the board in the final year of their appointment.

STUDENT TRUSTEE (TERM)

Soraya Rofagha (1997–1999)
Allyson M. Lowe (1998–2000)
Jaclyn M. Nowakowski (1999–2001)
Kevin R. Filiatraut (2000–2002)
Joseph A. Shultz (2001–2003)
Paula A. Habib (2002–2004)

Members of the National Academy during the Kirwan Administration

ELECTED BEFORE THE KIRWAN ADMINISTRATION

Kenneth G. Wilson, Physics, National Academy of Science (1975)
Paul G. Shewmon, Materials, National Academy of Engineering (1979)
Jose B. Cruz Jr., Electronics, National Academy of Engineering (1980)
Leo A. Paquette, Chemistry, National Academy of Science (1983)
Robert A. Rapp, Civil and Environmental, National Academy of Engineering (1988)
Charles C. Capen, Veterinary Medicine, Institute of Medicine (1992)
John D. Kraus, Electronics, National Academy of Engineering (1992)
Robert G. Kouyoumjian, Electronics, National Academy of Engineering (1995)
Robert H. Wagoner, Materials, National Academy of Engineering (1995)
Albert de la Chapelle, Molecular Virology, Immunology, and Medical Genetics, National Academy of Science (1997)

ELECTED BEFORE THE KIRWAN ADMINISTRATION BUT RECRUITED DURING THE KIRWAN YEARS

C. Bradley Moore, Chemistry, National Academy of Science (1986)
James C. Williams, Materials, National Academy of Engineering (1987)
Avner Friedman, Mathematics, National Academy of Science (1993)

ELECTED DURING THE KIRWAN ADMINISTRATION

Clara D. Bloomfield, Medicine, Institute of Medicine (2000)
Liang-Shih Fan, Chemical Engineering, National Academy of Engineering (2001)
Janice K. Kiecolt-Glaser, Psychiatry, Institute of Medicine (2001)
W. S. Winston Ho, Chemical Engineering, National Academy of Engineering (2002)

Distinguished University Professors Named during the Kirwan Administration

Gregory A. Caldeira, Political Science (1999)
Frank C. DeLucia, Physics (2000)
Joseph H. Lynch, History (2000)
Charles C. Capen, Veterinary Biosciences (2001)
Matthew S. Platz, Chemistry (2001)
Linda J. Saif, Food Animal Research (2002)
Lonnie J. Thompson, Geological Sciences (2002)

Wexner Prize Recipients

Gerhard Richter, painter (1998)
Louise Bourgeois, visual artist (1999)
Robert Rauschenberg, visual artist (2000)
Renzo Piano, architect (2001)

Major Building Projects Begun during the Gee Administration and Completed during the Kirwan Administration

1998

The Jerome Schottenstein Center
Fisher College of Business–Phase I (Max M. Fisher Hall and John B. Gerlach Graduate Programs Building)
University Hospitals Emergency Department

1999

Fisher College of Business–Phase II (The Schoenbaum Undergraduate Program Building, Raymond E. Mason Hall, and The John K. Pfahl Executive Education Building)
McPherson Chemical Laboratory Rehabilitation
Tuttle Park Place Garage (formerly Northwest Parking Expansion)
Lima Campus–Life and Physical Sciences Building
The Longaberger Alumni House
OARDC–Horticulture/Entomology Greenhouse

2000

The Dorothy M. Davis Heart and Lung Research Institute
The Younkin Success Center (formerly Neil Hall Renovation)
Baker Hall Renovation
Stillman Hall Addition

2001

Ohio Stadium renovation (plus Ohio Stadium Scoreboard in 2000)
Parker Food Science and Technology Building
Jessie Owens Track
ATI/OARDC–Center for Education and Economic Development

2002

Rodger D. Blackwell Inn at Fisher College

Major Building Projects Begun during the Kirwan Administration

The Stanley J. Aronoff Laboratory of Biological Sciences*
Biomedical Research Tower
Austin E. Knowlton Architecture Building
Psychology Building
Ohio 4-H Center
Oval Restoration
Page Hall Renovation
Peter L. and Clara M. Scott Laboratory (Robinson Lab replacement)
Physical Sciences Research Building
The Richard M. Ross Heart Hospital
Veterinary Medicine Academic Building (replacement for Sisson Hall)

* Started under Gee; completed under Holbrook

William Oxley Thompson Memorial Library (renovation)
Hagerty Hall Renovation

Commencement Speakers

September 3, 1998	Donald B. Shackelford, chair, Fifth Third Bank of Columbus
December 11, 1998	Clark Kellogg, college and professional basketball TV commentator
March 19, 1999	Richard D. Klausner, M.D., director, National Cancer Institute
June 11, 1999	Dumisa B. Ntsebeza, acting judge, Cape High Court of South Africa
September 2, 1999	John F. Wolfe, chairman, publisher, and CEO, the Dispatch Printing Company
December 10, 1999	Gregory S. Lashutka, mayor, City of Columbus
March 17, 2000	David Citino, professor, Department of English, The Ohio State University
June 9, 2000	J. C. Watts Jr., member, U.S. House of Representatives
August 31, 2000	John E. Pepper, chairman, Board of Directors, The Procter & Gamble Co.
December 8, 2000	Jo Ann Davidson, Speaker, Ohio House of Representatives
March 16, 2001	Bunny C. Clark, professor, Department of Physics, The Ohio State University
June 8, 2001	William H. Cosby Jr., comedian and actor
August 30, 2001	David Satcher, M.D., U.S. surgeon general
December 7, 2001	Ken Lee, professor and chairperson, Department of Food Science and Technology, The Ohio State University
March 22, 2002	David L. Brennan, chairman, Board of Trustees, The Ohio State University
June 14, 2002	George W. Bush, forty-third President of the United States

Honorary Doctoral Degrees Awarded

SEPTEMBER 3, 1998

Humane Letters	Marie M. Clay
Science	Vera Cooper Rubin
Natural Resources Management	Ismail Serageldin
Business Administration	Donald B. Shackelford

DECEMBER 11, 1998

Humane Letters	Adalet Aụaoglu
Humane Letters	Leonard B. Meyer

MARCH 19, 1999

Science	Chung-Hsin Chung
Science	Richard D. Klausner
Education	Lee Y. Dug
Science	Eugene P. Odum

JUNE 11, 1999

Science	Elias Burstein
Science	Lawrence J. DeLucas
Business Administration	David W. Longaberger (posthumously)

SEPTEMBER 2, 1999

Science	William V. Lumb
Humane Letters	William G. Ouchi
Journalism and Communication	John F. Wolfe

DECEMBER 10, 1999

Laws	Gregory S. Lashutka
Humane Letters	Ilse Lehiste
Business Administration	John G. McCoy

MARCH 17, 2000

Political Science	Robert D. Putnam
International Poicy	Sir Brian Urquhart

JUNE 9, 2000

Science	Robert Coleman Richardson
Science	Richard J. Solove
Humane Letters	William Julius Wilson

AUGUST 31, 2000

Humane Letters	Jules B. LaPidus
Science	R. S. Paroda
Business Administration	John E. Pepper

DECEMBER 8, 2000

Public Administration	Jo Ann Davidson
Sociology	William H. Form
Musical Arts	Michael Murray
Humane Letters	Frank Wobst

MARCH 16, 2001

Public Service	Henry Brognard Betts
Business	Betty Frank Schoenbaum
Business Administration	Ratan N. Tata
Engineering	Hiroyuki Yoshino

JUNE 8, 2001

Science	Lester R. Brown
Education	William H. Cosby Jr.
Landscape Architecture	Daniel Urban Kiley
Business Administration	Raymond E. Mason Jr.

AUGUST 30, 2001

Science	Raphael Mechoulam
Science	Clayton D. Mote Jr.
Science	David Satcher
Science	Karen K. Uhlenbeck

DECEMBER 7, 2001

Science	John N. Bahcall
Music	Paul E. Bierley
Science	F. Albert Cotton

MARCH 22, 2002

Science	Wilford R. Gardner
Humane Letters	Theodore M. Hesburgh
Science	Ray D. Owen

JUNE 14, 2002

Public Administration	George W. Bush
Science	Walter E. Massey
Business Administration	George M. Steinbrenner II
Social Science	Marta Tienda

Highest GPAs, 1998–2002

SUMMER 1998

Jeffrey Iding (Cincinnati) 4.0

AUTUMN 1998

Shannon Michelle Novosad (Centerville) 4.0

WINTER 1999

Makkari Cheng (Hilo, HI) 3.96
Robin Timmons Craft (Plain City)

SPRING 1999

Matthew Green (Cambridge) 4.0
Thomas Lewis (Waverly)
Debra Merold (Kenton)
Kari Mount (Knoxville, TN)
Leonid Trostyanetsky (Reynoldsburg)

SUMMER 1999

Marilyn Campbell (Mansfield) 3.98
Colleen McCarthy (Canfield)

AUTUMN 1999

Melissa Adam (Fort Jennings) 3.98
Thad Summersett (Convoy)
Erin Tunis (Worthington)
Jane West (Columbus)

WINTER 2000

Adele Robbins (Pataskala) 4.0

SPRING 2000

Tasha Castor (Westerville) 4.0
Sara Darst (Newark)
Ryan Geiss (Columbus)
Lynnsay Leesburg (Portsmouth)
Nathan Nelson (Lima)
Beth Paumier (Louisville)

Anne Spicker (Ashland)
Ann Tellep (Solon)
Brooke Whittaker (Toledo)
J. D. Wylie (Worthington)
Rebecca Zell (Bellefontaine)

SUMMER 2000

Shawn Brueggemeier (Columbus) 4.0

AUTUMN 2000

Ellen Doughty (Adams Mills) 4.0

WINTER 2001

Jamie Goodman (Columbus) 3.99

SPRING 2001

Lauren Baylor (Brecksville) 4.0
Jennifer Burkhart (North Olmsted)
Grace Fuller (Cleveland)
Tessa Majewski (Pickerington)
David Quarfoot (Richardson, TX)
Jennifer Stecker (Martins Ferry)
Jeffery Stoller (Van Wert)
Jessica Weeks (Shaker Heights)

SUMMER 2001

Curtis Tuggle (Cardington) 3.97
Gretchen Davis (Canfield)

AUTUMN 2001

Carrie Kincaid (Cincinnati) 4.0

WINTER 2002

David Reinhardt (Marysville) 4.0
Diana Ruggiero (Hilliard)

SPRING 2002

Bryan Cairns (Granville) 4.0
Karoline Gilbert (Uniontown)

Regan Snider (Celina)
Leigh Mowrer (Westerville)

Members of Foundation Board during the Kirwan Administration

Honorable Daniel G. Amstutz
Vincent T. Aveni
John W. Berry Jr.
Edwin M. Cooperman
Jameson Crane
Lois Ann Crane
John W. Creighton Jr.
Samuel B. Davis
Richard J. Denman
Ruann F. Ernst
Joseph J. Gasper
John B. Gerlach Jr.
Herbert Glimcher
Ray J. Groves
Edward E. Hagenlocker
Virginia S. Hull
E. William Ingram III
William M. Isaac
Alexis A. Jacobs
Ralph E. Kent
John W. Kessler
Charles Klatskin
James D. Klingbeil
H. Frederick Krimendahl II
Abba G. Lichtenstein
William G. Lowrie
John Lucks
Thomas A. Mann
Robert E. Martini
General Raymond E. Mason Jr.
John G. McCoy
Lou Ann Moritz
Michael E. Moritz
Douglas E. Olesen
Floradelle A. Pfahl
Corbett Price
Robert F. Reusché
David A. Rismiller
Patricia A. Robinson
Ralph Rockow
John E. Sandefur
John J. Schiff Jr.
John J. Schiff Sr.
Betty Frank Schoenbaum
Thekla Reese Shackelford
David B. Sharrock
John M. Shepherd
Alex Shumate
Barbara Trueman
Frank Wobst
John F. Wolfe
Jacqueline F. Woods

PRIVATE SUPPORT (IN MILLIONS) DURING THE KIRWAN ADMINISTRATION

Year	*Total Gift Activity*
1998–99	$153.4
1999–2000	$174.3
2000–2001	$179.5
2001–2002	$210.6
Total	$717.8

MEMBERS OF THE HOLBROOK SEARCH COMMITTEE

James F. Patterson (chair), trustee
Robert M. Duncan, trustee
Karen L. Hendricks, trustee
Dimon R. McFerson, trustee
Bruce E. Bursten, chairperson and professor, Department of Chemistry
Susan W. Fisher, professor, Department of Entomology and secretary, University Senate
David O. Frantz, professor, Department of English
Jacqueline J. Royster, professor, Departments of English and African-American and African Studies
Marilyn Brewer, professor, Department of Psychology
Fred Sanfilippo, senior vice president for Health Sciences and dean, College of Medicine and Public Health
James C. Williams, dean, College of Engineering
Marsha Robinson, graduate student, Department of History
Eddie Pauline, president, Undergraduate Student Government
Soraya Rofagha, professional student, College of Medicine and Public Health
Jerry A. May, vice president for Development and president of University Foundation
Mac A. Stewart, vice provost for Minority Affairs
Dan Heinlen, president and CEO, The Ohio State University Alumni Association
Willa N. Young, chair, University Staff Advisory Committee

About the Author

Chris Perry served as Brit Kirwan's speechwriter at Ohio State from January 2000 through June 2002. Born on New York's Long Island and educated at Princeton (B.A.–Politics) and Columbia (M.S.–Journalism), he has worked as a journalist, political consultant, magazine editor and publisher, public relations executive, and freelance writer. Besides Kirwan, he has worked with several CEOs at DuPont, as executive assistant to Delaware governor Russell Peterson, and as assistant to the U.S. secretary of commerce, Elliot Richardson. He is the author of the Delaware Heritage Commission's oral history book about Governor Peterson. He lives in Andover, Vermont, with his wife, Nancy, a trainer/facilitator now in real estate. They have two children and two grandchildren.

Academic Plan

Preface

The Ohio State University aspires to become one of the world's great public research and teaching universities. This Academic Plan is the initial roadmap for the journey to academic excellence. With few exceptions, we expect the initiatives identified herein to be realized in the next five years. At the same time, implementation of this plan will be a continuing process, and the pace at which we progress will depend upon a number of circumstances, including the availability of financial resources.

The plan is divided into the following primary sections:

- **Vision.** Our vision for the future of The Ohio State University;
- **Setting the Stage.** A candid assessment of our current position, strengths, and weaknesses;
- **Strategies and Initiatives.** Six core strategies and 14 initiatives to help achieve academic excellence and move us substantially toward our overarching goal;
- **Facilitating Actions.** Additional changes that are necessary to release the full creativity of the University and successfully implement the strategies and initiatives;
- **Continuing Activities.** A brief summary of continuing activities that while extremely important, are not part of this plan;
- **Resources.** A strategy to acquire the resources necessary to support this plan; and
- **Scorecard.** Benchmarks we will regularly consult to monitor our progress.

TABLE OF CONTENTS

Preface 1

Executive Summary 2

The Ohio State University Vision 4

Setting the Stage: Context and Strategies for the Academic Plan 5

Strategies and Initiatives:

Build a World-Class Faculty 10

Develop Academic Programs that Define Ohio State as the Nation's Leading Public Land-Grant University 11

Enhance the Quality of the Teaching and Learning Environment 12

Enhance and Better Serve the Student Body 13

Create a Diverse University Community 14

Help Build Ohio's Future 15

Facilitating Actions:

Obtain Increased State Support 16

Improve the Organization and Delivery of Instruction 16

Increase Organizational Flexibility 16

Improve the Faculty Work Environment 17

Continuing Activities 18

Resources 19

The Academic Scorecard 22

Executive Summary

The Ohio State University aspires to be among the world's truly great universities—advancing the well-being of the people of Ohio and the global community through the creation and dissemination of knowledge. Ohio needs a great teaching and research university for a rich flow of ideas, innovation, and graduates from a wide variety of disciplines. Ohio also needs a great university to be what The New York Times has called a "revving economic engine" that spurs strategic growth in the new Information Age economy.

Any review of the comparative data makes it clear that our focus must be on building academic excellence. For while the University needs to continuously improve in many areas, we will never be a great university without dramatically enhancing the reality and perception of our teaching and learning as well as our research and scholarship - and without enhancing the service activities that flow from our excellence in these endeavors.

Over recent years, we have focused on four core elements: Becoming a national leader in the quality of our academic programs; being universally recognized for the quality of the learning experience we offer our students; creating an environment that truly values and is enriched by diversity; and expanding the land-grant mission to address our society's most compelling needs.

These core elements are reflected in the six strategies and 14 supporting initiatives that follow. While the University will undertake many more initiatives over the next five years, these are considered the most transformational.

Strategy: Build a World-Class Faculty

1. Over the next three to five years, recruit at least 12 faculty members who have attained or have the potential to attain the highest honors in their disciplines, concentrating these appointments in areas of strategic focus.

2. Implement a faculty recruitment, retention, and development plan - including a competitive, merit-based compensation structure - that is in line with our peer institutions.

Strategy: Develop Academic Programs that Define Ohio State as the Nation's Leading Public Land-Grant University.

3. Continue the Strategic Investment approach by competitively funding initiatives that build programmatic strength and open new fields. Build on existing capabilities and capture opportunities specific to Ohio State and to Ohio. Maintain ongoing multidisciplinary initiatives where appropriate and develop new initiatives that draw on University-wide strengths to attack major problems of the next quarter century. Create multidisciplinary centers that can attract additional faculty in key areas, helping reduce student-faculty ratios in high-demand fields.

4. Significantly increase space dedicated to funded research beyond what is currently planned. Include a multidisciplinary building devoted to high-quality research space as well as to office and meeting space.

Strategy: Enhance the Quality of the Teaching and Learning Environment.

5. Transform the Library into a 21st century Information Age center within the next five to ten years.

6. Upgrade the quality of our classroom pool space and enhance the appearance of the campus facilities and grounds.

7. Provide faculty, staff, and students with the latest technology tools for leadership in teaching, research, and career development within the next five years.

Strategy: Enhance and Better Serve the Student Body.

8. Within the next three years, make admissions to Ohio State selective throughout the year for new freshmen and for all transfer students.

9. Create a rich educational environment for undergraduates. Increase course accessibility, reduce class sizes, and establish at least ten scholars programs within five years - expanding opportunities for students to live with those who share common interests and enhancing students' academic success and sense of community. Provide academic programming, advising, and career counseling within these communities.

10. Provide ample need-based and merit-based aid for undergraduates and a competitive financial aid and fellowship support package for graduate and professional students to improve Ohio State's graduate and professional matriculation rate.

Strategy: Create a Diverse University Community.

11. Hire at least five to ten women and five to ten minority faculty at a senior level each year for five years through the Faculty Hiring Assistance Program (FHAP) and other initiatives.

12. Recruit, support, and retain to graduation larger numbers of academically able minority students.

Strategy: Help Build Ohio's Future.

13. Significantly strengthen the scope and effectiveness of our commitment to P-12 public education, with a special focus on the education of underserved children and youth. In so doing, work with the State of Ohio and selected local school districts. This initiative will be a University-wide partnership, with the College of Education in the lead college role.

14. Become the catalyst for the development of Ohio's technology-based economy. Increase collaborations with the private sector to enhance research, successfully transfer University technology, and provide experiential learning and career opportunities for students.

To successfully implement this ambitious agenda, the University must take four Facilitating Actions: Obtain increased state support, improve the organization and delivery of instruction, increase organizational flexibility, and improve the faculty work environment. The Plan identifies specific steps to meet these needs.

Over the next five years, the University expects to invest in the range of $750 million in new and reallocated resources to implement this Plan, with spending scaled up or down depending upon actual funding. The Plan identifies potential sources for the needed revenues. A set of strategic indicators will help measure our progress.

The Ohio State University Vision

A successful strategic plan requires two fundamental components. First, the plan must be designed around a strong, compelling vision that provides context and identifies overall direction and goals. Second, the organization needs strategies to achieve that vision and the capacity and will to execute those strategies.

The most meaningful statements of vision are comprised of four elements - a statement of the organization's core purpose; an illumination of a few core values that represent its true essence; a significant overarching goal, which the organization is fully committed to achieving; and finally, a description of what the organization would be like should it succeed in achieving its overarching goal in a way that is consistent with its purpose and values.

The vision statement that follows succeeds the original mission-vision statement adopted by the University in 1992, which was intended for review on a decennial basis. The new vision statement was developed initially by a group of Ohio State administrators, deans, and faculty. Subsequently, it was revised based on comments from faculty, staff, and students as well as representatives from the extended Ohio State community. This vision stands today as the underpinning and conceptual framework for the strategies and initiatives outlined in the plan that follows. It also reflects the values and aspirations of a broad cross section of the University community.

Purpose

To advance the well-being of the people of Ohio and the global community through the creation and dissemination of knowledge.

Core Values

- Pursue knowledge for its own sake.
- Ignite in our students a lifelong love of learning.
- Produce discoveries that make the world a better place.
- Celebrate and learn from our diversity.
- Open the world to our students.

Overarching Goal

The Ohio State University will be among the world's truly great universities.

Future

The Ohio State University will be recognized worldwide for the quality and impact of its research, teaching, and service. Our students will be able to learn and to advance knowledge in all areas. As a 21st century land-grant university, The Ohio State University will set the standard for the creation and dissemination of knowledge in service to its communities, state, nation, and the world. Our faculty, students, and staff will be among the best in the nation.

Academic excellence will be enriched by an environment that mirrors the diverse world in which we live. Within this environment, we will come to value the differences in one another along with the similarities, and to appreciate that the human condition is best served through understanding, acceptance, and mutual respect. Throughout the learning process, our faculty and staff will find the highest levels of fulfillment and satisfaction as they collaborate to educate and support a student body recognized for its scholarship and integrity.

Students will have the opportunity to learn on our campuses or from locations around the world through the innovative use of technology. The quality of our physical facilities and grounds will be consistent with our world-class status. Extracurricular activities will support the personal growth of all members of our community. Our intercollegiate athletic programs will routinely rank among the elite few.

Graduation rates for all students will compare favorably with the nation's best public universities. Most of all, our graduates will be among the most sought after by the world's best employers and will become leaders in their communities and accomplished professionals in their chosen work. We will lead Ohio to a dynamic knowledge economy, and our research, widely known for its multidisciplinary programs, will help solve the most challenging social, cultural, technical, and health-related problems.

The excellence of our programs will be recognized by the highest levels of public and private support. As a result, The Ohio State University will earn an intensity of alumni loyalty and of public esteem unsurpassed by any other university.

Setting the Stage

Context and Strategies for the Academic Plan

The Ohio State University is a major public comprehensive teaching and research university with strong core values and high aspirations. We have a bold new vision. To realize that vision, we are calling for an investment in the range of $750 million in new and reallocated resources over the next five years. This total is in addition to funds already committed in continuing services and previously identified capital projects. It depends upon enhanced state allocations, increased federal support for our research, continued success in raising private funds, and our commitment to a new spirit of entrepreneurial endeavors.

With this vision, and supported by such resources, we have the potential to improve significantly. We can better serve our students, faculty, staff, community, and state through even more effective research, teaching, and service. We can achieve the goals in our vision statement. In short, we can become one of the world's truly great universities.

This Academic Plan - the first iteration of what will be an ongoing planning process - is designed to launch us toward our ambitious goals. In this section of the plan, we address the following questions:

- Why does Ohio need a truly great teaching and research university?
- What do we mean by "academic excellence?"
- How far are we from that ideal?
- What challenges must we overcome to attain our goals?
- What are the internal and external factors that will influence our journey?
- And, finally, what are our core strengths?

Why Does Ohio Need a Great University?

For centuries, civilization has depended upon universities for a rich flow of ideas, innovation, and graduates from a wide diversity of disciplines - from the humanities and social sciences to physical sciences, technology, and the professions. These intellectual and human resources have long been vital to Ohio's social, economic, and civic success. They remain so today, when the need for ideas, innovation, and graduates is greater than ever.

A top-tier university will be a center of excellence for the very best high school graduates - providing a broad, diverse population of students with access to a rich campus experience and offering lifelong learning opportunities to traditional and non-traditional students alike. It will also be a center of excellence for graduate and professional education, research, and scholarship - creating knowledge and innovation that fundamentally improve learning and the way people live. It will excel in the arts and sciences, dynamically enhancing the way our graduates understand and experience their world. And it will be a land-grant university that serves Ohio citizens in a multiplicity of useful ways.

One very important role for Ohio State is to spur Ohio's economic growth. Increasingly, our nation's most dynamic economies - areas such as Silicon Valley - are connected to great research universities. In writing about our nation's most economically successful regions, The New York Times said that, "If there is one never-absent factor at work, it is the proximity of a research university shifting from ivory tower to revving economic engine." Ohio needs such a "revving economic engine" to succeed in the 21st century Information Age economy - a university that spawns innovation, generates new technologies and ideas, and produces talented graduates for successful commercial enterprises.

The university we envision will transfer knowledge and ideas to boost the state's fortunes. It will also help meet the state's need for ever-larger numbers of workers in such disciplines as biotechnology, information technology, and other high-growth fields and critical professions. It will prepare Ohio citizens to govern themselves effectively and to lead satisfying and rewarding lives. And since Ohio is irreversibly linked to the global economy, the University will prepare its graduates to live and work in a socially and economically diverse world.

The issue is not whether Ohio will continue to have a large, academically diverse state university that educates thousands of its residents. Clearly, it will. The issue is whether Ohio will have a truly great university, the kind of top-tier university that Ohio and its people need and deserve. We are determined that it will.

What Is Academic Excellence?

The sine qua non of a great university is academic excellence, as measured by the quality of the research, scholarship, and graduates it produces along with their collective impact on the larger society. To be a great university, the prevailing culture must demand excellence in all endeavors. That excellence can only be achieved when all parts of the University - administration, faculty, staff, students, and alumni - are committed to the highest standards of performance.

In today's world, academic excellence requires elements and experiences beyond those traditionally associated with universities. For example, an excellent education today requires an understanding of diversity and how diversity can enrich our learning and our lives. It also requires an understanding of how theory and practice meet, an understanding that can be enhanced through a rich array of service, outreach, and partnership opportunities. Academic excellence also requires state-of-the-art infrastructure and a talented and highly motivated staff.

How Far Are We From Our Ideal?

To create a plan that enables The Ohio State University to become an academically excellent institution, we need to assess where we stand today - comparing our current position with our peers, including a number of aspirational peers. These nine benchmark Research I universities - Arizona, Illinois, Michigan, Minnesota, Penn State, Texas, UCLA, Washington, and Wisconsin - were selected for their general comparability.

The following brief snapshot of Ohio State's current position in selected key areas was compiled from a variety of sources, including Strategic Indicators 2000 prepared by the University's Office of Strategic Analysis and Planning and the Research Commission Report.

While some of these statements underscore the rigorous challenge before us, the path to excellence must begin with a candid acknowledgement of our current position. In no way does any particular current ranking detract from the outstanding record of accomplishment that The Ohio State University has compiled over the years - nor the high quality and quest for continuous improvement that distinguishes it today. We should also note that no ranking system exists for some of our most outstanding academic programs.

Academic Quality and Scholarship

- The most recent NRC rating (1992) placed nine Ohio State programs in the Top 25, tying us for the last position among our benchmark universities. In its most recent report on selected academic areas, U.S. News & World Report rated four Ohio State academic Ph.D. programs in the Top 25, ranking us eighth among benchmark institutions. (The four programs are Chemistry, Physics, Political Science, and Sociology.) In professional graduate programs, we fare somewhat better and approach the middle of the pack among our benchmark universities.
- We rank poorly in undergraduate student pre-college preparation levels relative to our benchmark universities. While entering classes are gaining in strength year by year - average freshman ACT scores have risen from under 23 to almost 25 since 1995 - incremental improvement will become more difficult as we progress.
- Graduate applicants and enrolled graduate students score above the national average. Yet even in some strong departments, Ohio State appears less able than some leading peers to attract graduate students from highly ranked undergraduate programs.
- Though absolute amounts of federal research dollars have increased for Ohio State and the benchmark universities, our portion of federal research dollars is below that of the benchmark universities. Overall, we lag benchmark institutions on virtually all key measures of sponsored-research success. However, we are moving steadily up the scale in industry-funded research, where we now rank fifth among U.S. universities.
- Despite recent improvements, we remain well below the mean of benchmark schools in publications and citations as well as patents and licenses.

Student Experience

- Ohio State is beginning to close the gap in freshman retention rate with the benchmark universities. However, the gap between the six-year graduation rate at Ohio State and its benchmark schools grew from 10 percent in 1996 to 14 percent in 1997 and remained there in 1999. This reflects classes admitted in the early 1990s and highlights the time it takes to register progress.

Campus Diversity

- Although our record has improved and compares favorably to most benchmark institutions, we are not satisfied with our progress. For example, we attract fewer underrepresented minority students than we would like, and retention and graduation rates for these students are low relative to the University's overall statistics.

- While we have a higher proportion of women faculty than our benchmark universities and are substantially better at attracting new faculty from under-represented minority groups, there has been little change in our percentage representation since 1990. The reason is that our turnover rate is too high.
- Staff diversity across all categories is close to the benchmark mean, although minority representation in executive positions lags the benchmark mean. The percentage of women and ethnic minorities among professional staff has remained relatively constant since 1990.

Outreach and Engagement/Community Service

- The Ohio State University Extension represents a $58 million annual commitment to Ohio's agriculture and natural resources, community development, family and consumer services, and 4-H Youth Development. We also make significant contributions to Ohio through our $800 million investment in healthcare delivery services and our growing support of Ohio's public school system. In short, we maintain one of the nation's best land-grant traditions, which continues to be a source of great strength and leadership for the University.
- While strengthening our work in these traditional areas, we need to bring a similar sense of commitment and leadership to issues that greatly challenge Ohio's urban communities in the 21st century - issues such as P-12 education, economic development, and community renewal.

What Challenges Must We Overcome?

In summary, we are far from our ideal. Today, Ohio State is perceived as having great athletics and good, but not outstanding, academics. We are viewed as big and bureaucratic but with a strong spirit, particularly among alumni. Allowing for many exceptions to such gross generalizations, that perception is fairly close to the mark. So where do we start?

Any review of the comparative data makes it clear that our focus must be on building academic excellence. For while the University needs to continuously improve in many areas, we will never be a truly great university without dramatically enhancing the reality and perception of the teaching and learning and research and scholarship we do - and without the service activities that flow from our excellence in these endeavors.

Although much has been accomplished in recent years, our academic reputation has not appreciably improved. The 20-10 Plan is designed to move Ohio State into the top-tier of America's public research universities by the year 2010, with 10 programs ranked in the top 10 in their respective disciplines and 20 programs ranked in the top 20. This is a bold objective and the essential starting point of our plan. It is an important benchmark in reaching our ultimate goal.

In addition, we will not succeed without explicitly defining expectations for other Ohio State colleges, schools, and departments that make significant contributions to the University - even if not targeted for the initial round of investment. The profiles of leading universities reflect strength that is broad and deep - not simply in a few disciplines but throughout the institution. They also offer market-competitive compensation for their faculty and staff. We must also recruit and maintain the finest possible faculty and staff and provide faculty and staff members with competitive compensation.

We must also upgrade the achievement level of our undergraduate student body.

As already noted, our six-year graduation rate lags our benchmark institutions. So does the preparation level of our incoming students, although we have made real progress in that measure over recent years.

Finally, there is strong support for improving the University infrastructure, with particular attention to the appearance of the campus and the cleanliness and quality of maintenance of campus buildings. We must challenge ourselves to create a campus environment that contributes to and is consistent with academic excellence.

What Factors Will Influence Our Progress?

The Academic Plan is a product not only of our vision and aspirations, but also of the environment in which we operate. This environment includes broad economic and societal trends as well as the pressures, opportunities, and resource constraints that confront higher education today. Together with the actions of benchmark universities, these forces help define how the University can best achieve its objectives.

1. Macro Trends

The Information Age economy. By Information Age economy measures, Ohio does not fare well. It ranks 32nd in the creation of high-tech jobs, 29th in the number of high-growth companies, 29th in venture capital investment, and 28th in Internet use. The state has been ranked 33rd overall in its path to the new economy. This may explain why Ohio's personal income ranking has declined from sixth in 1960 to 22nd today and why, over the last 20 years, Ohio's economy has grown more slowly than the total U.S. economy. Successful Information Age economies uniformly rely upon top-tier research universities. Conclusion: Ohio State must help the state transition to the Information Age economy by becoming the state's "revving economic engine."

Globalization and demographics. America is becoming much more global and diverse, requiring employees with greater knowledge of other countries and cultures along with greater language capabilities. In addition, America's demographic composition is changing fast. By 2020, there will be 10 percent fewer whites and 30 percent more non-whites in the U.S. work force. By 2050, the Caucasian population will drop to around 50 percent. Ohio State has made some but not enough progress in its diversity and international initiatives. Conclusion: Ohio State must become more diverse so we can prepare our students for success in this more diverse nation and must enhance and coordinate our international studies and programs to prepare students for a more global economy.

Urbanization. In 1900, almost 40 percent of the U.S. population lived on farms. By the end of the century, the figure stood at less than two percent. Today, 20 percent of the nation's farms produce 80 percent of our food output. Ohio State's agricultural outreach is exceptional. We are moving to make similar contributions in other broad areas. Conclusion: We must expand our land-grant mission to serve urban as well as rural populations.

Technology. No change factor is more evident than the continuing and ever-more-rapid growth of technology, which affects not only what is taught but how, e.g. online learning. While this is not an area of current strength at Ohio State, we must help our students - whatever their field of study - become fully conversant with the latest available technology. We cannot be a great university without making major progress in this area. Conclusion: We must equal or surpass our benchmark institutions in the use of technology for teaching, learning, research, and overall effectiveness.

Continuous and rapid change. Today's continuous and rapid change affects all institutions but is particularly challenging for universities, which are better structured to respect tradition, conserve established areas of excellence, and adopt proven changes than to move quickly and flexibly to seize opportunities. Our peers are beginning to adapt to this new environment, and we must not be left behind. Conclusion: We must accelerate our decision-making process, become receptive to more innovative ideas and partnerships, and make organizational and process changes that will enhance our effectiveness.

2. Funding Realities

While reaching our goal is not just a matter of resources, it will be impossible to succeed without additional resources - along with continuously enhanced efficiency and effectiveness, greater productivity, and an ongoing reallocation of funds based on current priorities. As the numbers below indicate, Ohio State receives and spends less per student than our benchmark institutions. Specifically:

- Ohio ranks 42nd nationally in the percentage of budget allocation to higher education - the lowest per student amount among Big Ten states.
- Our FY2000 annual resident undergraduate tuition and fees total $4,110 - five percent below the average for benchmark institutions. In Ohio, we rank ninth among 13 public-assisted universities in tuition and fees - 6.3 percent below the state average although our academic reputation ranking is well above any other Ohio university.
- State appropriations per student FTE remain barely at 1991 levels in constant dollars.
- Our overall Total Education and General (E&G) Expenditures are 81 percent of the benchmark average - up from 77 percent in the early 1990s.
- While current fund revenues per student FTE average 20 percent below the mean for benchmark institutions, we have begun to close the gap in recent years. The potential exists to reach the benchmark mean by the middle of this decade.

Ohio is a large and prosperous state that is not supporting its institutions of higher learning at the level necessary to compete effectively in an Information Age economy. We need to help the people and leaders of Ohio better appreciate the many ways that The Ohio State University benefits the state - and the large additional benefits that could be realized.

What Are Our Core Strengths?

Can we succeed? Is our vision realistic? As challenging as it will be to reach our goal, the quest is not quixotic. To be counted among the top ten public research universities in the nation is achievable. For Ohio State can rightly claim great strengths in many areas, strengths that it can leverage to its advantage. These include:

- Several programs that already qualify as "top tier";
- A dedicated faculty, many of whom are internationally renowned;
- A vibrant and strong student body that improves every year;
- A talented and committed staff;
- A comprehensive array of programs with a potential for increased interdisciplinary research, instruction, and service;
- A large body of alumni whose loyalty and school spirit are unsurpassed;
- Private giving that is a model among public universities;
- An exceptionally strong position within Ohio, where we are the state's "flagship" university and enjoy a strong level of community support;
- A land-grant tradition that is among the strongest and most effective in the nation; and
- A pervasive commitment to excellence.

With these strengths, and the initiatives that follow, we can move aggressively toward our vision of academic excellence.

Strategies and Initiatives

Over recent years, The Ohio State University has focused on four core elements:

- Becoming a national leader in the quality of our academic programs;
- Being universally acclaimed for the quality of the learning experience we offer our students;
- Creating an environment that truly values and is enriched by diversity; and
- Expanding the land-grant mission to address our society's most compelling needs.

These core elements were fundamental to the preparation of this plan. They are reflected in the six strategies and 14 supporting initiatives that follow. Consistent with our vision and circumstances, these strategies are to:

1. Build a world-class faculty.
2. Develop academic programs that define Ohio State as the nation's leading public land-grant university.
3. Improve the quality of the teaching and learning environment.
4. Enhance and better serve the student body.
5. Create a more diverse University community.
6. Help build Ohio's future.

It is important to emphasize that the University will continue to be engaged in a wide array of useful and important initiatives, only a few of which are reflected in this Plan. The initiatives and resource plan contained herein are designed not simply to sustain progress, but to accelerate it over the next five years - to take the University to a higher level of performance. They represent a manageable number of items with the potential to fundamentally transform the University.

In developing this Plan, we have drawn on the thoughtful and thorough work of the Research Commission; the Reports on Undergraduate, Graduate and Professional Experience; the Diversity Action Plan; the President's Council on Outreach and Engagement; and numerous other documents.

Strategy:

Build a World-Class Faculty

Academic excellence begins with high-quality faculty. Faculty not only enhance the University's teaching and programmatic reputation but also attract the highest quality students at all levels. More than any other single factor, attracting and keeping exceptional faculty members will help us become a great university.

In its 1998 report, The Ohio State University Research Commission found that, compared to benchmark institutions, Ohio State has few faculty who have attained the highest honors and that our total faculty complement in critical disciplines is low when compared to our benchmark peers. Relative to peer institutions, for example, Ohio State has no disciplines ranked in the first quartile of the NRC or USN&WR rankings, and only three of 38 disciplines in the second quartile of the NRC rankings. Clearly, every faculty hire is important. The ability to hire a dozen or so exceptional senior faculty of international acclaim over the next five years will significantly enhance our reputation and complement our efforts to hire the very best faculty at every level.

But no strategy to enhance faculty quality will succeed without compensation that is competitive with our peer universities. Today, our faculty compensation does not rank in the top half of our benchmark institutions.

To address these challenges, we will:

1. Over the next three to five years, recruit at least 12 faculty members who have attained or have the potential to attain the highest honors in their disciplines, concentrating these appointments in areas of strategic focus. Implementation: Begin immediately to recruit 2-3 internationally eminent, National Academy caliber faculty members per year. Cost: \$3.6M in continuing funding for salary and benefits and \$15M in one-time funding for start-up packages.

2. Implement a faculty recruitment, retention, and development plan - including a competitive, merit-based compensation structure - that is in line with our benchmark institutions. Implementation: Adopt a 2-3 year merit-based plan to match the average faculty salaries at our benchmark institutions, which requires an increase of 2.5% beyond the 4% baseline. Provide competitively funded enhanced support for our most promising junior and senior faculty. Cost: \$13.5M in continuing funding over the next five years.

Strategy:

Develop Academic Programs that Define Ohio State as the Nation's Leading Public Land-Grant University.

Academic excellence requires that the quality and reputation of our academic programs rival those of our benchmark institutions. While we lag these institutions in the number of programs that are highly rated in the NRC and USN&WR rankings, our 2010 Plan provides a roadmap for success. As already noted, that plan is designed to move Ohio State into the top-tier of America's public research universities by the year 2010, with 10 programs ranked in the top 10 in their respective disciplines and 20 programs ranked in the top 20.

In the last three years, the University has identified 13 programs that within the next few years will receive $1 million each in additional continuing funding - a level of continuing support that is equivalent to an endowment of $260 million. Already, our recent emphasis on focused investment has fostered programmatic development in areas of strategic importance. By continuing to "invest for success," we will create top-quality academic programs that will move us toward parity or better with our peer institutions.

We must also invest in research space. Although significant improvements in research space are either planned or will be coming online soon, Ohio State remains well below the benchmark institutions identified by the Research Commission in providing the infrastructure needed for modern research. With enhanced research facilities, we will be better able to recruit and retain faculty and to increase the volume of funded research.

Finally, great research universities typically house a number of nationally prominent research centers that flourish outside traditional disciplinary boundaries. These centers initiate cutting-edge research and educational opportunities that are oriented around important problems rather than disciplines. Often, such world-class centers connect with the community through outreach and technology transfer. Strong multidisciplinary and interdisciplinary centers also help attract and retain exceptional faculty and attract and retain to graduation talented students. Many of the major research opportunities of the future, particularly in the international arena, will require such multidisciplinary collaboration.

The following initiatives, and the two that precede them, are closely linked in purpose and must be closely linked in execution. For example, quality research space and equipment must be available to effectively recruit and retain faculty and to develop multidisciplinary institutes and centers.

To meet these challenges, we will:

3. Continue the Strategic Investment approach by competitively funding initiatives that build programmatic strength and open new fields. Build on existing capabilities and capture opportunities specific to Ohio State and to Ohio. Maintain ongoing multidisciplinary initiatives where appropriate and develop new initiatives that draw on University-wide strengths to attack major problems of the next quarter century. Create multidisciplinary centers that can attract additional faculty in key areas, helping reduce student-faculty ratios in high-demand fields.

Implementation: Fund 3-5 initiatives each year that will capture a unique opportunity within a discipline, create an interdisciplinary program, or link a range of disciplines for a coherent attack on a highly complex area. Fund at least one program of each type in each year. Fund each initiative at a level that allows it to become one of the nation's leading programs. Cost: While support for personnel, facilities, and equipment can vary widely by research area, a typical threshold level for a multidisciplinary center is approximately $1-3M in continuing funds and up to $10M in one-time costs. Total: $9M/yr in continuing funds for five years for faculty and staff salaries and operating expenses and $30-50M in one-time funds for start-up support.

4. Significantly increase space dedicated to funded research beyond what is currently planned. Include a multidisciplinary building devoted to high-quality research space as well as to office and meeting space. Implementation: Allocate $250M by FY05 through prioritized capital budget requests to enhance research activity and pursue funding from multiple sources; maximize the use of Ohio Board of Regents' matching funds to enhance the research equipment base on campus; and increase support for maintenance. Cost: About $250M in one-time funds plus $3.8M/yr in increased operating costs. This level of investment will fully equip approximately 250,000 assigned square feet of new research space. [Note: Meeting the University's total need in this area may require comparable sums over the next 20 years.]

Strategy:

Enhance the Quality of the Teaching and Learning Environment.

Academic excellence is dependent upon many factors, including up-to-date infrastructure and leading-edge learning tools. One major driver for this infrastructure need is technology, which is transforming teaching and learning along with many other aspects of University life and operations. Another is the need to renovate, update, equip, and maintain classrooms and instructional laboratories and to maintain an attractive campus environment. While it will require a number of years and significant resources to bring all University facilities into the modern age, we need to jump-start the process and instill a sense of urgency in achieving that objective.

We should also recognize that the development of distance learning programs can help us benefit students from around the world while reducing the need for costly physical facilities. In addition, following a period of transitional investment, distance learning programs have great revenue-raising potential.

To begin this process, we will:

5. Transform the Library into a 21st century, Information-Age center within the next 5 to 10 years. Implementation: Combine fund-raising with support from state capital funding budgets over the next several biennia. Cost: $20-30M in one-time costs plus $2.5M in acquisitions over the next 5 years. (Cost assumes that the private, fund-raising portion of a $60-70M library renovation will be $20-$30M.).

6. Upgrade the quality of our classroom pool space and enhance the appearance of the campus facilities and grounds. Implementation: 1) Build 25 state-of-the-art classrooms (5/yr for 5 years) in addition to the 85 for which funding is in place while enhancing classroom cleanliness and providing modern equipment. 2) Add Project Cleaning Teams (each with 8 custodians and a supervisor) to augment today's custodial staff as well as high-intensity grounds maintenance to the seven most highly visible areas of the campus. Total Cost: $2.9M in continuing funding and $1.9M in one-time funding for updated classrooms.

7. Provide faculty, staff, and students with the latest technology tools for leadership in teaching, learning, research, and career development within the next 5 years. Implementation: Focus on distance and web-based education programs, comprehensive student support, on-campus Internet connectivity, infrastructure, remote connectivity, and a data strategy to improve coordination, quality, and accessibility of information and response times. Seek sponsored-research support to evaluate the effect of new technologies and teaching methods on student learning. Create web-based and distance learning programs that can reduce the incidence of closed courses in high-demand areas and provide improved state-of-the-art Information Technology capabilities to improve the quality of academic advising and other student support services.

Cost: $10M in one-time funds for technology-enhanced learning, $50M in one-time funds for Student Information System, $6M in continuing and $2.5M in one-time funds for shared technology infrastructure, and $1M in continuing and $5M in one-time funding for enterprise data strategy. Totals: $7M in continuing funds and $67.5M in one-time funding.

Strategy:

Enhance and Better Serve the Student Body

To be an academically excellent institution, we must recruit and retain to graduation an excellent and diverse undergraduate, graduate, and professional student body. More talented and better-prepared students require less remediation, face fewer academic difficulties, and graduate in higher numbers and in a shorter time-span. Better prepared students also help attract better faculty, grants, and awards and enhance the University's academic reputation.

Since the University began admitting fall quarter undergraduate students on a selective basis in 1987, and particularly recently, the quality of preparation of the incoming class has improved. We must now accelerate our efforts to recruit and retain to graduation an excellent and diverse student body. Today, only about half of our new undergraduate students (the fall freshmen) are admitted selectively. To continue this improvement, we must implement our enrollment plan and extend selective admission to all incoming students - freshmen entering in winter and spring as well as all transfer students.

In moving forward with the implementation of a selective admissions policy, it is important to preserve our land-grant role in serving the people of Ohio. In part, that role includes providing access for qualified students regardless of their economic need, an issue that is addressed in Initiative #10 below. Our land-grant mission also assures access to the University to any student who can attain the preparation and skills needed to succeed at Ohio State. The regional campuses will continue to provide open access to students and provide them with the opportunity to complete Ohio State University degrees - to a limited extent at the regional campuses and more generally at the Columbus Campus. We will also continue our efforts to improve articulation agreements with community colleges and to provide financial aid to qualified transfer students.

In addition, we need to better serve the better-prepared students who are entering Ohio State. Thus far, we have increased our emphasis on enhanced student life and improved student support services. It is now time to focus more on academic enhancements, including greater course accessibility, smaller classes, more undergraduate research opportunities, additional honors and scholars programs, and more and higher quality advising and career counseling. We also need to utilize instructional technology and changes in the budget process to more quickly and effectively respond to academic program choices in emerging areas, such as Information Technology and Management.

Finally, the Research Commission found that, "Even in some strong departments, OSU appears less able to attract graduate students from highly ranked programs than some leading peers." To attract the best, we must improve the fellowship packages we offer since our standard one-year fellowships are less attractive than those of many competing institutions. In focusing on recruiting higher ability, better-prepared graduate and professional students, we should target candidates from highly ranked undergraduate institutions. In the process, we must assure a growing proportion of diverse graduate and professional students.

With these goals in mind, we will:

8. Within the next three years, make admission to Ohio State selective throughout the year for new freshmen and for all transfer students. Implementation: Move in stages to selective admission for transfer students and those admitted in winter and spring quarters. More effectively utilize the regional campuses as alternate entry portals. Enhance relationships with community colleges for the recruitment of sophomores, juniors and seniors.

Cost: The net financial impact of these changes is difficult to predict. Over the short run (next 3-5 years), tuition and state instructional support are likely to decline along with the number of newly-admitted freshman and transfer students. Over the longer run (next 4-7 years), increases in student retention, increased state instructional support for upper-level courses and better enrollment planning could generate additional revenue. Recognizing this situation, the Enrollment Management Steering Committee developed a number of alternative scenarios to model the net impact of these changes. The estimate included in this plan - a five-year revenue loss of $2.5M in continuing funds and $10M in one-time funds - is in the middle range of these estimates. Actual results must be monitored and carefully managed as the plan is implemented to appropriately balance academic goals and financial implications.

9. Create a rich educational environment for undergraduates. Increase course accessibility, reduce class sizes, and establish at least 10 Scholars programs within five years - expanding opportunities for students to live with those who share common interests and enhancing students' academic success and sense of community. Provide academic programming, advising, and career counseling within these communities. Implementation: One program was created last year. Add 3 programs in 2000-2001; 5 programs

in 2001-2002; and 1 program in 2002-2003. It's projected that 5,300 students will be involved in scholar programs by 2005-2006. Cost: $5.3M in continuing costs.

10. Provide ample need-based and merit-based aid for undergraduates and a competitive financial aid and fellowship support package for graduate and professional students to improve Ohio State's graduate and professional matriculation rate. Implementation: Adjust need-based aid funds commensurate with increases to undergraduate tuition. Implement the relevant recommendations of the Research Commission Report and the G-QUE (Graduate Quality of University Experience) and I-QUE (Inter-professional Quality of University Experience) reports.

Cost: An additional $0-10M for undergraduate student financial aid, depending on the extent to which tuition increases exceed the cap. $5.34M in continuing costs, as follows: 125 additional first-year graduate fellowships @ $16,800 ($2.1M); 125 additional dissertation-year graduate fellowships @ $16,800 ($2.1M); 25 professional student fellowships @ $16,800 ($420K); and increased graduate fellowship stipend level from $1,200 to $1,400/month to match $16,800 annual level ($720,000).

Strategy:

Create a Diverse University Community

A growing body of research links diversity and academic excellence. We now know that students learn better in a diverse setting. In fact, college students who experience the most racial and ethnic diversity in the classrooms and in informal interactions on campus become better learners and better citizens. As a result, students who attend a truly diverse university are better prepared to live and work in a multi-cultural society and a global economy.

To create this rich learning environment, Ohio State must recruit and retain greater numbers of women and minorities into faculty, staff, and administrative positions - especially senior positions. Such senior faculty arrive with tenure and serve as role models and mentors for their junior counterparts. We must also recruit and retain to graduation greater numbers of ethnic minority students and create a culture of inclusiveness that respects and values differences. We must assure that all groups are represented in campus diversity policy and that the newly established Women's Place receives adequate support. In our efforts to support P-12 education, we must enhance the pool of minority students who can succeed at Ohio State. Finally, we must ensure that deans, department chairs, and other leaders are held accountable for their part in increasing campus diversity.

A series of specific goals and initiatives are included in the University's Diversity Action Plan. We strongly support them all. Consistent with this Academic Plan's focus on academic excellence, we have highlighted the following items. We will:

11. Hire at least 5-10 women and 5-10 minority faculty at a senior level each year for 5 years through the Faculty Hiring Assistance Program (FHAP) and other initiatives. Implementation: Modify the FHAP by focusing funding on two especially important needs. One is to help departments with small pools of women and minority candidates. The other is to help units that have been successful in increasing diversity to hire senior-level faculty.

Cost: $250-500K/yr for 5 years for a total of $1.25 - $2.5M in additional continuing costs.

12. Recruit, support, and retain to graduation larger numbers of academically able minority students. Implementation: Increase investment in relevant programs and more effectively coordinate efforts of academic departments and colleges with the Offices of Admissions, Financial Aid, Enrollment Management, and Minority Affairs. Improve the climate for diversity through seminars, courses, and programs along with the establishment of a multicultural center and support of the Women's Place.

Cost: $3M for additional new freshman recruitment and merit scholarships; $2.5M for recruitment and scholarships for able transfer students from community colleges; $1.5M for academic support programs; and $800K for improving the climate for diversity. Total: $7.8M in continuing funding over 5 years.

Strategy:

Help Build Ohio's Future

Since our founding in 1870 as a land-grant college, Ohio State has proudly and effectively served Ohio and its people - educating hundreds of thousands of Ohioans and applying our base of knowledge and skills to economic and societal needs. Our pro-active outreach and engagement initiatives integrate teaching, scholarship, and research. They also connect our research results to community needs and to the global marketplace - a dynamic aspect of academic excellence. And while few would contest Ohio State's past and present success, economic and social trends have changed contemporary community needs. In response, we must expand our land-grant mission.

Ohio State's current outreach agenda reaches across every facet of the University. Outreach programs number in the hundreds. For example, our agricultural extension programs offer economic development information and educational opportunities in every county of the state. Our continuing education programs, supplemented increasingly by distance learning, make lifelong learning a reality for all citizens. WOSU broadcasts radio and television coverage of public affairs and other matters of important public interest. Through the John Glenn Institute for Public Service and Public Policy, and through other targeted interdisciplinary policy initiatives, the University is studying policy issues and encouraging public service. Faculty, staff, and students help people in the campus neighborhood with health, educational, and legal problems.

In recent years, Ohio State has added to its traditional focus on areas such as agriculture by initiating campus-wide outreach efforts in technology-based economic development, community healthcare delivery and neighborhood revitalization (Campus Partners). We are now adding an additional area of campus-wide concentration, which is the improvement of primary and secondary education. This is an area where we can serve our community, state, and nation while strengthening the pipeline for potential university students.

In economic development, TechPartners provides the infrastructure and entrepreneurial environment to commercialize technology generated at the University for the benefit of Ohio and its people. Involving three University offices and four non-University organizations, this collaboration is helping to build a greater Ohio presence in the new Information Age economy. Among these partners are SciTech, the Science & Technology Campus Corporation, a research park connected to the University. Over the long term, Tech Partners' collaboration with business and government will increase research funding, attract and retain entrepreneurial faculty, involve students in experiential learning, increase inventions and licenses, attract venture capital funding, and help to build Ohio's economy.

To launch this education initiative, and accelerate TechPartners, we will:

13. Significantly strengthen the scope and effectiveness of our commitment to P-12 public education, with a special focus on the education of underserved children and youth. In so doing, we will work with the State of Ohio and selected local school districts. This initiative will be a University-wide partnership, with the College of Education in the lead college role. More specifically, we will:
* Strengthen initial teacher preparation and teacher professional development through collaborations between arts and sciences and education faculty.
* Build cross-college collaborative initiatives in math/science education, early literacy, and education leadership.
* Work with Columbus and other urban school districts to develop "best practice" P-12 learning strategies.
* Establish Ohio State as a vital source for education policy and school improvement in Ohio and the nation.

Total Cost: $500K/yr in University-based funding for campus-wide activity, which will leverage additional monies from foundations and business.

14. Become the catalyst for the development of Ohio's technology-based economy. Increase collaborations with the private sector to enhance research, successfully transfer University technology, and provide experiential learning and career opportunities for students. Implementation: Make SciTech a national leader in technology transfer and University-related enterprise development. Position TechPartners as a nationally recognized vehicle to increase the University's competitiveness; attract top faculty, students, and research funding; and create a tangible positive impact on Ohio's economy.
* Complete development of a seamless University-wide strategy that dovetails with internal and external partners and constituencies and that integrates separate marketing and communications activities.
* Execute plan strategies, e.g., educational outreach to University and technology communities and co-sponsorship of major events that reinforce technology initiatives.
* Aggressively support activities that can "leapfrog" Ohio State into a position of national prominence in technology partnerships, particularly broad-scale involvement with companies that enhances research and experiential learning opportunities for students.

Total Cost: $500K/yr in University-based funding for campus-wide activity, which will leverage additional monies from foundations and business.

Facilitating Actions

Facilitating Actions describe changes that are necessary if the University is to successfully implement the strategies and initiatives that are listed above. At this time, we have identified four such Facilitating Actions, each of which is described briefly in this section:

- Obtain increased state support.
- Improve the organization and delivery of instruction.
- Increase organizational flexibility.
- Improve the faculty work environment.

Obtain Increased State Support

As described earlier in this plan (Setting the Stage), Ohio devotes proportionately less in State funds to higher education than many other states. To become a great University, we will need additional funding as well as greater productivity and budget restructuring. This funding must come from a variety of sources, e.g., government, industry, private donors, tuition, and increasing entrepreneurial activity on our part. But it all begins with the level of State support and the flexibility to better control our own destiny.

Therefore, working individually and in concert with other Ohio colleges and universities, we will endeavor to:

- Achieve a State subsidy that is at least at historical levels;
- Enhance performance funding through the Research Challenge and Success Challenge;
- Obtain relief from the State tuition cap;
- Attract strategic investments in technology-related research and development (the Ohio Plan); and
- Obtain reimbursement for debt service in life sciences and biomedical research (tobacco fund and DOD initiative).

Improve the Organization and Delivery of Instruction

To improve students' academic experience, we must also reexamine our academic timetable, our undergraduate curriculum, course availability, and majors. Several structural changes are important in this regard. For example, of 88 Research I universities, only 15 use the quarter calendar. The trend is toward semesters, which give students more time for in-depth study, ease the transfer process, provide efficiencies, and save money. Faculty who have taught under both systems report many operational benefits under the semester system. While opinions vary on this issue - especially among students - many faculty and administrators believe that this change should be implemented.

In addition, the extensive and complex General Education Curriculum, which was appropriate for an open-admissions university where many students arrived with educational deficits, may no longer be appropriate for today's better-prepared students. A thoughtful redesign of the curriculum, the enrollment of more freshmen directly into academic colleges, and a First-Year Experience program that coordinates support for students in their early months at Ohio State will help students get the courses they need and want, make transfers from one major to another as seamless as possible, and help students graduate within four years. Such changes are best accomplished as part of the quarter-to-semester shift. Thus, we will:

- Subject to appropriate consultation, shift from quarters to semesters within four years and work with the faculty to undertake a concurrent simplification and streamlining of the General Education Curriculum (GEC) process.

Implementation: Undertake a thorough review of the academic calendar and the undergraduate curriculum: majors, the GEC, and the individual courses that make up both.

Increase Organizational Flexibility

The forces of change described in Setting the Stage require today's institutions to be more flexible and capable of responding more quickly to internal and external events. In the case of Ohio State, implementation of this Academic Plan would be significantly enhanced by greater flexibility in four important areas:

- Continue to rationalize college and departmental organization on an ongoing basis to assure an optimal organizational structure to serve our students and operate as effectively and efficiently as possible.
- Move toward compensation systems offering greater variability according to the individual competitive needs of a department or college.
- Allocate faculty positions in line with current needs, e.g., allowing units to utilize clinical faculty.
- Restructure the budget process to more clearly align resources with academic goals.

Implementation: The President and Provost will work with the University's governance structure over the next 1-2 years to seek greater flexibility in all four areas. The Faculty Senate is already considering the rationalization issue.

Improve the Faculty Work Environment

To be as productive as possible in their research, and perform at an outstanding level in the classroom, faculty need a supportive environment and a minimum of impediments. To improve the faculty work environment, we will:

- Encourage individualized faculty work loads.
- Recognize work load efforts of faculty who supervise large numbers of doctoral students (already done in some departments).
- Enhance professional leave opportunities by encouraging faculty participation in the leave system and rewarding faculty who use this time productively.
- Encourage faculty entrepreneurship through opportunities for seed grants and other small grants to faculty, particularly in areas where external funding sources are limited.

Continuing Activities

This plan does not include every activity that will take place at Ohio State over the next five years - opting instead for a more focused and manageable list of initiatives. As already noted, the initiatives and facilitating actions herein are only a few of many important activities that are ongoing at the University, some of which carry substantial price tags to which we are already committed. However, the initiatives noted in this document, in the aggregate, should also play a major role in moving the University toward its vision.

Over recent years, a handful of excellent planning documents have made scores of useful recommendations on ways to improve the University. For example, The G-QUE (Graduate Quality of University Experience) and I-QUE (Inter-professional Quality of University Experience) reports contain many excellent recommendations on improving life for graduate and professional students. We expect many of these recommendations to be implemented. The same holds true for the Research Commission Report, recommendations from which are being implemented over a period of years.

Recently, the University issued an excellent Diversity Action Plan with many compelling recommendations. We are committed to implementing these recommendations, including the creation of a Council on Diversity, more support for The Women's Place, and accountability measures such as Diversity Council Report Cards and administrative evaluations.

We face many challenges in seeking to become a truly great public teaching and research university. Among them is a more meaningful system of faculty and staff development, along with improved professional development to benefit our students, including more and better training for graduate teaching associates. We also need a more systematic, campus-wide approach to planning that improves constancy of purpose and alignment of goals while improving follow-through. There are many good ideas for new multidisciplinary programs, including a proposed Institute for the Study of Race and Ethnicity in the Americas. While it is not specifically highlighted in the Plan, we are working hard to better prepare students, faculty, and the community for the global community of the 21st century. And just as market-competitive compensation is necessary to recruit and retain an excellent faculty, so is it essential to recruit and maintain a top-quality staff.

Many exciting initiatives are under way to help us contribute to Ohio's future. Three such outreach efforts coincide with the Ohio Board of Regents' current statewide priorities: Economic development, healthcare delivery, and improvement of primary and secondary education. A fourth area of ongoing emphasis is Campus Partners. Education and economic development were discussed earlier in the report. Regarding the others:

- **Healthcare Delivery.** We are committed to becoming one of the nation's leading academic medical centers by combining research excellence in cancer, cardiology, and other fields with state-of-the-art healthcare delivery. The Ohio State Academic Medical Center's mission of teaching, research, and patient care increasingly extends beyond campus laboratories, clinics, and hospitals to the people of Ohio and sometimes the world. Initiatives range from a $60-70 million Heart Hospital scheduled to open in 2003 (complementing our new Heart & Lung Research Institute) to the Collaborative Task Force for Healthy Communities - 16 University specialists in areas such as public health, oncology, cardiology, pulmonary disease, and psychology. Task Force members will work closely with the Columbus Department of Health and the Ohio Department of Health to establish principles and practices that will bring about a healthier city and state population.

- **Campus Partners.** A partnership of The Ohio State University, the City of Columbus, and the neighborhoods of the University District, Campus Partners is a nonprofit community development corporation committed to revitalizing those neighborhoods. In so doing, it creates an improved environment for students and faculty, provides opportunities for experiential learning, protects the University's investment, and improves a section of Columbus that has declined in appearance and safety. One objective is to facilitate greater cooperation and coordination to improve neighborhood public services, e.g., crime reduction, more effective trash collection, better code enforcement, etc. Another is to increase the level of home ownership in the University District. And still another is to complete the University Gateway Center, a $100 million, mixed-use urban redevelopment project.

Resources

Preliminary Cost Estimates

Listed below are preliminary cost estimates for the highest priority components of the Academic Plan. These numbers represent an early estimate of the magnitude of funds required over a five-year period commencing in FY2002. These preliminary estimates are intended to inform a discussion regarding priorities and funding sources. They are not intended as a commitment, guarantee, or entitlement. Further refinement is necessary as part of the iterative nature of a good academic planning process.

Preliminary Cost Estimates for the Academic Plan (in millions)

Initiative	Continuing Funds	One-time Funds
1. Eminent senior faculty	$3.6	$15.0
2. Fac/staff recruitment, retention	13.5	0
3. Strategic invest/multidisc prog*	45.0	30-50
4. Research space	3.8	250.0
5. Library	2.5	20-30
6. Classrooms	2.9	1.9
7. Technology	7.0	67.5
8. Selective admissions	2.5	10.0
9. Undergrad learning experience	5.3	2.5
10. Student financial support	5.3-15.3	0
11. Women/Minority faculty hires*	3.8-7.5	0
12. Minority student rec/ret/grad	7.8	0
13. P-12 education	0.5	0
14. Technology partnerships	0.5	0
Total	$104.0-117.7	$396.9-426.9

* Strategic investment projects generally require a 1:1 match by colleges and departments from reallocated funds. The FHAP program generally requires a 2:1 match by colleges and departments from reallocated funds. These and other matches are reflected in the totals.

Note to Preliminary Cost Estimates. These expenditures are based upon a projection of available funding over the first five years. The initiatives can be scaled up or down depending upon actual funding.

Possible Available Resources for Support of the Academic Plan

This section describes additional resources that could be available to support the priorities of the Academic Plan. This is not a prediction, but rather a series of scenarios designed to show the effects of various assumptions. This estimate deals with gross numbers only and does not address timing constraints or restrictions on how funds might be used. All figures are based on a five-year time span commencing in FY2002.

The fundamental assumption underlying these numbers is that the University will be able to secure additional resources beyond inflation to invest in academic priorities. These resources are expected to be generated through a series of initiatives that are presented in a range of possible scenarios. Actual figures could be higher or lower. It is important to remember that receipt of almost all of these funds, with the exception of private gifts, is dependent on legislation of one kind or another. How much the University will actually receive in FY2002 and FY2003 will not be known with any degree of certainty until passage of the next biennial budget in June of 2001.

Baseline Growth. This assumes that current trends continue (revenue growth of about 5 percent with annual compensation increases of 4 percent). Figures below are an estimate of uncommitted funds available after continuing operations are funded.

Continuing $50-75 million
One Time $50-75 million

Tobacco Funds. These funds have already been appropriated. This assumes that Ohio State will receive $35-45 million (25-30 percent) of the statewide share of $150 million to be distributed over the next five years for biomedical research and technology.

Outside the Box. This scenario concludes that a combination of initiatives including a shift of Development funding from the General Fund to endowment earnings, Research Challenge, and other initiatives will produce $65-85 million in one-time funds.

Reallocation. This scenario assumes a centrally driven reallocation of $25.5-$30.5 million over the next five years. Reallocation funds include the matches for Strategic Investment ($20 million) and Women/Minority faculty hires ($2.5-5 million) as well as administrative cost reductions of $3-5 million.

Tuition Cap Relief. This scenario is predicated on an adjustment to the tuition cap at the Columbus Campus. Funds created by this adjustment would become one part of the resource base necessary to build academic excellence in undergraduate programs. The adjustment proposed would be the equivalent of three to four percentage points above the cap for each of the next four or five years. Such an adjustment would require legislative approval, and if fully implemented, could produce approximately $32 million in additional funds annually. Of this $32 million, $10 million would be earmarked for additional funding for student financial aid to offset the impact of tuition increases on those students who are least able to pay. The remaining annual income of $22 million would be targeted to the portion of the Academic Plan directly related to the improvement of undergraduate education. If legislative approval is not granted, net additional revenues would be zero. Thus, the projected net income from this initiative for the Academic Plan is estimated to range from 0 to $22 million. Under the new budget system, a substantial portion of the above-cap tuition revenue will be shared with generating colleges, and the Office of Academic Affairs will assure that these revenues are used in a manner consistent with the goals of the Academic Plan.

Ohio Plan. The Ohio Plan is a joint initiative of Ohio's colleges and universities and the Ohio Board of Regents that is still in the development stage. It is designed to be a breakthrough initiative for a partnership between higher education and the State of Ohio. This scenario assumes that Ohio State will receive between $150 million and $250 million over five years as its share of the proposal.

Private Gifts. This assumes private giving that provides $4-5 million in continuing funds and $300 million in one-time funds over five years that can be directly applied to initiatives in the Academic Plan.

Distance Learning. The University lags its benchmark institutions in the creation and dissemination of distance-learning programs. Fortunately, the substantial resources that will be required to seed distance learning programs over the next several years have the potential for significant net earnings in the longer term. Cost and revenue profiles for this initiative will be developed within a new strategic Information Technology plan to be prepared by the incoming Chief Information Officer.

Enterprise Development. The University is investing in a number of private sector partnerships which over a period of years are expected to generate revenue from royalties, patents, license fees, sponsored research, and other activities. As with distance learning, a revenue estimate for these activities is not possible at this time.

Known Commitments. Funds available are adjusted downward by $25 million in continuing funds and $200 million in one-time funds for known and emerging commitments that do not currently have an identified funding source.

Possible Available Resources For Support of the Academic Plan (in millions)

Initiative*	Continuing Funds	One-time Funds
Baseline	$50-75	$50-75
Tobacco funds	0	35-45
Outside the Box	0	65-85
Reallocation	25.5-30.5	0
Tuition Cap Relief	0-32	0
Ohio Plan**	0	150-250
Private Gifts	4-5	300
Known Commitments	(25)	(200)
Total	$54.5-117.5	$400-555

* As already noted, Distance Learning and Enterprise Development are also expected to generate a currently unidentified amount of revenue.

** This estimate is based upon the current proposal. If that changes, the estimate will be scaled back accordingly.

SUMMARY

These preliminary scenarios produce between $54.5 million and $117.5 million in continuing funds and between $400 million and $555 million in one-time funds to support academic plan initiatives beyond maintenance of existing programs. However, these scenarios are not the equivalent of spendable resources. Additional refinement and, in many cases, enabling legislation, are necessary before resources of this magnitude are considered available.

Implementation Process

The above charts demonstrate that there could be a gap between our aspirations and available resources, particularly in continuing funds. We will know much more once next year's State budget is adopted. Should such a gap exist, alternatives include finding other funding sources and/or scaling back or stretching out the implementation of various initiatives.

At the end of each academic year, we will review our accomplishments and compare them with the benchmarks outlined in the next section of this plan. We will also reassess the continuing and one-time expenditures necessary to implement the Plan along with currently available resources. Based on this reassessment, we will set priorities and establish our agenda for the year ahead. This process will take place during the summer in Year One of the State budget biennium and in the spring during Year Two.

The Academic Scorecard

Most data presented in the Academic Scorecard come from data previously collected for OSU Strategic Indicators in academic year 1999-2000. Where available, benchmark information is provided. In academic year 1997-98, The Ohio State University selected the following universities as its primary set of benchmark institutions: University of Arizona, University of California-Los Angeles, University of Illinois at Champaign-Urbana, University of Michigan, University of Minnesota, Pennsylvania State University, University of Texas at Austin, University of Washington, and University of Wisconsin-Madison. This set of benchmark universities is the basis for comparison data reported on the Academic Scorecard. Where institutional benchmark information is unavailable, national averages are reported if available.

The measures on the Academic Scorecard do not represent all specific actions and goals associated with the Academic Plan. As measures are refined, the Academic Scorecard may change and evolve to more closely reflect the specific actions, goals, and resource allocations implemented by The Ohio State University.

Information regarding the sources of data or the calculation of most measures in the Academic Scorecard can be found in the comprehensive appendix to the Strategic Indicators 2000. The Strategic Indicators 2000 document is available for review at:

www.rpia.ohio-state.edu/strategic_analysis/strategic_indicators.htm.

Strategy	Strategic Indicator	Ohio State	Benchmark Universities	OSU Change from previous reported year
Build a World Class Faculty			Benchmark Average	
	1. Academic Honors and Awards (1992-99)	32	39	17
	2. Market Share of Publications (1996-98)	0.41	0.5	-0.01
	3. Market Share of Citations (1996-98)	0.52	0.81	0.08
	4. Market Share of Federal Research Dollars (1998)	0.82	1.48	-0.03
	5. Average Faculty Compensation (FY2000)	$70,350	$72,330	$3,460
Define Ohio State as Leading Public Land Grant			Benchmark Average	
	1. US News Academic Reputation Score (1999)	3.8	4.08	0.1
	2. US News Academic PhD programs among the Top 25 (1999)	4	8.4	NC
	3. US News Professional programs among the Top 25 (1999)	7	7.3	NC
	4. NRC Academic PhD programs among the top 25% (1992)	9	20	NI
Enhance the Quality of the Teaching & Learning Environment			National Average	
	1. % of Faculty Satisfied Overall (1999*)	71.1	73.2	NI
	2. % of Students Satisfied with Instruction and Courses (1998**)	58	65	NI
	3. % of Students Satisfied with Campus Facilities (1998**)	62	75	NI
Enhance and Better Serve the Student Body			Benchmark Average	
	1. % of Freshmen in the Top 10% of H.S. Class (1999)	29	50	3
	2. Freshmen Retention Rate (1999)	81	89	2
	3. Six-year Graduation Rate (1999)	56	70	NC
	4. Average GMAT score for MBA students (1999)	638	644	NI
	5. Average LSAT range for Law students (1999)	153-160	157-163	NI
			National Average	
	6. Average GRE verbal score for graduate students (1998)	545	505	-1
	7. Average GRE quantitative score for graduate students (1998)	655	621	7
	8. Average GRE analytic score for graduate students (1998)	637	586	1
	9. % of Students Satisfied with Student Support Services (1998**)	47	51	NI
Create a Diverse University Community			Benchmark Average	
	1. % of Women Faculty (1997)	29.9	28.6	NC
	2. % of African American, Hispanic, and Native American Faculty (1997)	5.38	5.62	0.38
	3. % of Minority Staff (1997)	23.2	24.5	-0.7
	4. % of African-American & Hispanic Students (1998)	10	11.6	1
	5. African-American Freshmen Retention Rate (1998)	74	88	4
	6. Hispanic Freshmen Retention Rate (1998)	74	87	2
	7. African American 6-Year Graduation Rate (1998)	37	51	-4
	8. Hispanic 6-Year Graduation Rate (1998)	49	58	11
Help Build Ohio's Future			Benchmark Average	
	1. Number of Invention Disclosures (1998)	75	155	4
	2. Number of Patent Applications (1998)	42	110	20
	2. Number of Patents Awarded (1998)	24	38	-3
	3. Number of License/Options Executed (1998)	26	44	2
	4. Number of Start Up Companies (1998)	0	4	NC
	5. Revenue from Income Generating Licenses (1998)	$1,758,533	$6,803,893	($474,138)
	6. Sponsored Research Dollars for Education (1999)	$13.1mil	$10.5 mil	NI
	7. Impact of P-12 Initiatives	TBD		

Index

20/10 Plan, 5, 23, 37, 53

Academic Affairs, Office of, 22, 26, 28, 100, 113, 114, 131, 252
Academic Computing Services, 86
Academic Enrichment initiative, 3, 46, 53, 56, 145
Academic Plan, 5–6, 35–138, 141, 144–45, 147, 153, 161, 171, 180, 212–14, 219, 233–54
Academic Technology Services, 86
Administrative Resource Management Systems (ARMS), 87, 174–75
admissions: open, 98, 104, 248; selective (or competitive), 3, 6, 90, 91, 98, 104, 145, 234, 245, 251
"Affirm Thy Friendship" campaign, 3, 20, 65, 155–62, 168
affirmative action, 111
Afrikan Student Union, 116, 117
al-Akhras, Ahmad, 186
Allen, David, 123, 127–28
Allen, Jan, 60, 163, 170
Alley, Keith, 31, 57, 59
Alumni Association, 164, 166–68
Alumni Distinguished Teaching Awards, 56
Alutto, Joe, 40, *64*, 129, 171, 212
American Center for Physics, 19
Anderson, Carole, 28, 103, 113, 114, *117*, 121
Andrews, David, 131
Apothekar, Howard, 186
Arthur G. James Cancer Hospital and Research Institute, 70, 71, 74, 76, 77
Arts and Sciences, College of the, 49, 56–57, 96, 116, 131, 237, 247
Asher, Herb, *30*, 65, 135, 163
Ashley, David, 113, 124
Association of American Universities, 166
athletes, scholar, 202–4
Austin E. Knowlton School of Architecture, 84–*86*, 224
Ayers, Randy, 188

Baeslack, William ("Bud"), III, 57
Baisden, Vernon, 183–84
Ballengee-Morris, Christine, 116
Baroway, Malcolm, 10, 169
Basinger, Mary, 23, 29, *30*
basketball, 6, 188, 199. *See also* Foster, Jim; Jerome Schottenstein Center; O'Brien, Jim; Taylor, Fred
Battelle Memorial Institute, 59–60, 128
Beck, Paul, *25*, 54
Bell, Karen, 46
Bellotti, Mike, 193
Berdahl, Bob, 10
Berry, John, Jr., 161, 230
Besanceny, Bryan, 107
Best Damn Band in the Land, 48, *49*, 198
Bhaerman, Dave, 36
Biancamano, John, 50
Bioinformatics Initiative, 61
Biomedical Micro ElectroMechanical Systems (BioMEMS), 125
Biomedical Research Initiative, 53, 59, 67–69, 147
Biomedical Research Tower, 47, 53, 67–69, 76, 138, 224
Black Cultural Center, 115, 116
Blackwell, Marilyn, 50, 52
Blackwell Inn, 99, 218, 224
Bloomfield, Clara, *74*, 223
Board of Trustees: and Academic Plan, 5, 35, 38, 41, 180; and admissions, 98, 102–3; and Biomedical Research Tower, 69; and budget, 148, 149–50; and Campus Partners, 134–36; and commencement, 107; and Cooper, 192; district plans of, 5; and fund-raising, 155–56, 160, 167; and Glenn, 66; and Institute on the Study of Race and Ethnicity in the Americas, 55; and International Affairs, 134; Kirwan and, 23, 45, 150, 151, 165, 210–12, 219; and medical center, 70–71; members of, 35, *42*, *164*, 168, 222; and MicroMD Laboratory, 125; and Office of Minority Affairs, 116; and Ohio Plan, 144; and

Outreach and Engagement, 133; personnel changes, 27; and presidential search, 6, 9–15, 21, 213–16; and public education, 131; and regional campuses, 104–5; and riots, 181–82; and salary increases, 46; and scholar athletes, 202; and sexual orientation, 120–21; and Strategic Investment Fund, 47, 146; and technology, 87, 129; and tuition, 152; and university's future, 3–5
Borror, Douglas G., 222
Boysen, Sally, 15
Brand, Myles, 10
Branin, Joseph, 81–82
Brannon, Tom, 104
Brennan, David, 10, 47, 150–52, *158*, 207, 208, 211–13, 219, 222, 225
Brillson, Len, 46
Brown University, 10, 99, 188
Bruce, Earle, 193, 195
Burns, Beth, 199
Bursten, Bruce E., 221, 231
Burtt, Harold E., 213
Bush, George H. W., *64*, 70
Bush, George W., 107–9, 111, 184, 225, 227
Business and Industry Contracts, Office of, 127
Business Technology Center, 126

Campus Partners, 99, 122, 131, 134–38, 183, 247, 250
"Carmen Ohio," 23, 155, 167, *198*
Carney, John, 221
Cassidy, Howard ("Hopalong"), 201
Celeste, Richard, 163, 176
Celeste, Ted, 11, 23, *24*, *42*, 123, 152, 166–67, 175, 178, 221, 222
Center of Science and Industry (COSI), 129
Center for Teaching Excellence, 86
Chamallas, Martha, 47–48
Chemical Abstracts, 88
Chism, Grady, 52
Chronicle of Higher Education, 81, 203
Chu, Rod, 142–43, 184
Citino, David, 186, 225
Cleveland-Bull, Kathy, 92
Coca-Cola, 101
Code of Student Conduct, 182
Coleman, Michael, 116, *117*, 125, 136–38, 182, *185*
Colley, Michael, 9, *42*, 222
Collins, Jim, 38–39
Columbus City Council, 135–36, 177
Columbus Higher Education Partnership, 131
Columbus Partnership, 129
Columbus Public Schools, 131
Columbus Technology Leadership Council, 128
commencements, 106–10; speakers, 225
Committee on the Undergraduate Experience (CUE), 5, 90, 92, 95, 102, 103
Communications Workers of America (CWA), 176–80
Community Connection, 131
compensation, competitive, 45–46, 103, 239
Compston, Michelle, *30*
Conlisk, Elizabeth, 163
Cooper, Dara, 113
Cooper, John, 191–93
Cormier, J. Briggs, *117*
Cosby, Bill, 107, *108*, 225, 227
Critical Difference for Women, 14, 119
Cuellar, Clara, 221

Davidson, Jo Ann, 151, *164*–65, 222, 225, 227
Davis, Dorothy M., 77. *See also* Dorothy M. Davis Heart and Lung Research Institute
Davis, Jim, 27, 87
Davis, William H., 77
Denman, Marte, *61*
Denman, Rick, *61*, 230
Denman Undergraduate Research Forum, 61, 96
DeRolph v. State of Ohio, 6, 143–44
Development, Office of, 47, 159, 160–61
DeWine, Mike, 163
distance education, 87, 244, 247, 252
Distinguished Scholar Awards, 56
Distinguished University Professors, 48, 49, 56, 223
diversity: in Academic Plan, 234, 238–40, 246, 250; accomplishments in, 115–121; commitment to, 18, 20, 23, 55, 100, 112; improving, 103, 114; Kirwan and, 111–12, 120–21, 157; lecture series on, 116; scholarship on, 54; Williams and, 99. *See also* affirmative action; Diversity Action Plan; Institute for the Study of Race and Ethnicity in the Americas; Minority Affairs, Office of; Multicultural Center; sexual orientation
Diversity Action Plan, 6, 99, 112–15, 118, 242, 246, 250
"Do Something Great," 171
domestic partner benefits, 120
Dorothy M. Davis Heart and Lung Research Institute, 48, 76, *77*, 224
Dottavio, Dominic, 106
Douce, Louise A., 97, 186
Drake, Jeanette, 208
Drug Delivery Initiative, 61
Duke University, 61, 69, 71, 72
Duncan, Robert, *42*, 104, 121, 164, 213, 222, 231

Eminent Scholar positions, 47
Englert, Brad, 175
Environment Initiative, 59
Ervin, James, 176
Eschenbacher, Deborah, 15
Evans, Donna Browder, 131

Faculty Council, 29, 37, 46, 50
Faculty Hiring Assistance Program (FHAP), 115, 234, 246, 251
Faculty Recognition Day, 48
Farrell, Dan, 31, 94
Farrell, Lynda, *30*
Fawcett Center for Tomorrow, 15, 99, 167, 173
Federlein, Anne Cairns, 106
Ferguson, David, 113
Ferrar, Joseph, 56
Ferrari, Mauro, 46, 60, 124, 125, *162*
Filiatraut, Kevin R., 222
First Year Experience Program, 95–96, 248
Fisher, Max M., *64*
Fisher, Susan, 40, 50, *51*, 52, 113, 213, 218, 231
Fisher College of Business, 49, 63–64, 84, 85, 116, 190, 214, 223, 224
Florida State University, 190
Foegler, Terry, 134
football, 161, 184, 185, 188–99, 201, 202, 204. See also Cooper, John; Tressel, Jim
Foster, Jim, 199
Foundation Board, 230
Fountain, Judy, 119
Fraley, Reed, 71, 76, 179
Frantz, David, 161, 190, 202–3, *218*, 221, 231
Fraser, Jane M., 221
Freeman, Mabel, 90, 92, *95*, 96
Friedman, Avner, 61, 223
Funk,William, 10, 11
Future of the City, 123

Garland, Martha, 26, *91*, 92, 93, 96, 97, 98, 121, 203
Gateway Project, 129, 134–37, 183, 213, 250
Gee, E. Gordon: as OSU president, 3, *4*, 5, 6, 10, 15, 21, 28, 31, 64, 66, 69, 84, 86, 90, 106, 119, 120, 122, 155, 160, 161, 168, 169, 174, 183, 200, 207, 214, 223; personality of, 20, 21, 30, 31, 161; at Vanderbilt, 99
Geier, Peter, 75
Geiger, Andy: and athletic facilities, 189; and coaches' contracts, 199; and Collins, 39; and Cooper firing, 191–92; and Kirwan, 15–16, 29, 188–89, 190, 195, 199, 202, 204; at Maryland, 188–89; and O'Brien firing, 204; and scholar athletes, 202–4; and September 11, 184; and Tressel hiring, 193–*96*, 197; and Younkin Success Center, 97
General Assembly (Ohio): and arena project, 135; and CWA strike, 176; and funding for research, 60; and higher education, 12, 143; and homosexuality, 120; Kirwan and, 20, 162–65; and regional campuses, 104; and tuition, 146, 150–52
General Education Curriculum (GEC), 52, 248
George, Eddie, 201, 202
Georgia Institute of Technology, 61
Gill, Deborah, 113
Glendening, Parris N. (Gov.), 15, 207–8
Glenn, Annie, *41*
Glenn, John, *65*–66
Gobe, Marc, 170
Goldschmidt, Pascal, 71–73
Graduate Quality of University Experience (G-QUE), 5, 102–3, 246, 250
Gray, Jon, 125
Greek system, 101
Greenwood, Jan, 214
Gregory H. Williams Dean's Fund for Excellence, 63
Griffin, Archie, 195, 201
Groves, Ray, 156–*57*, *158*, 160, 230
Gruden, Jon, 194
gymnastics, 199, *203*, 204

Habash, Matt, 182
Habib, Paula A., 222
Hagerty Hall, 83, 225
Hale, Frank, 115–16
Hale Center, 115, 116
Hall, Bill, 97, 99–102, 107, 181–83
Hall, Kermit, 54, 90, 221
Hamilton, Ann, 47
Hammel, Chris, 48
Harbrecht, Sandra, 39, 188
Harris, Walt, 194
Harvard University, 66, 70, 129, 135, 186
Hayes, Ed, 5, 57, 123
Hayes, Woody, 193, 195
Healy, Bernadine, 5, 11, 70, *74*, 221
Heinlen, Dan, 167–69, 221, 231
Hendricks, Karen, 19, 104, 212, 213, 222, 231
Hermanoff, Michael, *162*
High Street, 135, 137, 183
Hill, Jesse David, 186
Ho, Winston, 46, 223
Hogan, Michael, 54, 98, 219
Holbrook, Karen A., 6, 28, 198, 204, 214–16, *217*
Hollingsworth, Richard, 107–8
homeland security, 59
homosexuality. *See* sexual orientation
honorary doctoral degrees, 225–27

Honors Program, 3, 18, 47, 57, 90, 92–94, 95, 245
Hoover, David, 170
Horvath, Les, 201
Human Learning Initiative, 59
Human Resources Management System (HRMS), 175
Humphries, Barry, 134
Huntington, Susan, 102

India, 166–67
Information Technology, Office of, 87
Information Technology Initiative, 59, 244, 245, 252
Institute for the Study of Race and Ethnicity in the Americas, 53, 54–56, 59, 147, 250
intellectual property, 60, 127
International Affairs, Office of, 134
Inter-Professional Council Quality of the University Experience (I-QUE), 5, 102–3, 246, 250
Inter-University Council, 129, 150, 152, 162, 184

Jack Nicklaus Museum, 189
Janowicz, Vic, 201
Japan, 167
Jennings, Edward H.: on Committee on the Status of the Colleges of the Arts and Sciences, 56; as interim president, 56, 98, 214, *215;* as OSU president, 3, 6, 43, 90, 115, 155, 163, 207; on presidential search, 10
Jerome Schottenstein Center, 6, 81, 99, 107, 188, 189, 197, 200, 223
Jesse Owens Hall of Fame, 201
Jesse Owens Memorial Stadium, 189, 200, 224
John C. and Susan L. Huntington Archive on Buddhist and Related Art, 102
John Glenn Institute for Public Service and Public Policy, 53, 65–66, 83, 163, 166, 247
John W. Wolfe Cancer Genetics Research Laboratories, 77
Johns Hopkins University, 61, 69, 70, 72, 73
Josephson, Gary, 176–77, 179

K–12 education, 60, 136, 143, 146. *See also* P–12 education
Kellogg, Clark, 202, 225
Kellogg Commission, 11, 32, 166
Kessler, Jack, 129, 230
King, John, *58*
Kirwan, Ann Elizabeth, 12, *13, 18,* 111, 212
Kirwan, Patty, 11–15, 17–18, *22,* 101, 119, 162, 165, 189, 208, 211, 212, 219
Kirwan, William E. ("Brit"), *vi, 4, 27, 30, 154, 157, 162;* and Academic Plan, 5, 35, 38–43, 46–47, 51; and alumni, 166–69; and ARMS, 175; and athletics, 189–91, 194–97, 199, 202–4; and Board of Trustees, 42, 150–51; and Campus Partners, 134–37; and commencement, 106–110; and compensation, 45–46; and CWA strike, 176, 179–80; and development, *62*–63, 156, *158*–59, 161, 213; and diversity, 54–56, 111–13, 115–16, 120–21, 157; and faculty, 30, *48,* 57–59; and family, 12–*14,* 208, *210,* 212; and Geiger, 15–16, 29, 188–89, 190, 195, 199, 202, 204; and Glenn Institute, 65–66, 83; and Greek life, 101; and Knowlton, 84–85; and Gov. Taft, *149;* hiring of, 15–*16,* 19–20, 21–*22,* 23, *24;* interviewing for OSU presidency, 9–12, 15; leaving OSU, 6, 58, 207–14, 216–19; and library renovation, 79–82; and marketing the university, 169–71; and medical programs, 67–76; and Outreach and Engagement, 132–34; and P–12 education, 130–31, 132; personality of, 21; and regional campuses, 106; and reorganization, 26; and research, 57–*61;* and riots, 181–83; and Scholars Program, 92–94; and September 11, 184–86; and sexual orientation, 120–21; State of the University address of, 40, 51; and state support, 141, 142, 144–45, 150–52, 162–65; and students, 92–97, 102; and technology, 123–29; and tuition, 64, 148–49; at University of Kentucky, 17, 101; at University of Maryland, 10, 15, 18–21, 101, 198; and university senate, *51*–52; and Wexner, 129; and women's issues, 119; working style of, 28–31
Kirwan, William E., III, 12, *14*
Kleberg, John, 183
Knight Commission report, 204
Knowledge Bank, 59, 88
Knowles, Sebastian, 79
Knowles, Tim, 117–18
Knowlton, Austin E. ("Dutch"), 62, 84–85, 213
Kohrt, Carl, 60
Korea, 167, 187
Koroscik, Judith, 40, *41,* 116, 170, 172, 219

Kozobarich, Jeri, 180, 221
Kremer, Steve, 92

Laaksonen, Emma, 199
Ladman, Jerry, 134
Larkins Hall, 102
Lashutka, Greg, 6, 23, *24,* 123, 128, 135, 225, 226
Learning Connection, The, 131
Lee, Valerie, *117*
Lewellen, Larry, 45, 176, 177, 179, 180
Lewis, Marvin, 194
Lima campus, 104, 106, 224
Livesey, Rob, 84–85
living-learning programs, 92, 94, 96, 99, 101
Longaberger, Dave, 168, 226
Longaberger, Rachel, *168*
Longaberger, Richard, *168*
Longaberger, Tami, 11, *42, 168,* 199, 221, 222
Longaberger Alumni House, 168–69, 224
Longaberger Foundation, 168
Lowe, Allyson, *42,* 222

Mager, Jim, *95,* 96, 98
Mandel, Josh, 23, 102
Mansfield campus, 104, 106
Marino, Mario, 128
Marion campus, 104, 106
Mason, Glen, 193
Massachusetts Institute of Technology (MIT), 61, 123
Mathematical Biosciences Institute, 61, 213
Mathematical and Physical Sciences, College of, 56, 61, 130, 132
Mathews-Mead, Jamie, 180
May, Jerry, *62, 157;* and "Affirm Thy Friendship," 20, 155–56, 168; on development staff, 160; and fund-raising, 159–61; and fund-raising for medical facilities, 76; Kirwan on, 159; and Knowlton gift, 85; on library renovation, 82; on Moritz, 62; on presidential search committee, 9, 11, 221, 231
McCollum, Jim, 165
McCue, Jerry, 129, 135
McFerson, Dimon, 35, 42, 70, 87, 165, 171, 211, 213, 216, 222, 231
Medical Center: Academic, 69–76, 216, 250; University, 68–69, 75–78, 119, 176, 177, 179, 199, 216
Medicine and Public Health, College of, 50, 61, 69–71, 76, 125
Meek, Violet, 106
Mercadante, Linda, 186
Merritt, Deborah Jones, 65
Metros, Susan, 88
Meyer, John, 160, 161, 213
Michael E. Moritz Scholars Program, 63
MicroMD Laboratory, 47, *125–26*
Milenthal, David, 169, 170
Miller, Jim, 64
Miller, Terry, 57, 58
Mills, Margaret, 186
Miner, Jack D., 221
Minnis, Alastair, 47
minorities. *See* diversity
Minority Affairs, Office of, 99, 115, 116–19, 246
Mirror Lake, 83
Moore, Brad, 40, 57–60, 68, 69, 123, 126, 127, 223
Morelli, Jill, 85, 190
Moriarty, Erin, *157*
Moritz, Lou Ann, 63, 230
Moritz, Michael E., *62,* 63, 230
Moritz College of Law, 49, 63
Moser, Bobby, 38, 87–88, 104–5, 132–33, *154,* 167
Mosley-Thompson, Ellen, 161
Motz, Joe, 200
Mount Leadership Society, 94
Moyer, Thomas, *168*
Multicultural Center, 99, 100, 101, 116, 246
Murray, Richard, 179
Murray-Goedde, Amy, 108

nanotechnology, 59, 68, 126
Napier, Bill, 11, 26, *42,* 163, 221
Natalie, Jamie, 199
National Academy members, 222–23
National Association of State Universities and Land-Grant Colleges, 19, 166
National Chung Hsing University, 167
National Science Foundation, 61–62
National Taiwan University, 167
NCAA, 10, 181, 190, 199, 203, 204
Newark campus, 104, 106
Nora, Lois, 38
Northwestern University, 58, 120
Nowakowski, Jaclyn M., 222
Nursing, College of, 88
Nutrition Initiative, 59

O'Brien, Colleen, 163
O'Brien, Jim, 6, 188, 199, 204
Ohio Agricultural Research & Development Center (OARDC), 224
Ohio Board of Regents, 3, 26, 47, 60, 87, 142, 144, 184, 243, 250, 252
Ohio Capital Corporation for Housing (OCCH), 138
Ohio Collaborative Research and Policy for Schools, Children, and Families, 130–31
Ohio College Library Center (OCLC), 81, 88
Ohio Controlling Board, 87
Ohio Department of Education, 132
Ohio legislature. *See* General Assembly (Ohio)
OhioLINK, 81

Ohio Plan, 60, 69, 144, 248, 252
Ohio Stadium, 48, 84, 107, 109, 177, 185, 189–90, 198, 199–*201,* 224
Ohio Union, 23, 99, 101, 116
OSU & Harding Behavioral Healthcare and Medicine, 76
Outreach and Engagement: initiatives of, 54, 104, 132, 134, 239, 247; Office of, 133; President's Council on, 5, 104, 122, 132, 242
Ouzts, Dale, 173

P–12 education, 130–32
Pagac, Fred, 194
Page Hall, 83, 224
Palazzi, Maria, 47
Palmer, Colin, 54
Park Medical Center, 77
Parsley, Lea Ann, 199
Parson, Alayne, 26–27, 30, 59, 83, 154
Party Smart program, 182
Pauline, Eddie, 99, 102, 186, 219, 231
Patterson, Jim, 11, *42,* 55, 104, 213–17, 219, 221, 222, 231
Patterson, Karen, 163
Payne, Thomas, *154*
Penn, Scoonie, 202
Pennsylvania State University, 36, 48, 61, 101, 123, 190, 199, 238, 254
Petterson, Jim, 11, *42,* 55–56, 104, 213–17, 219, 221, 222, 231
Pharmacy, College of, 88
Pichette (Ashe), Janet, 26, 187
Pinchuk, Barbara, 116
Pizzuti, Ron, 161–62
Platz, Mat, 49, 223
powell, john a., 54–*55*
President's Council on Women's Issues, 119
public safety, 180–84

Randall, Alan J., 221
Ratcliff, Roger, 47
Ray, Edward J. ("Ed"), *58, 62, 72, 154;* and Academic Plan, 37, 38, 40, 41, 43; and ARMS, 175; background of, 22; and branding, 170; and Committee on the Status of the Colleges of the Arts and Sciences, 56; and compensation, 45–46; and diversity, 113, 116, 117–18; and Faculty Recognition Day, *48;* and honors, 95; information technology, 87; and Institute on the Study of Race and Ethnicity in the Americas, 54; on Kirwan, 28, 29, 82; and Knowlton gift, 85; and leadership agendas, 5; named provost, 21, *25;* and regional campuses, 106; and reorganization, 26; and Selective Investment for Academic Excellence, 47; and state support, 152–54; and teach-in on terrorist attacks, 186; and union strike, 179; and university senate, 49–50
Regan, Gerry, 50
regional campuses, 104–6
Research, Office of, 54, 59, 61, 124, 125
Research Challenge, 47, 142, 144, 248, 251
research park, 3, 122, 124–26, 247
Rhimes, Ilee, 87
Rhodes, Frank, 24–26, 28, 52, 70
Rice, Condoleezza, 9
Rich, Barbara, 116, 118
Richard M. Ross Heart Hospital, 76, 77, 236
Rideout, Chris, 97
Riedl, John, 106
Rieland, Thomas, 173
Ries, Carol, 107
Riffee, Kate, 97, 202
rioting, 180–83
Ritterbusch, Todd, 128
Robinson, Patricia A. Duke, 82
Robinson, Randall, *113*
Robinson, Robert, 89
Robinson, Ryan, 102
Robinson, Thomas E., 82
Rofagha, Soraya, *42,* 222, 231
Rogers, Nancy Hardin, 28, 63, 133, 186
Ross, Elizabeth ("Libby"), 77
Royster, Jacqueline, 54, 231
Rudd, Nancy, 26, 28
Rudman, Sally V., 22

Sadee, Wolfgang, 47, 59
Saltz, Joel, 47, 60
Sanfilippo, Fred, 40, 50, 67–69, *72*–77, 123, 231
Sanfilippo, Janet, 133
Schoenbaum, Betty, 131, 227, 230
Scholar Maximus Competition, 83, 90
Scholars Program, 57, 92–94, 234, 245
Schuerger, Robert ("B. J."), 102, 178
Schuller, David, *74*
Science and Technology Campus Corporation (SciTech), 31, 123–27, 138, 247
Science Village, 47, 125
Sedmak, Daniel, 70–71
Selective Excellence, 3, 53
Selective Investment for Academic Excellence, 47, 53, 56, 61, 63, 148
Senate, University, 5, 29, 37, 38, 40, 44, 49–52, 56, 144, 182
September 11 (9/11), 146, 184–87
sexual orientation, 114, 120–21
Shackelford, Thekla ("Teckie"), 156–*57,* 159
Shaw, Stephanie, 113
Shkurti, William J. ("Bill"), 6,

26, 28, 29, 45, 46, 79, 142, *143,* 144, 153, 164, 175, 179, 190, 221
Shultz, Joseph A., 222
Shumate, Alex, 10–11, 15, *16,* 19, 21, 129, 161, 164, 212, 221, 230
Siedentop, Daryl, 130
Sigafoos, Kam, 119
Sisson, Richard ("Dick"), 5, 21, *22,* 23, 47, 57, 66, 116, 221
Skestos, George, 9, 11, 19, *42,* 73, 221, 222
Slane, Dan, *42,* 73, 136, 219, 222
Smith, Ora, 31, 123, 124, 126, *127*
Smith, W. Randy, 26, 38, 40, 104, 106, 131, 166
Snyder, Barbara, 28, 51
Sofia, Zuheir, *42,* 75, 222
Solove, Richard, 62, *74,* 76, 226
Solove Research Institute, 76
Spielman, Chris, 194
Spirit of Women Park, 119
St. Pierre, Ron, 132
Stadium Scholarship Dormitory, 200
Stanford University, 9, 15, 39, 66, 188
Stanton, Frank, 213
Steinbrenner, George, 161, 200, 227
Steiner, Curt, 60, 163
Stewart, Mac, 27, 112, *117,* 118, 231
Stewart, Todd, 59–60
Stoddard, Dick, *30,* 40, 121, 165–66
Stoops, Bob, 194
Strategic Investment Funds, 3, 47, 61, 78, 97, 125, 146, 147, 153, 170, 234, 243, 248, 252
strike, union, 176–80
Student Affairs, Office of, 92, 94, 98–102, 103, 106, 113, 131
Student Athletic Support Services, 97
Strider, Eileen, 87
Studer, William, 81
Success Challenge, 144, 248
Sullivan, Leon, 112, 187
Sylvan, Donald, 186

Taft, Bob, 6, 60, 125, 142, 144, 146, *149*–52, 163, 165, *185*
Taiwan, 167
Taliaferro, Adam, 199
Tashjian, Lee, 38–39, 108, 129, 163, 169–71, 179, 191
Task Force on Technology, 123
Taylor, Fred, 199
technology, information, 86–89. *See also* Information Technology Initiative
Technology Commercialization Corporation, 126
Technology Licensing, Office of, 127
Technology Partnerships, Office for, 127
Third Frontier Initiative, 60, 69
Thompson, Lonnie, 161, 223
Title IX, 189
tobacco settlement funds, 60, 69, 145, 147, 163, 248, 251, 252
Tokyo University, 167
Toogood, Diane, *30*
Transportation Initiative, 59
Tressel, Jim, 185, 193–99
Trethewey, Virginia ("Ginny"), 6, 26, *27,* 28–30, 35, 39, 85, 120, 151, 175, 177, 179, 187, 190
tuition, 64, 91–92, 97, 102, 141–42, 145–50, 152, 210, 212, 240, 245, 246, 248, 252
Tyson, Laura, 9
Tzagournis, Manuel, 70, 71, 73, *74,* 75

Undergraduate Curriculum Review Committee, 52
Undergraduate Student Academic Services, Office of, 96–97
Undergraduate Studies, Office of, 96
UNITS, 87
University of Arizona, 36, 238, 254
University of California system, 9; Berkeley, 9, 22, 40, 48, 57–58, 124, 156, 186; Los Angeles (UCLA), 22, 24, 36, 87, 156, 238, 254; Merced, 57; San Francisco, 59
University of Cincinnati, 60, 97
University of Colorado, 127
University of Georgia, 215, 216
University of Illinois, 36, 101, 148, 156, 238, 254
University of Indiana, 10, 120, 123
University of Kentucky, 16, 17, 101, 132, 189, 208
University of Maryland, 9, 18–19, 67, 75, 188, 208, 211
University of Michigan, 36, 48, 69, 83, 101, 120, 142, 156, 186, 191, 238, 254
University of Minnesota, 36, 54, 61, 120, 156, 193, 195, 254
University of Nebraska, 190
University of Notre Dame, 186
University of Oregon, 10, 193
University of Southern Illinois, 100
University Staff Advisory Committee (USAC), 180
University Teacher Education Council, 131
University of Texas, 10, 21, 36, 129, 238, 254
University Technology Services, 86–87
University of Washington, 9, 36, 216, 238, 254

University of Wisconsin: Madison, 36, 238, 254; Milwaukee, 130
U.S. News & World Report, 18, 36, 50, 78, 81, 96, 189, 238

Van Brimmer, Rick, 187
Veres, Mike, 87
Veterinary Medicine, College of, 213, 224
Voinovich, George V., 6, 11, 12, 20, 22, 142, 163, 168

Watts, J. C., 107, 225
Wells, Bill, 77
Wells, Jackie, 77
Werth, Paul, *162*
West Campus, 3, 122, 124
Wexner, Les, 15, *64,* 129, 135
Wexner Prize recipients, 223
Whitacre, Caroline, 52, 68
William C. Davis Baseball Stadium, 189
William Oxley Thompson Memorial Library, 79–83, 190, 225, 234, 244, 251
Williams, David, 97, 99, 101, 113, 114, 136, 190, 221
Williams, Greg, 54, *62,* 63
Williams, James, 124, 126, 223, 231
Wofford, Richard, 180
Wolfe, John F., 77, 129, *185,* 225, 226, 230
Wolfe Study Abroad Scholarships, 134
Women's Place, 119, 246, 250
World Media and Culture Center, 83
WOSU, 172–73

Y2K, 174–76
Yonsei University, 167
Young, Willa, 180, 231
Youngstown State University, 194, 195
Younkin Success Center, 97, 99, 101, 202, 224

Zimpher, Nancy, 97, 130, 222
Zweier, Jay, 48

www.ingramcontent.com/pod-product-compliance
Lightning Source LLC
La Vergne TN
LVHW091036080826
845145LV00002B/523

* 9 7 8 0 8 1 4 2 5 7 4 5 6 *